DIRTY SWEET DUET

paige press

DIRTY SWEET DUET

Laurelin Paige

NEW YORK TIMES BESTSELLING AUTHOR
LAURELIN PAIGE

Copyright © 2019 by Laurelin Paige

All rights reserved.

No part of this book may be reproduced in any form or by any electronic or mechanical means, including information storage and retrieval systems, without written permission from the author, except for the use of brief quotations in a book review.

Editing: Erica Russikoff

Proofing: Michele Ficht

Cover: Laurelin Paige

ISBN: 978-1-957647-26-5

ALSO BY LAURELIN PAIGE
WONDERING WHAT TO READ NEXT? I CAN HELP!

Visit www.laurelinpaige.com for content warnings and a more detailed reading order.

Brutal Billionaires

Brutal Billionaire - a standalone (Holt Sebastian)

Dirty Filthy Billionaire - a novella (Steele Sebastian)

Brutal Secret - a standalone (Reid Sebastian)

Brutal Arrangement - a standalone (Alex Sebastian)

Brutal Bargain - a standalone (Axle Morgan)

Brutal Bastard - a standalone (Hunter Sebastian)

The Dirty Universe
Dirty Duet (Donovan Kincaid)

Dirty Filthy Rich Men | Dirty Filthy Rich Love

Kincaid

Dirty Games Duet (Weston King)

Dirty Sexy Player | Dirty Sexy Games

Dirty Sweet Duet (Dylan Locke)

Sweet Liar | Sweet Fate

(Nate Sinclair) Dirty Filthy Fix (a spinoff novella)

Dirty Wild Trilogy (Cade Warren)

Wild Rebel | Wild War | Wild Heart

Men in Charge

Man in Charge

Man for Me (a spinoff novella)

The Fixed Universe

Fixed Series (Hudson & Alayna)

Fixed on You | Found in You | Forever with You | Hudson | Fixed Forever

Found Duet (Gwen & JC) Free Me | Find Me

(Chandler & Genevieve) Chandler (a spinoff novel)

(Norma & Boyd) Falling Under You (a spinoff novella)

(Nate & Trish) Dirty Filthy Fix (a spinoff novella)

Slay Series (Celia & Edward)

Rivalry | Ruin | Revenge | Rising

(Gwen & JC) The Open Door (a spinoff novella)

(Camilla & Hendrix) Slash (a spinoff novella)

First and Last

First Touch | Last Kiss

Hollywood Standalones
One More Time

Close

Sex Symbol

Star Struck

Dating Season
Spring Fling | Summer Rebound | Fall Hard

Winter Bloom | Spring Fever | Summer Lovin

Also written with Kayti McGee under the name Laurelin McGee
Miss Match | Love Struck | MisTaken | Holiday for Hire

Written with Sierra Simone
Porn Star | Hot Cop

This book may contain subjects that are sensitive
to some readers.
Please visit www.laurelinpaige.com/dirty-sweet for content
warnings. May include spoilers.

SWEET LIAR

ONE
DYLAN

"What the fuck was that?!" Weston, my business partner, exclaimed from the front passenger seat of my service car as we pulled away from the curb.

Restraining myself from directing the driver—a habit of mine, surely not useful now when I'd been out of New York City for so long—I looked behind me out the rear window at the two figures we'd left behind. Donovan Kincaid, another one of my partners at Reach, Inc. along with Weston King, was chasing down a girl who worked in the office—Sabrina Lind.

I had only just met Sabrina this evening. The woman was pleasant, smart, straightforward. Had a good head on her shoulders. Weston and I had dined with her and her younger sister and had just been finishing up when Donovan had come in, all blustering and noble and knightly.

"Donovan called himself her *boyfriend*," Weston said incredulously, recalling the scene we'd just left. "Was I the only one who heard that? I can't be *that* drunk."

It had been an out-of-character declaration for the usually tight-lipped and brooding Donovan, but I'd seen this side of him before, many years in the past. The last time he had given a woman his heart.

If anyone asked me, he was wasting his time with this one. Sabrina had said several things over dinner that suggested she was no longer entertained by the circus that surrounded romantic notions.

"I heard it," the young woman sitting next to me answered.

Now this one—Audrey, the younger sister whom I'd volunteered to see home—a man would have a much easier time trying to woo *her*. She'd made that clear over dinner as well.

Too bad she was *that* kind of girl. The kind of girl who wanted a man to love her before she lifted her skirt. Otherwise...

I turned my head slightly, imperceptibly, and slid my eyes down her form, pausing on the sweet curve of her breasts, watching her chest rise and fall with her breath. My gaze had traveled this journey several times this evening, but now I was lucky enough to have the added view of her legs, which had been hidden under the table before. They were long and toned, a little curve in just the right place.

"I heard it," she said again, "and it was *so* romantic."

The swoon in her voice made me chuckle. God, she was young. Younger than whatever ridiculous young age she actually was. Who the hell even believed in romance anymore?

"I don't understand," Weston muttered, combing his hand through his hair. "I'm Donovan's best friend. I knew he was sleeping with her, but I didn't know he was her boyfriend. I didn't know he was *into* her. *I* was supposed to be into Sabrina. When did this happen? Where have I been?"

Oh. That was right. *Weston King* believed in love and relationships.

He turned his head to look at both of us in the backseat. "I'm seriously asking here."

I glanced at Audrey. Her expression said that she had been in the know, but her lips were sealed.

That left me to console my partner. "You've probably been too distracted with that Dyson pussy you've been banging," I was definitely still intoxicated. I didn't normally use such crass language in front of a lady. Especially such a *young* lady.

"Hey," Weston said, pointing a stern finger in my direction. "Elizabeth is not just some pussy I've been banging. I'm going to marry her."

Never mind that their engagement was part of a business ruse. Despite the fact that it counted for nothing, Weston seemed to have grown fond of the girl—even as he bemoaned the loss of Sabrina.

It was exhausting.

"You're exhausting," I told him.

"*I'm* exhausting?" He seemed baffled by the idea that he would exhaust anyone.

"The entire lot of you. More exhausting than the flight across the pond. All of you are intelligent creatures normally. I wouldn't have gotten into business with partners who gave in to the whims and fancies of human nature. It takes a clear head, your feet on the ground, your priorities straight, to be as successful as we have been with our company.

"But now the lot of you have gone and eaten some fruit from the tree of temptation. Drank the potion number nine. Watched one too many Netflix Christmas specials, because you've suddenly all descended into the ridiculous camp of men who fall in love with women."

"Wait," Weston halted me. "I never said I was in love with Elizabeth Dyson, I only said I was going to marry her."

"You spent the entire dinner pining after her. *Pining*, Weston King. Surely pining is a sign of love." I turned to the audience member that I knew would be on my side.

"Yes, indeed," Audrey nodded, with a bob of her head that was somehow both girlish and sexy as hell. "Pining is Love 101. If a girl came to me and said the guy had told her he was pining after her? That's like popping the question."

"Exactly like," I said straight-faced. I was being sarcastic, of course, but the girl did make me want to smile.

Among other things.

I stretched my arm across the back of the seat bench, casually, making myself comfortable. Not making a move. No, not that.

"I am not in love with Eliza—"

"And on top of your pining..." I said, speaking loudly over Weston. His denial, which he was surely about to deliver in full, was infuriating and, frankly, patronizing, and I refused to listen to more than a second of it. "We have Donovan, who declares a relationship with a woman on a public street, for crying out loud, in front of his partners. I thought for sure that man, of all of you, had reason." He must have forgotten how miserable he'd been the last time he'd given his heart, albeit ten years ago.

Soon enough, he'd remember.

"And then we have Nate," I continued. A man of varied sexual pleasures and interests, Nathan Sinclair had been another fly I'd never expected to drop. "When I'd had drinks with the man last night, he was talking about one particular woman like she hung the moon. Soon it will just be me and Cade."

I leaned closer toward Audrey, since she probably didn't know anything about our fifth partner who headed the Tokyo office. "No one will ever love Cade, even if he goes pansy on us. That's a man that even a mother wouldn't love. He's one of my best friends. I ought to know."

Weston harrumphed from the front seat, completely indignant, but I noted a hint of optimism, as though he hoped I were right about his future, and that he'd be leaving the bachelor life for good.

He really had gone bananas over that Dyson girl. Poor sucker.

I stole another glance at Audrey, curious at how badly I'd offended her with my speech, love-cheerleader that she was.

But when I turned in her direction, I hadn't expected that she'd already be staring at me. The flush in her round cheeks as she looked quickly away sent a jolt to my todger.

I should have been ashamed of myself.

But I wasn't.

She was a very attractive young lady. I couldn't help how my body reacted. I'd been respectful. For the most part.

"This is me," Weston said, pointing out the window to his building.

My driver pulled over next to a large bank of snow. To be fair, the entire street was banked with snow, lingering from the storm the day before.

"Guess I'm going snowshoeing," Weston said with a sigh. He stepped out of the car and immediately cursed, the door slamming before I could make out the full extent of his blaspheme.

I leaned over Audrey, and not just because I wanted to smell the rose bouquet in her perfume, but so that I could roll the window down and call after my partner.

"Have a good Thanksgiving," I said, "if I don't see you again before the holiday." He was flying off somewhere later in the week—Utah or Kansas—the United States Midwest was always a blur to this Hampshire native.

"You too, friend. It was good seeing you. If even briefly. And nice meeting you, Audrey." He turned, stepping into the snow. "Fuck. These were a brand-new pair of Giacomettis."

"You can put them out with the rubbish, along with your balls. Since you're obviously not using *them* anymore." I rolled up the window before he could throw back a dig of his own, but he got me with a simple flip of the bird.

I sat back in my seat, accidentally grazing my hand along Audrey's bare knee.

Perhaps, not so accidentally, but I played it perfectly—the shocked drawback from the touch and an immediate apology, stammering so that she would indeed believe that the brush was innocent. With all the predators these days, I certainly didn't want to be confused for one.

Or at least I wanted to be my own breed of predator. The kind that knew when to behave. Though the shock of the touch had sent fire through my blood, it wouldn't be followed up with any pouncing.

We drove in silence for several minutes, a thick silence. Too thick. Too heavy, making the car hot and stuffy and tense.

I loosened my tie and stole another glance in her direction. She seemed to be lost in her own thoughts. Had I offended her after all with my touch?

Then I remembered the conversation from before Weston exited the car. That was more likely the cause of any hard feelings.

Normally, I would brush the whole thing off. Let her be offended. I wasn't changing my stance on romance to please her.

The tension between us, though, wouldn't dissipate. It seemed filled with more than just the words of what I had said. It was growing and breathing, and I felt the need to claw through it, the way you claw through bedsheets when they've twisted around you during a nightmare.

"You've been quiet," I said. Obvious. To the point. "Have I rained on your love parade?"

She twisted her head in my direction, her eyes catching a reflection of a streetlight making them spark in the darkness.

"You can't rain on my parade," she proclaimed with a smile, as though she were Barbara Streisand herself. "I am firm in my faith." She swiveled a little more in her seat, angling herself so that her body was pointing in my direction. "Are you quite sure that you're firm in your disbelief?"

Heat traveled down my spine, liquid and molten. That's what this tension was, then—not of a disgruntled nature, but of the sexual. I'd been attracted to her, yes. I hadn't allowed myself to believe it might be mutual.

I studied her face. She had light almond eyes that were deep set in a pear-shaped face, her pallor flawless. Not a single line marred her skin. She was lovely. Delicious, I imagined. Fresh, like a peach. Her bee-stung lips, turned up on both sides below her apple cheeks, portrayed her as innocent.

I liked believing she was that innocent. It made it more fun to imagine what those lips could be taught. What they could be introduced to.

I'd sworn off love years ago, but not sex. Never sex. And Audrey Lind was all sorts of temptation, the kind I knew better to stay away from. She was too romantic. She was too American. She was too young. *Much* too young. I was definitely old enough to be her father. Probably.

Definitely.

I didn't want to think about that.

She was also the sister of a subordinate, which felt highly inappropriate, especially since I was only in town for the week. Donovan might have gotten involved with the staff, but at least he'd seemed serious about it. A fling was another thing altogether, not as polite.

And none of that mattered since she was so very young.

"You're hesitating," she said, her smile broadening as though she'd won some sort of trophy. "Are you unsure of your answer?"

I had to remind myself of the question. "No. My commitment to refute love and relationships in all forms remains unwavering." My eyes flickered to her plump lips. The delectable mouth.

"I wonder if you're lying." Before I could offer a protest she went on. "Which isn't why I was quiet. I was thinking about Weston's situation. Not the current one, but how he was before he met Elizabeth. I'm normally not into players, but he's reformed. And his past has advantages."

Her words were a fishhook. If I were a smart little fishy I would swim away as fast as I could.

I was a smart fishy. I was.

But I liked to swim as close to the bait as possible. Just to see what it was.

"What exact benefits does Weston King have in being a former playboy who now thinks he's head over heels for a woman he's fake-engaged to? The first woman he's ever spent more than a weekend with, might I add." It was one of the messiest messes I had ever imagined.

"Well. Um." Her eyes fluttered downward and her cheeks darkened a bit. "Weston figured out what he was doing before he fell for Elizabeth. So when they were together, it was...you know." She rubbed her lips together—believe me, I was watching everything she did with that mouth. "In the bedroom, I mean."

"Are you saying that you are not...? That you haven't...?" I cleared my throat, floundering a bit with how I was asking this near-stranger about her virginity. It was like the opening of a poorly written porno.

Holy mother of God, I was going to be fantasizing about this for quite some time.

"Oh, no," she said in a rush.

And to my relief. I couldn't handle the weight of knowing that and later having to get out of the car to see her to the door of her apartment building.

"I'm not that innocent," she went on. "I've had boyfriends. Two serious. Long-term, each of them. Very committed, very in love with both of them. And, maybe, even, either one of them could have been the guy. You know, *The* Guy? The Forever Guy?"

The fairy tale. Yes, I knew that story.

She was in a car now with me though. Not *with me*, but she wasn't with anyone else either, from what I'd gathered during the night. So those fairy tales had obviously ended. The way that every fairy tale eventually does and life returns back to reality.

"So what happened?" I asked, guessing she was about to reveal the flaw in her religion.

"Our sex life happened. Or didn't happen. My friends used to tell me about all these filthy, hot, dirty things they were doing with their boyfriends. Really sexy, adventurous things. You know the way girls share everything. And my guys? Missionary. Every time. I swear to God. Once the boredom in the bedroom became obvious, it seeped elsewhere in our relationships. No matter how much I hinted or pushed to explore new things, my guys were always as ignorant as I am."

My trousers were suddenly much too tight. Oh, the things I could show her. The ways I could *be* with her. If every man had only ever been on top of her, rutting around inside like some horny little teenager—had she ever even had an orgasm? My body pulsed with the want to show her the sweetness of expertise.

But that couldn't happen. For all the reasons I'd gone through before. Whatever those reasons were. They had left my mind at the moment, but there had been many. Good reasons.

Yet, even as I knew where this little car ride *couldn't* go, it seemed we were suddenly closer to each other. Audrey had unbuckled her seatbelt and smoothly slid across the bench toward me, and I hadn't even noticed.

I swallowed.

"I think your story of two men who could've been the one but ended up not, proves your theory of there *being a one* at all as flawed." My voice was still surprisingly steady. Fortunately. It didn't belie the pounding of my heart, the tingling of my skin. The rock hard state of my cock.

"No way. The One still exists. The theory isn't flawed. I had simply jumped to conclusions too soon. Maybe because I wanted it too much. Maybe because I wasn't ready yet. I still most definitely believe in kismet."

Her hand was on my thigh, like a hot iron burning through the material of my trousers to the skin underneath. It was a warning sign. A flash of silver threaded through a dead worm.

She lifted her delicate face up toward me, blinking her eyes innocently. "I'm pretty sure I can convince you kismet exists too, if you'll just do one thing."

Swim, fishy.

I didn't swim. "What's that?"

"Kiss me."

TWO
AUDREY

"Kiss you?" he asked, and the wariness in his tone almost made me doubt myself.

Almost.

Actually, not even almost. More like, I wondered if I *should* doubt myself.

But I didn't. I didn't doubt myself at all. Why should I, really?

I'd always been confident. I'd had the good fortune of being raised first by a father who instilled power in me, and then an older sister who made sure I felt my worth. Ironically, Sabrina had often lacked faith in herself, probably because, as the oldest, she had felt the burden of filling the woman-of-the-household role at such an early age, our mother having died young and then our father only a handful of years later.

And, to be honest, mothering wasn't Sabrina's strong suit. It made sense that she struggled with her self-esteem, as she'd been thrown into that role when she'd never asked for it. I loved her grotesquely, exactly the way she was—strong, opinionated, and smart as hell—but she tended to be *too* strong for much of the traditional world. *Too* opinionated. *Too* smart. Weren't women supposed to be dainty and quiet and demure? Sabrina didn't buy into that, and I so very much appreciated her paving the way for me to walk behind her with my head held high, no matter what form of femininity I wore.

So I felt pretty secure with myself for the most part. I knew who I was—talented, but not quite talented enough to pursue a career based on selling my artwork. Smart enough to understand the chemistry and archeology that went into my nearly completed masters of art conservation. Attractive—no one would ever confuse me for a model, but I did turn heads. I certainly wasn't desperate. I got to choose who I paid attention to, and when I liked someone, I told him. I had no reason to play hard to get.

But even though I was fun and romantic, I never felt like I wasn't grounded or that I needed someone else to anchor me. I especially never needed a man for that.

Yet, I did *like* having a man in my life. When I had a boyfriend, the world spun around him. I was a love-with-the-whole-heart kind of gal. I didn't enjoy being alone, and never had. There's a comfort in knowing someone will always catch you when you fall that Sabrina had never been able to replace. I'd been single now going on five months. That had been purposeful. After the last relationship that had blossomed and thrived everywhere except the bedroom, I'd decided something had to change.

Finishing school, though, had been the priority, and I hadn't thought much about how I was going to bring about that change.

Until tonight.

Since I was visiting Sabrina in New York for Thanksgiving break, I'd intended to give her all my focus, not expecting that *her* head would be wrapped up in a guy. Not that I was resentful. She deserved some happiness.

Just...her preoccupation with Donovan left me free to, well, *notice*. Notice Sabrina's boss—the tall, sophisticated, much older Brit with the chiseled jaw and brown wavy hair. Notice the way his eyes melted like chocolate as he got more buzzed on wine. Notice how his gaze lingered on me throughout dinner, despite the two other people present. Notice the crackle and the spark of electricity that traveled between us.

Notice how he noticed me.

And, wow, was he fantastic to look at. And listen to. And be noticed by. It made me beam and pulse. A lot like when Mr. Gregori, my favorite art teacher, acknowledged my work in class. That was what Dylan felt like—a professor. A very sexy, very hot professor. The kind of professor who could teach a girl a thing or two. The dirty professor who obviously had naughty thoughts about his young student but was decent enough not to act on it. He let those thoughts simmer and stew instead.

It wasn't like any other attraction I'd felt before. There was no pretense. No expectation. Just this raw, primal interest drawing me to lean in, to angle my body toward him. Drawing me to be bold.

Drawing me to have Ideas.

"Yes, kiss me," I repeated, my hand on his thigh. I swear I could feel the temperature of his skin rising through his pants.

Still, he made no move to grant me my request.

"Am I supposed to fall in love?" he asked, studying me with an intensity that made my heart beat against my ribs like a caged madman.

Gosh, he was noble. Wrestling with propriety even as his desire pressed against the wall he'd so firmly built around himself.

Or perhaps he feared that wall wasn't as sturdy as he proclaimed.

"Are you worried about it?" I challenged.

His eyes never left me. "Of course not."

"Then what are you afraid of?"

His restraint broke, and his mouth swooped down on mine like a wolf descending on its prey. There was no foreplay. No sweet seduction. Just hungry determination as he placed a hand at the back of my head and attacked with fierce ardor. He was firm and aggressive. He was skillful and demanding. He was in charge.

Silly, stupid, willing lamb that I was, I latched myself to him, throwing my arms around his neck and licking at the greedy plunge of his tongue between my lips. I wanted his taste of wine and smoked bass to be *my* taste, to be the only taste I could remember. I needed to drink him and devour him the way he seemed to need to drink and devour me.

We were frenzied and sloppy, our teeth crashing against each other at times, our breath coming in irregular measures. It felt as though the whole of time had been reduced to this moment, the entirety of the universe reduced to the three square inches that belonged to his mouth, and even as existence was shrunk down to this tiny form, there was nothing missing. Everything, *everything* I could ever want or need or desire was found in the electric field of this kiss.

Soon, I became aware of more, my attention spreading through my body like heat with the sunrise. My breasts felt heavy and my nipples tight. My belly swirled like a cyclone was tearing across its insides. Lower, between my legs, my core throbbed and ached. I was wet and empty, my thighs vibrating with need.

Desperate to ease the growing hum, to touch more of him and be touched, I swung my leg over his lap to straddle him and gasped when I landed on the steel ridge bulging from his pants. My hips bucked automatically, pressing my pussy against the outline of his cock. Again, again, needing to feel the exact shape of him, hoping to still the buzz that only seemed to grow louder with each stroke.

It was humiliating how eager I was. How urgent. How impetuous. How deeply romantic all of those things had suddenly become.

But then Dylan's hands were under my skirt, his fingers digging into my ass as he tilted my hips up along the length of him, deepening the notch of his cock, and I realized he was just as eager. Just as urgent. Just as impetuous.

And he knew what I needed. Knew exactly how to give it to me.

I felt myself get wetter. Felt him thicken against me. A frantic mewling sounded in my ears, and it took me several seconds to recognize it was coming from me. It was an entirely new and thrilling experience. Our lips stayed locked as we grinded and humped, a tight ball of tension growing deep in my belly. I'd never been so intimate with someone during a first kiss let alone the first night we'd met. Never felt so close to orgasm with all of my clothes still on. Never been on the verge of begging for sex from a near stranger—

The sound of a throat clearing brought me tumbling out of ecstasy.

Dylan broke his mouth from mine and peered around me. "Yes?"

The driver. Oh my God, I'd forgotten about our driver.

"This is the street," the forgotten driver said. "There's snow piled up against the curb. I've driven down the entire block, and there isn't a spot that's clear."

Dylan turned his head to look out the window, verifying the driver's claim. "Circle around the block, and let her off at the corner then," he said.

"Yes, sir."

The rhythmic click-click of the turn signal filled the silence.

My cheeks felt hot as I forced myself to meet Dylan's eyes. The need and urgency from only a moment ago still screamed between us, impossible to ignore even as my pulse began to settle.

Should I invite him up?

I wanted to.

But it was my sister's apartment. And he was my sister's boss, and there seemed to be a dozen things wrong with that situation.

Would he invite me to his hotel?

Also improper for as many reasons, and I saw from his expression that he'd gotten hold of himself enough to understand his obligations.

I shouldn't have felt so disappointed. I'd only meant for it to be a kiss. A kiss to find out if what I'd been considering was really something that might work.

Now I knew it could definitely work.

"You said I'd believe in kismet after that," Dylan said. "Was something supposed to happen?"

I could have smacked him. Trying to play like I'd had zero effect on him when his cock was still as hard as stone underneath me.

Fortunately, I wasn't that easily deterred. "Yes. Now you give me your phone number."

He only hesitated for a fraction of a second before pulling out his cell phone and unlocking the screen. He handed it to me. "Text yourself."

I shivered. How could a person make something so innocent sound so naughty?

Because he was experienced, that was how. Because he knew things that I didn't. Because he was The Professor.

I quickly shot myself a text from his phone then handed it back just as the car came to a stop. "I'll talk to you tomorrow," I said, climbing off his lap.

And maybe because I'd moved too quickly, because I'd surprised him, or because he was curious, or maybe because he was hard and horny and not in his right mind, he didn't argue about my parting remark.

Instead he sat somewhat dazed as I slid across the backseat, opened the door, and disappeared into the night. I was dazed too, but I'd never been more confident in myself.

THREE
DYLAN

I stared after Audrey, dumbfounded, as she walked to her building. My lips still burned from our kiss. My cock still ached and throbbed from her grinding on my lap. And I, like a fool, clung to her final words, "I'll talk to you tomorrow."

Fuck, how I wanted her to ring me. Wanted it like a teenage boy waited by his phone for the call from the pretty girl. The idea of it made me nervous and excited and...stupid.

That's what I was. Stupid.

Because even if she did ring me, there was no way I could accept her call, except to tell her that I was sorry for the egregious way I'd acted in the car.

Yet I *wasn't* sorry. Not truly. Not at all.

"Fantastic," my driver said dreamily, breaking my stupor.

I looked forward to find him also staring after Audrey.

Irritated, I scolded him. "What are you looking at?" He was even older than I was. It was inappropriate for *me* to be eyeing her. It was disgusting that *he* was. How I could feel both a fatherly protection and an indecent attraction to the girl, I had no idea.

That was a therapy session for another day.

"To the hotel, sir?" he said, moving his eyes back to the road where they belonged.

I didn't answer right away, staring at the mobile still in my hand. I'd had no texts from my son. When I'd seen him at lunch, I'd suggested we go out for a late movie tonight. He'd said he'd get back to me. I'd felt the sting of rejection, but he was thirteen now—independent and awkward. Moody, too. Even though I traveled across the ocean to see him, he wavered these days from wanting to see his dad and wanting to spend all his free time with his friends. I remembered this age. Remembered parenting this age. My stepdaughter, Amanda, had been thirteen when I'd married her mother. I'd done this teenager thing before.

So I understood.

We were at a delicate phase, Aaron and I, and I knew it. I didn't want to press, wanted him to reach out to me if he wanted to spend the evening in my presence. I'd known somewhere inside of me that I would be blown off. I wouldn't have gotten inebriated if I'd expected otherwise.

Disappointment sounded in my tone nonetheless when I finally replied. "Yes. The hotel."

The car signal clicked rhythmically as we waited at a light to turn uptown. I sunk back in my seat, letting myself remember, for a moment, the person I'd been when I'd wed. I'd felt so much older marrying a woman ten years my senior, but I was really such a child then, only twenty-five.

My, how I'd grown up since.

And now my thoughts turned back to Audrey, younger than I'd been when I'd married, but just as enthusiastic and charmed with love and life as I'd been.

I opened my texts and found where she'd sent herself a message.

> A million people in the city, and you and I met. That's kismet.

I laughed out loud. My driver was spot on—she *was* fantastic. Fantastic and trusting and young and that was enough reason to delete both her number and the whimsical message from my phone.

But I saved it instead. Not because she'd hooked me, but because I needed to know it was her when she called. If she called.

She *wouldn't* call.

She couldn't have been more than ten years older than Aaron. Why would a girl her age have any interest in me? Our encounter had been one of the moment. It had been dark, and we were alone and tipsy and aroused by good conversation. Nothing else. It would be forgotten by tomorrow.

Though if she really could forget that kiss...

I was still thinking about the malleable way her lips fit to mine when I reached my hotel room on the Upper East Side. I'd forgotten and left the Do Not Disturb sign on my suite door when I'd left for the day so the bed was still rumpled and the pot for tea was still sitting on the desk. Sloppy and cluttered weren't usually my style. An embarrassing space to bring a woman back to, not that there was one with me now. Not that I'd thought about asking Audrey to accompany me to my room.

If I had, would she have said yes?

She may have, and I would have devoured her. Would have spent the whole night showing her all the ways a man could please a woman, ways that she yearned for but couldn't yet imagine.

Fantasizing about it made my earlier hard-on return. I took off my suit jacket and hung it on the back of the desk chair before

I sat in it myself, fumbling with my belt, eager to play this daydream out with my cock in my hand.

But just as I got my zip down, I stopped, a sickening wave of guilt rolling over me. It felt crass and wrong to beat off to thoughts of this girl who could be my daughter. Even though she'd never know that I'd done it, it was degrading and a violation of sorts.

I zipped up my trousers and stood. I loosened my tie and then moved to the buttons of my shirt, undressing furiously. I needed a shower. A *cold* shower, that was what would take care of this.

Just as I dropped my shirt on the desk chair with my jacket, my mobile rang.

My heart leapt so high, it was practically in my throat as I scrambled to look at my screen, hoping it was *her* name that I'd see lighting up on the caller ID.

The name I saw instead caused me to let out a groan.

With resignation, I clicked the accept button and answered. "Hello, Ellen." Ellen Rachel Wallace Starkney Locke. She was just Ellen Wallace again now, having shed both the name I'd given her and the one she'd received in her previous marriage. Eight years had passed now since the paperwork had become final on our divorce, and still, she made my blood boil every time I had contact with her.

"I haven't even spoken yet, and you already have a tone," she greeted me, with a tone of her own. So nasty. So like Ellen.

Now there was a boner killer.

"Yes, I think I earned the right, don't you?" I didn't need to bring up her past sins against me. She knew them.

"Honestly, Dylan," she said, letting out an audible sigh. "Move on. I have. It's time you joined me."

I pinched the bridge of my nose. She was a liar. She hadn't moved on. She was still stuck underneath the emotional avalanche that had fallen upon her the day Amanda had died ten years ago. Instead of facing her pain, Ellen had buried it, becoming rotten and disconnected as she did.

If she'd really moved on, if she'd let herself heal, would she and I be apart today?

I couldn't imagine it. Didn't even want to anymore. Because I *had* moved on—moved on from her and any notion of happily ever after. She'd proven to me that love always died, and I'd accepted it. *She* was the one in denial.

I didn't want to go there with her, though, not tonight. "Why are you calling, Ellen? Anything you have to say could have been said to me tomorrow when I pick up Aaron."

"That's what I'm calling about. Aaron won't be able to see you until the afternoon. Oh, and then he has Latin lessons at four, so it will be evening, actually, before you can get him."

I ran my palm through my hair and clutched a handful tightly in frustration. "Christ, Ellen. He can't skip Latin one week while his father is in town? I flew from another continent to spend this time with him."

"Lessons are paid for in advance. There are no makeups. Latin is a foundational language, and it's so important these days."

No. It wasn't. Not as important as spending time with his father.

But there was no rationalizing with the helicopter tiger mother that was Ellen Wallace. "And why is it I can't see him during the day? I chose this week to visit because he had time off from school."

"While he doesn't have school this week officially, tomorrow the teachers will be in the classrooms available for makeup work and tutoring. I signed Aaron up for the full day."

I leaned against the desk, my knuckles curled. Aaron didn't need tutoring or makeup. He had a three point four grade point average. This was Ellen being spiteful and stubborn.

"Cancel it. I can tutor him."

"On seventh-grade advanced chemistry?" she retorted patronizingly. "Even if you could understand it, he needs a lab."

"Why is a thirteen-year-old even taking advanced chemistry? Aaron doesn't have a scientific bone in his body. Are you shoving these classes down his throat?"

"I'm insuring his future," Ellen said, raising her voice.

"Ensuring that he's going to hate you one day, if not already. Cancel the tutoring."

"It's too late. He's signed up. And I'll not let you get in the way of his success."

"*His success*," I echoed incredulously. He was still just a boy. Did she ever give him a chance to just be a kid? I was so angry, I went low. "I'll pick him up myself. I'll sign him out from the school as soon as you drop him off."

"It would be kidnapping. They won't let you take him without my authorization." She was just as nasty as I was. Nastier.

"I'm not on the school's parental records? We'd always agreed it would be both of us in case there was ever an emergency!"

"I reconsidered. If there was an emergency, you'd be too far away." She sounded proud of herself. "I have my sister listed as emergency now. And Donovan Kincaid is there as a backup to her."

I had to stop myself from kicking the chair, and only because I was concerned that I'd break a toe with as hard as I wanted to kick it. "Donovan Kincaid doesn't know what to do with a kid. This is you trying to keep him from me, like you always do." This conversation reaffirmed my decision to get a second apartment in New York City—so that I could visit more often and have more access to Aaron.

"I'm not keeping him from anyone. You are delusional."

"And you're ice. Cold and bitter and mean. Exactly the qualities that drove me to leave you." Maybe I was going there after all.

"You didn't leave me because I was cold and bitter. You left because I cheated on you." She'd destroyed my heart with her betrayal and she almost sounded like she was gloating.

To hell with her.

"You were ice cold and bitter before that. It simply took the act of you cheating on me to recognize that I couldn't..." I paused and inhaled deeply. I didn't need to relive this. I didn't want to remember how deeply I'd once believed in her. In us.

"That you couldn't save me?" she finished for me. "Couldn't make me whole again? Is that what you were going to say?" She was callous and cruel as she pointed out how naïve I had been to think that I could love her better.

Yes, Ellen, we are in agreement there.

I'd been stupid in those romantic notions. I was wiser now. And I didn't see any point in returning to naivety, regardless of the pull my heart occasionally gave.

"I'm picking Aaron up from school when he's done with the day," I said firmly, refusing to dwell on the past any longer. "I'll make sure he reviews his Latin before I drop him off at home. And, by God, Ellen, you better have me approved to retrieve him or I'll get my solicitor involved." Then, before she could refute me, I said good night and clicked off the phone.

What a goddamned shrew.

I was energized with rage, my heart racing with the power of it.

But underneath my temper was a dangerous longing. A yearning for a different time. A time when I could afford the innocent enthusiasm for human connection. Before I knew how cruel people could be. Before I understood the downfalls of being vulnerable.

What a rose-colored world it had been—a prettier, more tolerable world—when I'd believed wholeheartedly in commitments and forever. When lust and love were two sides of the same coin. Sex, an expression of feelings rather than just a pleasurable release.

I longed to be free of the reality that I wore like chains around my neck.

And then! Then I could ask a girl back to my hotel room without caring about age differences or impropriety or what state my suite had been left in. I could get lost in the breathlessness of her kiss, not worrying about anyone's feelings or what might inevitably happen if I put my trust in her embrace. I could imagine it so vividly, what it would be like to be that kind of a man again, what it would be like to kiss a girl like Audrey, undress her, teach her. Make love to her.

My trousers were bulging again with the fantasy. I was throbbing and thick. I couldn't make it to the shower if I tried.

I shoved down my trousers and pulled out my cock, fisting it with my right hand as I sat down on the chair. With my eyes closed, I remembered vividly the weight of Audrey on my lap, remembered the pleasurable burn of her rubbing up and down along the imprisoned length of my hard-on. Remembered the press of her breasts against my chest, her nipples so taut they spiked through the layers of clothing between us. Remembered her mouth as it gave in to my wicked desire, my tongue caressing and schooling her at once. My lips memorizing her and debauching her.

My palm stroked angrily across the inflamed skin of my cock, faster and faster, punishing myself even as the pleasure built and built and built, like static on a balloon when rubbed against a headful of hair. Like stockinged feet, trudged across the carpet. Like too many plugs jammed into a wall socket, my orgasm surged through me with electrical shock. Cum spilled out over my fist as I tugged and tugged, past the point of comfort, until everything inside me had fallen in thick ropes across my bare stomach, dirty and filthy and obscene.

I sat for several minutes, staring at the mess I'd made, my hands shaking from the release as, little by little, the delirious flash of bliss dissolved into cold, hard reality.

I was alone. I would always be alone.

I'd learned the hard way that alone was the most sensible way to live.

There was no benefit of vulnerability. There was no "making love." There was no reason to trust. Hearts were for pumping oxygen through the body. They didn't break. They beat on.

Audrey had called me a liar when she'd suggested that I secretly believed in her religion of romance, but she was wrong.

I wasn't a liar. I was a man who could no longer believe in the lie.

FOUR
AUDREY

"He *kissed* you?"

Of course I told my sister.

I told her as soon as she walked through the door. Mostly, because I wanted to be sure it wouldn't be a surprise if Dylan said anything to her, but also because I shared everything with Sabrina.

Well, almost everything. I never actually talked about sex with her, but that was because she had a barrier like a thirteen inch cement wall surrounding her when it came to the subject. Talking about sex made her tense and agitated. I'd decided that meant she was either asexual or into some weird stuff in the bedroom. Not that I'd knock her either way.

"More like *I* kissed *him*," I said, since I'd initiated the whole thing. I didn't want her to get the wrong idea about the situation. Because there had been absolutely nothing wrong about that kiss at all—except that it had been too short.

Just remembering the way Dylan's mouth fit so perfectly against mine brought a swarm of butterflies to my tummy.

"You *kissed* my boss?" Sabrina seemed to be having a hard

time wrapping her head around the fact. Obviously she was stuck on her own relationship with the man.

But I'd already thought about that.

I kicked off my shoes and pulled my knees underneath me on the couch. "Dylan is not actually your boss. He's more like your boss's equal, if you want to be technical." And, to be fair, she herself was sleeping with a different man who was her boss's equal. If there wasn't an issue there, why would there be an issue with me?

She dropped her coat and purse on the back of the sofa and put a stern fist on her hip—one of the postures she took when she was assuming a motherly role with me. "If you want to be technical, he's old enough to be your father."

I rolled my eyes. "He is not. He's just experienced and wise." To be honest, I wasn't actually sure of Dylan's age.

"He's twenty years older than you."

Huh. I'd guessed more like fifteen. "Maybe I have a thing for dads." I didn't, I didn't think, but I *could*. Could I? Was that the comfort I'd been unable to replicate with my previous boyfriends? "Don't knock my kink. I don't knock yours." I was possibly more defensive than I needed to be.

Sabrina's jaw slammed shut, and she got that tense, agitated way she did when sex conversations turned a spotlight on her.

So then she was definitely into some weird bedroom stuff. Interesting.

Finally, she sighed. "Fine. I won't knock the age difference." She came around to the front of the couch and sank down next to me. "I don't actually care what you're into anyway, as long as it's consensual. I just don't want you getting hurt. Dylan doesn't seem into relationships. You get that, right? Not to mention that you live on entirely different continents."

I had been defensive before, but now I was incensed. "It was just a kiss! God. I'm not planning to marry the guy." I stretched my legs out in front of me and studied my toes so I didn't have to look at her. She was being dramatic.

Even though it *hadn't* been just a kiss.

It had been the *best* kiss. It had been grinding and thrusting and heavy petting. It had told me everything I needed to know about Dylan—that he was skilled and sensitive and seduceable. It had been the stars aligning, bringing a man who needed to be reminded to let his emotions loose together with me, a woman who needed practice getting physically loose.

But Sabrina was skeptical. "Just a kiss," she repeated.

Did I mention she was being dramatic? Just because I'd fallen hard and fast for a few men that didn't work out didn't mean that I didn't know how to protect myself. It didn't mean that I wanted to change who I was, either. I was a girl who felt things. I knew who I was. I knew what I was made of—big emotions packed into a little body. And keeping all those feelings pent up in such a small space was impossible. I couldn't stuff my passion into some dark corner of my soul the way Sabrina did. I lived from the heart. I loved with my entirety. I loved frequently and deeply, and if that meant I hurt sometimes—or a lot of times—so be it. My heartbreaks shaped me into who I was.

And I *liked* who I was.

All that being said, love wasn't the reason I was drawn to Dylan. He was an opportunity that I couldn't pass up, a choice I almost couldn't help but make. Opportunity knocked, but Fate had seemed to be at the door as well.

Seeing how the conversation had gone so far, though, I really didn't think Sabrina was in a place to understand the whole truth.

I settled for partial honesty, peering up at her with a sigh. "I felt bad for the guy. All that doom and gloom. 'Love's dead. Grump, grump.' He needed something nice for a change."

She narrowed her gaze. "So you thought you'd kiss him and

that would show him. Make him magically believe in hearts and romance again?"

"Shut up." Now she was just being mean. Would she always think of me as the little girl she had to parent? She wasn't my mother. And little girls grew up eventually.

I slumped in my seat and pouted. "You think I'm naïve."

She gave me a look that said she very much wanted to lecture me, but when she leaned toward me, it was just to kiss me on the head. "I think you're amazing," she said.

And I grinned at her. Not because she'd told me I was amazing—she was my sister; she was sort of obligated to think that—but because *she* was amazing. She'd basically been my mother since she was thirteen years old. I knew it took an effort for her to let me make my own choices, make my own mistakes. I was proud of her for fighting against her instincts.

Maybe her latest relationship was changing her for the good.

Which reminded me, she and I had parted this evening when she'd left with her "boyfriend," and all we'd talked about since she'd gotten home was me.

I wasn't amazing, after all.

I nudged her with my shoulder. "Hey. Tell me what happened with Donovan."

We spent the next half an hour talking about her night and *her* kiss—seems I hadn't been the only Lind girl to get some action from a Reach CEO. Then, after I'd convinced her to look on the bright side about her romantic situation, I said good night and slipped into her guest room.

It wasn't even ten o'clock, still early, considering that I was used to staying up until two in the morning most nights with my graduate studies, but Sabrina had to work in the morning, and I didn't want to be the reason she was dragging her feet come six a.m.

I was hardly tired, though. The buzz from the dinner's wine

had long ago worn off, and there was a new energy stirring in me. An excited energy. An energy that had me fidgeting and restless in the queen bed I had all to myself.

The excitement was over Dylan and the freaking insane way he knew how to use his mouth. I could imagine those lips elsewhere on my body—along the curve of my jaw, down my neck. Lower, lower. Lower still.

I'd had men go down on me, but I'd never had one give me an orgasm. I bet Dylan knew how to satisfy a woman that way. I could tell by how he controlled our kiss with his tongue. He was more alpha than he appeared, with his brooding British act. It was refreshing, considering how many guys I'd been with who had been all around nice guys, including under the covers. Too nice. So nice they didn't know when to add a little pressure or another finger or even a hair tug.

Dylan was polite, but he wasn't nice. He was respectful, but he was also aggressive. He'd practically had me coming just from our makeout session, and he hadn't even gotten his fingers inside my panties.

If that was what an older man could do, I was never planning to date a guy my age again.

I turned on my sexiest Spotify list and replayed the memory, letting the heat and electricity rush through my body like it had when I had been with Dylan. My panties were damp again. The space between my thighs ached, and if I weren't in a bed that didn't belong to me, I would have put my hand down and rubbed the desire away.

Instead, I just held the feeling, held the buzz, let it gather within me until every part of my skin was humming and alive. It made for a restless sleep when I shut the lights out hours later, after I'd taken a shower and sketched a bit in my notepad.

It would be worth it, though, I was sure of it. And it wouldn't be long until I got relief, if everything went the way I hoped it would.

I WAITED until Sabrina had left before coming out of my room for breakfast. I didn't want her to drill me about my plans for the day, and boy, did I have plans.

First, I hustled over to a boutique lingerie shop nearby Sabrina's Midtown apartment. They were on holiday schedule and opened early, so I got what I needed and was at the register well before ten.

With my purchases "in hand," so to say, I finally pulled out my phone to get ahold of Dylan. Sure, I could have texted him before I'd gone shopping, but I didn't want to seem desperate, contacting him before the sun had reached a decent place in the sky. Because I wasn't desperate. I was *eager*. There was a difference, I was sure.

I had, however, composed my text the night before so it was ready to go with just a press of the send button.

> Happy Tuesday! Did U sleep OK?

Polite, harmless. A message that wouldn't scare him off.

Still, he took his time answering. Almost seven whole minutes. Thankfully there was a Starbucks next door so I had a Venti chai tea and a place to sit by the time he responded.

> I slept well, thank you for asking. And you?

I giggled softly at his formality.

> Well enough.

If tossing and turning to a night full of erotic dreams was considered well, anyway.

> What are ur plans for today?

> I have an appointment with an estate agent to look at an apartment.

I practically squealed. He'd mentioned at dinner that he was looking to buy a place in the city so he could visit his son more often, a place he could eventually give to his son, if he wanted it. But I hadn't realized he would actually be looking today.

> Oh, goody! I'll join u. Tell me where?

While he'd taken his time responding to each of my texts so far, this one came in almost immediately.

> Ah, no. I don't think that's a good idea.

I wasn't at all discouraged. I was expecting his hesitation. He was a proper man, after all, and oftentimes the things that happened in the dark seemed less than proper in the light of day.

> It's an excellent idea! U can't get a place w/out a 2nd opinion & I have very good taste.

> I'm sure you do, but I have this handled.

I sipped from my tea, considering what tactic to take next.

> Come on. Rn't U curious about the kismet?

> Still playing that game, are you?

He hadn't said no, which meant he *was* curious. How could he not be? I'd felt his *curiosity* poking at me last night while I straddled his lap.

This text had also come in right away. Which meant I was right about my assessment of Dylan Locke so far—the man responded well to taunting.

I could do taunting. I could do it very well.

Find out.

Two little words. They'd do the trick.

Bingo.

Less than a minute later I had an address and a time to meet him. I knew I had taunting down. It was in other areas that I lacked expertise.

For the time being, anyway.

FIVE
DYLAN

I thought she'd be less dangerous in the sunlight.

I was wrong.

She walked into the lobby of the apartment building in Sutton Place, dressed in a red flowy thing that stopped mid-calf and a stylish coat that hit mid-thigh. Her tawny brown hair was loose around her shoulders. But the piece de resistance was the high-heeled black boots that disappeared under her hem. After fantasizing about her the night before, it was impossible not to imagine those shoes wrapped around my waist—wrapped around my face—her body naked and trembling. She was sex on heels, and I was a goner.

But lust wasn't the only reason I found myself fascinated with her. She and I had shared an evening together, shared the same space, shared the same air, and yet the life that oxygen breathed into her was much different than the life breathed into mine. She inflated into someone animated and vivacious while I was left hollow and shriveled and wrinkled—metaphorically if not exactly literally. It intrigued me. It was like the old adage about onlookers unable to look away from a train wreck, only I was the train wreck, and I couldn't stop looking when something so unblemished and uncorrupted walked past.

I'd been like her once, hardened by the lessons of reality over the years. While I felt surely she'd have her own dose of truth in time, the thought made me grim. Couldn't she be spared from the spoils of heartache? If I were a praying man, or even a man who wished for impossible things, I may have spent a great deal of time asking for just that. For Audrey Lind to leave this world as is, unscathed. Unbitter.

Still a believer.

"It's a fantastic part of the city!" Audrey exclaimed, skipping a greeting while I remained transfixed on the bubblegum pink of her lips. "I've never been to the Upper East Side. It has so much more charm than I'd expected."

"Yes, well, I wanted to be within walking distance of both Aaron's home and school." I hadn't thought particularly much about the borough except that it suited Ellen—snooty and elitist. I'd focused so much on that angle that I'd forgotten there were charms to the city that were untainted by my ex.

Audrey began an earnest inspection of the building, circling around me to take everything in. "First impressions are good. The lobby is clean, well-furnished. Both a doorman and a security desk—that's a nice touch." She frowned suddenly. "It's strange that they have a reprint of John Constable as the major focal point."

I tilted my head at the hanging art. I hadn't noticed the familiar piece before she pointed it out, and I wouldn't have remembered the artist's name without her mention of it. The original was hanging in the National Gallery, if I remembered correctly. It depicted a man with his hay cart and horses in the River between Essex and Suffolk counties. There was a peace and beauty in the image that I couldn't put into words.

"You don't like it?" I was surprised at her indignation at such an unsuspecting painting.

She turned her frown on me. "John Constable? I love his work. He's quite a snob about your homeland, but he showed that landscape images are not just beautiful but also powerful. I'm just curious why a luxury building would choose a cheap recreation of a famous art piece—albeit in a rather hefty frame—rather than purchasing something unique and original by a local artist. It would definitely class up the place, and it seems that is what they're going for. Maybe I should give the suggestion to the doorman." She'd already taken two steps toward the door before she finished talking.

Who did that? Who had thoughts on everything—lovely thoughts and bold thoughts, on art and luxury apartment buildings—and then proceeded to share them with no inhibitions?

Who was this woman?

And what was she doing in my life?

"Audrey, why are you here?"

My question halted her task. She spun around in my direction. "Hmm?"

"Why are you here?" A simple but pressing question.

Slowly, with a subtle grin, she strode toward me, her heels clicking on the marble floor. "You invited me. Don't you remember?"

"I'm pretty sure that's not how that went." My eyes searched aimlessly over my shoes as I attempted to recall how we ended up there together. It all happened so quickly, my hands responding to her texts without giving my brain a chance to weigh in. "No, you lured me."

"I *lured* you? How is that possible when I'm the one who has joined *you* on your day's plans? It seems, Dylan Locke, that you may have lured *me*."

Her expression was so convincing, I momentarily doubted

myself. "No, no. I most definitely didn't lure you. You lured me with your talk of fate and finding out what it had to do with us."

"Kismet," she corrected.

"Yes, that's right. *Kismet*. You dangled the word out in front of me the way a fisherman dangles a—"

"Hook?" she guessed.

I narrowed my eyes. "*Lure*."

Her smile widened. "That's amazing that a simple text message could hold that much power over you. Why do you think that is, do you suppose?"

And that was the real question, more important than why she was here. The question about why I was tempting myself with something I was never going to believe in. About why her particular lure was so irresistible. The question I'd hoped she'd be able to answer because I was at a loss.

A question that wasn't getting answered now either because the estate agent I had an appointment with was currently walking toward me with his hand stretched out.

"Mr. Locke? Jeff Jones, nice to meet you." He finished his handshake with one hand and immediately his other passed over a business card, which I immediately pocketed without looking at. I knew everything I needed to about the man from our encounter thus far. He was a salesman, a charmer. Trendy with his trimmed beard and fitted suit. Good-looking, perhaps, but if I'd had my guess, he'd had work done. His jaw was too square. His nose too straight.

All that mattered was that he had the ability to put in a competitive offer, and the ambitious air surrounding him suggested he could.

"Sorry I'm running a tad bit late," he went on, talking in that fast New York style I still hadn't become accustomed to even after the years I'd lived here. "I had a closing this morning that ran long. There are no showings on the books today for this unit, though, so we'll have plenty of time to spend in the apartment."

His focus turned to Audrey then, and his voice suddenly shifted in tone. "Well, hello there...?"

"Audrey," she said, offering her hand in greeting.

"It's a pleasure, Audrey." The smarmy way Jeff Jones held Audrey's hand, said her name, and stared too long made me want to sock him in his too perfect nose. He was too old to be flirting with her. Jeff Jones had to be at least...

At least my age.

That realization was a punch, all right. In my gut.

And that was just a warm-up to the next blow. "Mr. Locke, I didn't know you'd be bringing your daughter. Glad to have you both here."

I felt my jaw drop and then lock up, frozen in horror.

At the same time, my cock stirred.

Audrey, fortunately, remained composed. Draping her arm over my shoulder, her eyes twinkled mischievously. "He wanted my opinion, didn't you Daddy? We're very close."

Very funny, my scowl said. I considered correcting her until it dawned on me the situation looked better this way. As long as no one noticed the bulging of my trousers every time she addressed me with the parental term, anyway.

Shopping for a flat with a girl half my age...what was I thinking?

Perhaps she wasn't as young as I gave her credit for.

The estate agent excused himself to grab the key from the lockbox at the security desk. As soon as he was out of earshot, I asked quietly, "How young are you exactly?"

Audrey batted her lashes in my direction. "Are you asking how old I am? I'm twenty-three."

I nearly choked.

Nineteen years between us.

I'd lost my virginity later than I'd wanted, at the age of seventeen. If I'd knocked that woman up, our child would still be older than Audrey Lind.

It was mortifying.

The realization didn't make me want to kiss her any less. It just gave me a sufficient amount of guilt about the desire to make kissing her again seem totally worth it.

I was still stewing about the years between us when Jeff returned and led us into the lift. He pushed the button for the thirty-second floor, chattering on about the building amenities and the maintenance upkeep.

I was barely listening.

"Are you okay?" Audrey whispered.

"Just thinking about how old I feel next to you." That wasn't exactly true. I was lamenting the difference in our ages, but she didn't make me feel old. She made me feel quite young. Younger than I deserved to feel. Her youth was contagious.

"Do you want to know how I feel next to you?" She linked her arm around mine. "Bold."

Bold. Jesus. I felt like I needed to loosen my tie, except I wasn't wearing one.

The lift opened on our floor, and Jeff Jones started out the door and down the hall, not paying much attention to us as we followed. Thank God. Since I still had Audrey's hand on my bicep. Her palm felt warm even through my jumper and the button-up underneath. Like a hot iron. Like a brand from the devil reminding me she might look like an angel but she'd been sent from hell.

Gently, I shrugged her off and doubled my steps to catch up to our estate agent.

My estate agent. There was no *our* here.

Jeff continued promoting the apartment's highlights as he unlocked the door and stood aside for us to enter. Instantly, I was pleased—both with the condition of the unit and the opportunity to concentrate on something other than the young woman attempting to rock my world. I was familiar with the layout of the two-bedrooms in this particular building. An acquaintance from my New York days had lived here, and wanting to purchase the same for myself, I'd diligently watched the realty notices from London until something came up. It was small in comparison to my flat in England, but exactly what I had in mind. Clean, simple. Well laid out. On property, there was a gym, a pool, billiards tables, a large courtyard. A gem in the city and for a decent price.

I opened the foyer cupboard and found it empty, save for a few stray hangers. Before I could close it again, Audrey was there, peering inside.

"Nice, sturdy bar," she said, tugging on the garment rod. She unbuttoned her coat and peeled it off.

Jeff Jones, gentleman that he was, immediately appeared at her side to hang it up.

I stood dumbstruck, seeing for the first time the entirety of Audrey's outfit. She was wearing a wrap dress. A sexy, fitted thing with only a tie separating her underclothing from the eyes of the world. *Kill me now.*

I had to turn away.

Pretending she wasn't there, I made my way through the rest of the apartment ahead of her, checking out the bathroom and the second bedroom before making my way to the main living area. The space was staged and styled with traditional furniture in fashionable colors, a look that I made a note to mimic after I purchased, with one addition—curtains. It was a corner unit, and the large windows surrounding the room delivered views of both the river and the city. Stunning as they were, the lack of window coverings meant no privacy. People in the building across the street could look right in if they had a mind to.

"Incredible!" Audrey gasped from behind me. She ran giddily to look outside, stopping several feet short of the actual windows.

"You don't feel the true impact without getting close up." I'd apparently forgotten my determination to pretend she wasn't there.

"That's okay. I'm good right here. I'm afraid of heights." She glanced quickly to Jeff Jones who'd entered the room with her. "You know that, Daddy," she added, remembering her ruse.

I hadn't thought she could be afraid of anything, daring and impetuous that she was. This new insight added to the enigma of Audrey Lind. Part wildling, part devil, part innocent, all contradiction.

"I thought you'd grown out of it," I muttered. Whatever was I doing, playing along?

And she was invading my space again, standing too close, smelling too good. Making my jumper feel too hot and my throat feel too tight.

I had to hurry this tour up.

Sticking my hands in my trouser pockets, I turned to the agent. "The website said this unit is up for lease as well as for sale. Rentals are allowed in the HOA amendments, then?"

Jones perked at the potential sale. "Yes. Is that of interest to you?"

"I'm not planning to be here year-round, so yes. I may consider leasing it out." Frankly, I was just as happy to leave it empty, a safe space for Aaron to hide out as he got older. Ellen would surely disapprove, which was half the appeal. "There's no one living here now?"

"Not at this moment. But!" He was winding up for his big pitch. I could feel it. "This unit has had several showings just in the last few days."

Not likely with the weather and the approaching holiday.

"If it gets rented out before an offer comes in, the lease will have to be dealt with in negotiations. It's another reason to act fast if you're serious about buying."

I'd have an offer in before the day was over, though I wasn't ready to admit it. But, even if I paid cash and rushed a closing, I wouldn't be in the unit before I left New York this time at the end of the week.

The idea of being in there sooner, to have the breathing room and get away from the stuffiness of the hotel, suddenly appealed to me. "I could, you're telling me, put in an offer and also apply for a lease at the same time."

"That's correct. If you want to try it out and see how it works before you decide to purchase, or if you want to move in right away, that's exactly what I'd recommend. You could be in here as soon as tomorrow, in fact."

Audrey edged up beside me, the heat of her a pleasant nuisance.

I felt my muscles tighten as I fought to remain focused. "It comes furnished?"

"Yes."

"I'd like to fill out a rental application." It was still early in the day. I'd push to be in by that evening.

"Sure, sure! I didn't realize you'd be interested in renting as well, so I didn't bring the application, but we can get that all settled if you just come with me to the leasing office. It's only a few blocks away. No more than a fifteen minute walk. Or if you'd rather grab a cab, it'll take just about as long."

I wouldn't rather grab a cab. And I wasn't interested in walking fifteen minutes in the snow and slush. I was irritated at the man's lack of foresight. Wasn't there an application at the desk along with the lockbox? What a professional faux pas.

The agent didn't seem to register my annoyance.

Audrey, on the other hand, read me completely.

"Mr. Jones," she said, her tone pure honey. "Jeff." She left my side to cozy up against the salesman, immediately triggering a rush of envy through my veins. I might have stopped her, even, if I weren't so curious about her motives.

"It's so cold outside today," she went on, swirling the tip of her finger in a giant O on the shoulder of Jones' suit jacket. "I've just started getting warm. You wouldn't mind terribly going and getting the application and bringing it back for us, would you? I know Daddy would love to have the extra time looking around the place."

Her coy manipulation, the sweet pout of her mouth, the damn use of the word *daddy*—I wouldn't be able to walk to the lift at this point, let alone to an office three blocks away.

I was a sick fuck. There was no doubt about it.

Jones hemmed and hawed. "Oh. I don't know about that. I'm really not supposed to leave you alone here."

He hadn't moved away from the girl, though. His dilated eyes and flushed face said he was under her spell and loving it. In front of her father, no less!

Fake father. But he didn't know that.

"Oh, but, Jeff!" Audrey batted her eyelashes. "He's going to buy it! Or, he will if he has the proper time to decide. There's a pretty significant commission on this unit, isn't there? I'd hate for you to lose out simply because of a silly, little rule."

She was good. So very good.

"Your daughter is sure convincing." Jones smiled nervously in my direction, appearing to be equally taken with her abilities. "Okay. All right. I'm sure it will be fine. I'll be back in about thirty minutes then?" He was headed to the exit, as though determined to be back as soon as possible.

At the foyer, he paused to look from me to Audrey with an anxious plea in his eyes. "Please don't do, well, don't...hurt...anything." I heard him muttering on to himself as the door shut behind him. Something that sounded a lot like *I better not regret this.*

Which left me with my own regrets, namely the seductress in my midst.

"That was quite impressive," I said, not quite sure if I should have gone with the man rather than be left alone with her. Alone. So near a bed. And other furniture that could be used for fornication.

She winked. "I have my talents."

Yes, she did. I was learning how skilled she was at wrapping men twice her age around her little pinkie. And now I was quite sure I should have left when I'd had the chance.

Still, she had me on that string, towing me toward her when I should be swimming away. Could I even swim away at this point? Understanding how my fate was tied up in her—never mind that it was because she masterminded the whole thing—I considered giving in to the pull.

I circled her, studying every delicious curve. "The thing I don't understand as of yet is why it was so important to you that he let us stay here?"

I stopped when I was facing her again so I had the full vantage point when she undid the tie at the side of her dress, shrugged it off her shoulders, and let it drop to the floor.

Audrey Lind in nothing but her high-heeled boots and the naughtiest pair of matching panties and bra I'd ever seen on a woman.

Goddamn, this apartment really needed curtains.

SIX
AUDREY

Dylan seemed to go pale. He normally had rather fair skin—probably because he was British and because his work habits didn't let him out in the sun too often—but now he was even whiter than usual.

Maybe it was a bit scandalous to just drop my dress the way I had. I could have talked to him about my plan first, but after the way he'd kissed me the night before, I didn't think conversation was necessary. I was certainly still buzzing from the feel of his lips and the sweep of his tongue. I thought a little skin would be all that was needed to reignite those passions in him as well.

Instead, it seemed to throw him into a state of shock.

"Audrey," he stammered, his eyes darting everywhere, then to me, then quickly to anywhere else but me. He was deliberately trying not to look, but it seemed he couldn't help himself. "What the bloody hell are you doing, girl?" He picked my dress up off the floor and brought it to me. "Put this on. Please. There aren't curtains. The whole city can see you!"

I glanced behind him at the windows. We were too high for anyone to see in through the street, and the apartments across the way didn't have the floor-to-ceiling glass that this unit had. It was unlikely anyone could see me from there either.

I took the dress from him anyway. Then tossed it over my shoulder to the ground. "I don't care if everyone can see me. I only care if you see me."

This made the color return to his face.

"And as for what I'm doing," I continued, stepping toward him, but before I could say more he interrupted.

"If you have more to say then could you please do it from the couch? Which is over there. A safe distance from me."

He muttered the last part so quietly that I wasn't even sure I was supposed to hear it.

It made me smile. He really was quite adorable. "If it makes you more comfortable." I shrugged.

"It does."

"Well, then." I didn't mind humoring him. And torturing him simultaneously. I sat on the sofa, crossing one leg over the other, hoping the slow, seductive routine didn't come off as clumsy and embarrassing. Just because I felt confident didn't mean I knew what I was doing. Hence this entire kismet project.

Dylan immediately lined himself up between me and the window, using his body to make up for the lack of blinds.

See? Adorable.

"As you were saying," he prompted.

"As I was saying." I took a breath in and let it out. "Here's the deal—I've had two serious boyfriends in my life. Two men that I've had sex with, and I didn't sleep with either of them until we'd said the L word. Which is to say, I don't do this. Ever."

"Mm hmm." His arms were crossed over his chest and he nodded furiously, as though urging me to go on.

So I did. "With both of them the sex was blah."

"Right. You didn't find either of them compatible. Yes, yes.

You told me this last night. I remember. How exactly does this lead to you standing naked in my flat?"

"Not your flat yet, Dylan," I teased. "And not naked. I have lingerie on. Purchased just for you." I uncrossed my legs, stretched them out in front of me, and leaned back on my palms so he could have the best view of my ensemble. "Do you like?"

"I, uh." He cleared his throat. "I do like. Very much."

The piercing gaze he hit me with made my heart trip and my skin prickle with goosebumps.

"But that doesn't explain the, um..." He gestured toward me with his entire hand. "This."

I chuckled. "I'm getting there. I was getting there last night, too, just, your lips became a distraction." Maybe I'd gone over the top in the flirtation department, but it didn't make the statement any less true. Besides, it was worth it to see the color in his cheeks deepen and the crotch of his pants expand while he let himself remember our kiss.

It was especially worth it because of how *much* his pants expanded. Dang, that man was hung.

After a distracted beat, I went on. "Anyway. After my last breakup, I decided that I needed to get the sex ed out of the way before I settle down. So. Isn't it kismet that I met you? An experienced man who is only interested in banging? Wouldn't you like to bang me now? Show me how it's done?"

He inhaled sharply then clutched his chest with one hand, wiping at his forehead with the other as he fell back against the glass behind him.

I stood up, panicked. "Dylan! Are you okay? Are you having a heart attack?" I rushed to him, but he waved me away and stumbled toward the couch.

"I'm fine, I'm fine. As long as you stay there, several feet from me, I'm fine."

Not his heart, then, but a good old-fashioned panic attack.

I gave him a lazy grin. "How many feet away? Like is this too close?" I stepped predatorily near him. "Or how about this?" Another step.

"It's all too close. All of it. You and me in this same flat is too close." He circled around the sofa, backing away from me as though I were a demon about to put a hex on him.

"Why ever would you say that?" I asked innocently, following every step he took. "If anything, I'd say we aren't close enough."

"No, no, no. This is not appropriate. This shouldn't be happening. You should have your clothes on, for God's sake. I shouldn't have even allowed you to come here."

His rant felt directed more to himself than to me, but I continued to engage. "That's a terrible thing to say! Aren't we having fun together? The whole 'daddy' game with your realtor? That was a good time, wasn't it?"

He laughed incredulously as he rounded back to the front of the couch, one arm held out before himself as if to ward me off. "A good time is not the term I'd... Okay, yes, it was a fun bluff, but... Your sister is an employee in my firm! You are twenty years my junior!"

"Is it really twenty?" I'd told him my age, but he hadn't mentioned his to me. Sabrina hadn't even been certain. Not that it mattered. The important thing was that we were attracted to each other. That we had chemistry. And we definitely had that, whether he wanted to admit it or not.

"Yes, I'm sure. Or, it's nearly twenty. Nineteen, to be precise."

"Nineteen." I thought about that for a minute, growing more comfortable with the idea by the moment. "That's kind of hot, isn't it? That a woman that you're interested in who is nineteen years your junior is throwing herself at you? Begging you to teach her a thing or two. Or seven."

I'd closed in on him while I was talking, trapping him against the armchair. He didn't realize until he'd tripped and fell backward into the seat, but he'd only caught the edge in his fall and immediately slipped to the ground.

And I slipped right into his lap.

I spread my legs, straddling him the way I had the night before. His breath came fast, but even, and his skin was hot to the touch as I swept my finger across his forehead, brushing away the hair that had fallen there. He locked his eyes on mine, the pupils darkening as they lingered in his stare.

"I'm supposing you don't need CPR," I teased. I was terrible, but he was too easy.

His gaze narrowed. "My heart is fine. It's my morals that I'm struggling with."

"Because I'm so young? Because of Sabrina?"

"Yes. Even if we can ignore that I'm your sister's superior I am definitely old enough to be..." He shook his head, unable to finish the sentence.

"My father? I told you I thought that was hot. Are you going to tell me it doesn't interest you at all?"

He didn't answer but swallowed, his Adam's apple bobbing with the action.

"Because I won't believe you if you do. There's definitive proof to the contrary."

He scowled even as I could feel his body relaxing underneath me. "What proof?"

"This bad boy." I ground my hips, rubbing against his erection, nearly moaning from the thickness of it.

"There's a near-naked beautiful woman sitting on him. He can't help himself. He has a mind of his own and is not always in agreement with my decisions." Contrary to his words, he stroked a single finger up my arm, sending a shiver down my spine.

Even this...even just the deliberate way he touched me was

more experienced than the men I'd been with. Boys, really, fumbling to get their cock inside me without any sort of prelude. My dirty professor was a *man*. Someone who knew exactly what to do with a woman. Who could show me how to handle him in return.

"He perked up long before I was sitting on him," I said, tilting my hips again.

This time he was the one to shudder. "You noticed that then?"

"It was quite hard to miss."

His lips turned up into a cocky smile as he drew his finger further up my arm, over my shoulder to the strap of my bra. He fiddled with the thin elastic, so leisurely, so carefully, that I thought I might explode when he finally touched me for real.

Once more, I tilted my hips back and then forward, tracing the stiff length of his cock with the damp crotch panel of my panties. I'd meant it to hurry him up, urge him into kissing me, but it felt so good that I was the one who threw my head back and sighed.

Next thing I knew, I was on my back, on the floor, my hands pinned above my head with Dylan stretched out above me.

Wow. That move was...wow. So manly and take-charge-like. So alpha and swoony.

Somehow, he was even more good-looking from this angle. His expression was serious and heated, the creases near his eyes intense as he focused on me.

My heart thumped against my rib cage, pounding, pounding at the possibility of what was to come next.

"You don't seem to need any lessons in the art of seduction," he said sternly. Fatherly, almost, except for the sexy, rough edge to his voice.

"You're right. I know how to seduce a man." I spread my legs, making room for him to settle in between my thighs. His eyes closed briefly as the ridge of his erection sunk down across my center. "What I don't know is how to tell a man what I like. How can I if I don't know what I like myself? If no one has ever shown me anything worth repeating."

He studied me silently for a moment. Every second felt like thirty as I measured time with the rapid lift and fall of my chest, waiting for him to make the next move, waiting for him to agree.

"And you think I can show you what you might like?" His gaze shifted to my mouth then back to my eyes.

I licked my lips in anticipation of the kiss he was obviously looking forward to as much as I was. "You've already shown me more than you can know."

His expression said he doubted that. "Assuming that's true...how do I know you won't fall for me in the process? You don't have a track record to prove you can separate sex from love."

Wasn't that a killer of a question?

He had every right to ask. I wasn't the least bit upset about it, though it did make me feel like the wind had been sucked out of my chest. Made me feel dizzy and unsure when just a moment ago I'd been drowning in confidence.

"I guess..." I started out tentatively, formulating the answer as I gave it. "I guess you *don't* know that. I guess I don't really know it either. I could try to convince you it isn't your problem—I'll be gone at the end of the week, and you'll be on the other side of the ocean—but I have a feeling you're the kind of guy that would very much think it was his problem, no matter where he was. You might not be fond of the love emotion, but you do recognize it in other people. That you acknowledge the weight it can carry might be what makes me feel so safe with you."

That was a revelation. I hadn't quite realized why I trusted him to be the guy to take on this task. We'd only just met. I shouldn't be this sure about him. But, just like he was afraid of how I'd react to this arrangement because I'd shown enough of myself for him to know it was a possibility, I also had seen enough of him to know I trusted him.

"I trust you," I told him. "I trust you to be careful with my body, and I trust that you won't lead me on in any way. That's a good start, isn't it?"

Before he could say anything, I pushed forward, my words tumbling out rapidly. "And what I can tell you for sure is that I don't have any *intentions* of becoming emotionally wrapped up in you. I *am* attracted to you. Crazy attracted to you. Turn-my-insides-into-mush kind of attracted to you, but I've always been able to separate attraction from real feelings. I've been crazy attracted to men before, given a few blow jobs to some of them, even, but I've only fallen in hard love with those two guys. Guys I *hadn't* slept with while the falling was occurring. Maybe that can help you trust me? It's not very reassuring, I suppose. I don't know what else to say. I hope that doesn't make you tell me no, though, because, Dylan, I *want* this. I want to learn from you. I want—"

He cut me off, crashing his mouth into mine. His lips were firm and persuasive, telling mine exactly where to move and what speed. Telling them when to open and take more. I responded eagerly, matching the strokes of his tongue with my own as soft whimpers escaped from my throat. My sounds made him groan and made me wet—wetter than I already was, that is. He swept me up with his kiss. He took me from the solid ground into a spiraling, dizzy windstorm.

He continued to hold my wrists above my head, which I found both highly erotic and frustrating at the same time. I wanted to caress his jaw. I wanted to slip my hands underneath his sweater. I wanted to draw the pads of my thumbs across his nipples and then trail my fingers down, down, down.

Unable to touch him the way I wanted, the rest of me became more antsy beneath him, as though trying to make up for my restrained hands. I squirmed and bucked, trying to get as much of my body to come into contact with his as possible. But he counteracted every one of my moves, bracing his body higher above me, holding himself away.

It took me a few minutes to realize he was purposefully taunting me.

Then it took me another few minutes to realize I really liked this too. I mean, I hated it. But as the torture continued, a tension built inside me, low and deep. A hum that spread through my core and out to my limbs. By the time he lowered himself to grind across my crotch, I was already halfway to an orgasm.

From there, the hum intensified quickly. Each thrust of his pelvis against mine sent me closer to the edge. He still had his pants on! I still had on panties, and yet he'd found the perfect spot, hit it on every stroke, making the hum swell and expand and consume and take over and buzz, buzz, buzz, and...

Suddenly it was all gone at the sound of a clearing throat.

Guess when I'd sent the agent away I'd forgotten that he'd also be coming back.

Whoops.

I wasn't sorry. I wasn't sorry at all.

SEVEN
DYLAN

I'd never lost an erection so fast.

Thank God, since it made it easier to scramble to my feet and distract Jeff Jones so Audrey could clothe herself privately. I was sweating and panicked as I diverted him back to the foyer. Behind me, I could hear the girl giggling.

It wasn't funny. It wasn't.

That she was laughing was a splendid example of why our age difference was a big problem. She was obviously not mature enough to handle matters that required adult responsibility. I was disappointed in myself for not being the adult from the start. If she hadn't been so tenacious, so assertive, so *beguiling*, I wouldn't have lost control of the situation.

And I *had* lost control. Really lost it. Almost gone too far, even.

The whole thing had left me flustered, and now there was a real chance I wasn't going to get this apartment.

"It's...I'm...this isn't at all what it looks like," I explained to the agent. I ran a hand through my hair, creating a floppy mess if

I were to judge by the uneven way it felt on my scalp. "I sincerely apologize. It was inappropriate and discourteous and—"

"Just tell me one thing," Mr. Jones interrupted. "She's not really your daughter, is she?"

"No! God, no." I thought about it after I'd answered, what that must have looked like to the man when he'd walked in on us. It had been bad enough that we'd behaved so badly in an flat I hadn't yet leased. The fact that he'd also thought we were father and daughter was...

Well. Maybe it *was* funny.

"I'm sorry. I don't know why we said that she was." The grin that had slid onto my face made my latest apology seem insincere.

Fortunately, Jeff Jones was smiling too. "It's fine. I understand. I'm sure I'd play that game too if I were with a woman so..."

"Young?" Yes, I knew she was too young. He didn't need to throw it in my face.

"I was going to say willing. But maybe her youth has something to do with it." He peered over my shoulder, which made me have to glance behind me as well, insuring he wasn't seeing anything he shouldn't be seeing.

He wasn't. Audrey was dressed now and was simply straightening the tie of her wrap.

That didn't stop Jones from leering at her. "You're a very lucky man, Mr. Locke."

"Yes. I am," I said sternly, subtly enforcing a claim on her that I didn't have. His leer bothered me. A lot. I probably wouldn't have responded so possessively otherwise.

His smile faded, and the man looked appropriately cowed. He opened his mouth and closed it twice, as though trying to discern the best way to react.

I put him out of his misery and nodded at the file in his

hands. "Are those the papers for the lease? Can I sign them now?"

"Oh! Yes. You may." He led me to the kitchen island where he spread out the contract in front of me. "Since we had you pre-approved before today, we've got all the finance and reference information that we need. You just need to initial the first two pages and put your John Hancock on the last, and I can hand over the keys right now."

He handed me a pen from inside the breast pocket of his jacket.

"And the terms of the contract are...?"

He used the pen to point to the paragraph answering my question. "Six months or until the unit is sold. If you're planning to purchase outright—"

"I am."

"—then you'll just want to make sure the sale goes through before the lease expires."

"I'll do that straight away." I took the pen and signed where he'd indicated.

When I was finished, Audrey sidled up next to me and clutched onto my arm. "Is it ours now?" she asked coyly.

I narrowed my eyes in her direction but didn't dispute the pretense that we were buying the flat together. It didn't feel necessary to confuse the agent any further, and besides, I was quite comfortable with the man believing Audrey was unavailable.

"Not quite yet, my dear, but we do get to have the keys now." I let the agent hand one to her so as not to destroy the latest ruse. I pocketed the duplicates. "Mr. Jones is going to put together an offer for us so we can buy the place outright."

"Sweet!" she exclaimed gazing up at me, and her eyes twinkled so spectacularly that I couldn't help imagining for a moment that we really were purchasing the place together. A pied-à-terre where I would teach her everything she wanted to know about her body and mine. As though she were a student, perhaps. The fantasy *was* "sweet." Delicious, even.

Too delectable to keep thinking about for too long.

I cleared my throat, forcing the fancy to dissipate from my head. "Do you need anything else from us?"

We briefly discussed an amount to offer the seller and decided the agent would pull up a few comps and get back to me before we confirmed the final number. I shook hands with him, watched with ire as he kissed the back of Audrey's hand, and then walked him to the door.

Once he was gone, I turned back to my companion and realized my mistake—I was again alone with Audrey. And this time there would be no one coming back to interrupt us.

Her expression said she'd realized the same thing. She didn't seem quite as upset about it as I was, though.

I thought quickly. "I shouldn't suggest this, but—"

"Yes. You should," she encouraged, stalking slowly toward me.

"Perhaps you'd like to join me somewhere for lunch."

Her face fell. "Oh. Then you aren't going to help me out after all?"

Jesus, she was enchanting. Magnificently so. The pout of her mouth, the way her top lip formed a sharp V, the liquid almond of her eyes—it was impossible to deny her. I'd be a liar to say that I could.

"I'm not saying that. I just think this might be a task best suited for a different time. I'm picking up my son this afternoon, and I need to stop by the office to chat with Nate and Weston and Donovan about a few things while we're all in the same place. Also, I have to bring my belongings from the hotel to the flat. Surely you have plans with Sabrina."

She let out a loud sigh, not unlike the teenage sighs I heard often enough from Aaron. "We're seeing a Broadway show tonight. I'm supposed to meet her at the office around four."

"Good. That leaves us time for lunch." I pulled her coat from the cupboard and helped her put it on. "We can work out an arrangement for the, er, the other thing from there."

She linked her arm through mine and beamed up at me. "Sounds like a plan, professor."

My trousers tightened at her newest title for me. Daddy? Professor? Did she know she'd hit the bullseye on my hot buttons?

If she didn't, her naivety certainly added to her allure.

And if she *did* know, as I expected she did, I had to wonder—what exactly could she possibly learn from me?

"I KNEW it would happen one day, honestly. He's a teenager now. He wants to spend his school breaks on skiing trips with his friends and playing marathon sessions of Fortnite, or whatever the game is he's into at the moment. He doesn't want to waste half of his holidays stuck in an aeroplane traveling to visit his boring old father." I paused to take a swallow of my champagne. It was early for alcohol, but Audrey had said the finding of my apartment had warranted a celebration, and as I'd already discovered, it was impossible to deny her whims.

Which was also why I'd spent the last ten minutes waxing on about Aaron. What a boring subject for a young female companion. Nothing could bring out the old man in me like reminding me of my teenager. I knew better than to bring up the topic, but as soon as the waiter had taken our order, she'd asked.

And she was compelling, that one was. She didn't have to ask twice.

To her credit, she'd remained engaged throughout my indulgent rant, asking questions, adding commentary. "He's so young," she said now—ironically, I thought. "This is just a phase of growing up. I remember feeling the same way at that age—not about my father. He died when I was thirteen. And then Sabrina left school to look after me, and I remember feeling so smothered. Like, I knew she'd sacrificed for me, and that should make me more appreciative, but I was a total pain in her behind. I resented her, for some reason. I didn't want her around. I mean, I *did*, but I didn't act like I did. I grew out of it—mostly. Aaron will too."

She really was lovely. Giving me advice on my son, who I felt more and more out of touch with as the years went by, was not something I expected at all in exchange for my help with her situation.

No, my reward for that was simply being the man she'd chosen as her tutor.

"He will. I know he will," I agreed. My stepdaughter had been the same way. At the time it had been hard to distinguish whether it was an age-related behavior or if it had been caused by my intrusion into her life. Amanda and I had gotten along well, but a new stepfather is always an adjustment.

I tapped my finger along the rim of the champagne glass. "Why do you think children resent the elders caring for them? Is there some secret club that requires that as an initiation into adulthood that I don't remember?"

She laughed. "Actually, sort of yes. You hit puberty, and your body is suddenly an adult body, which doesn't mean you make adult choices yet, but you *think* you do. And here's this person who—in my case—isn't much older than you, and she's in charge of all the rules, and some of them are ridiculous, and you know that she's wrong about everything, even if she did set her future aside to be there for you, and how can you not resent that? Then you grow up a little more and realize, oh, fudge. She was right about almost everything."

She ran her tongue over her bottom lip and brought her point back to me. "In your case, you don't live with Aaron every day. Yet you still have automatic authority over him, and he has to believe he knows better than you. And maybe he does sometimes, but he can't possibly realize all the times he doesn't. All you can do is give him lots of space to express what he feels. And then more space to let him feel it. And all the while you'll be there, hanging back, but close enough to protect him if he needs it."

"Sage advice." I meant it too. She was as wise as she was dear, it appeared. "I hope that's exactly what I'm doing with buying the flat. I don't want to force him to be with me, but I still want to be near him, when I can. I'll come for Christmas and spring break, and I'll spend as much of the summer as I can over here. It's only three years until he graduates from high school, and if he decides he really wants to go to NYU like he says he wants to, then he'll have a place to live that isn't with his mother. It would be cruel to expect him to live with that monster a minute longer than he has to."

Usually I wasn't that awful about Ellen to other people, particularly people who were practically strangers, but Audrey was a good listener, and I was not on the best terms with my ex as of late. The chance to be honest was simultaneously refreshing and concerning.

Audrey's eyebrows rose. "A monster? So she's the awful creature that poisoned you into believing you had to be a pessimist to survive the world."

"I'm not a pessimist—I'm a realist. I'm sure it's difficult to tell the difference when you're as unrealistically optimistic as you are—"

"Hey, now!"

I smiled to let her know I was teasing. Mostly. "But I promise you that the glasses I'm looking through are quite clear. There was no poison except truth."

"The worst poison of all." Her cheeks were pink and her eyes bright, and I suspected she was yanking my chain, but it was hard to care. Her attention was pleasant enough to make up for any mocking.

She must have felt guilty for it, though, because she grew serious then. "I'm sorry. I don't know her at all. Or your situation. She's probably a terrible beast. I can't imagine any other reason a woman wouldn't get along with you."

And now *I* felt guilty.

"No, she wasn't a terrible beast. Not really." Even with her affairs, even though she'd stopped loving me long before I'd stopped loving her. "She was broken and in grief, and it's easier to believe that she was a shitty human being rather than facing the fact that I couldn't make things better for her. That I wasn't a strong enough anchor to hold onto her. That I hadn't loved her enough to replace the things she'd lost."

I'd never said that before. Not out loud. Not really to myself, even, except in the wake of consuming several glasses of bourbon.

Audrey blinked at me sympathetically. "Wow. That's heavy. Does it feel good to be able to admit that?"

"No." It *didn't* feel good. It felt extremely shitty, but it did feel authentic, and that felt meaningful. "I'm glad I said it, though." I threw back the rest of my champagne, hoping to cover up the awkward aftertaste of my confession.

When that didn't work, I deflected. "And now it seems you know the source of my bitterness, what's the source of your *not-bitterness*?"

"My parents," she said quickly.

This surprised me, mostly because I hadn't expected she'd have an answer at all.

"My father, actually," she corrected herself. "I was only nine when my mother died, so memories of her and them together is a bit hazy, but what I do remember is how much he loved her. How he doted on her and took care of her and adored her, even after her death. He had such respect and devotion for her ghost that it almost felt like she was still there when she'd gone. He kept her present. He didn't date after her, and he had every reason to be sad and miserable without her—raising two girls on his own, especially—but his love for her kept him happy and upbeat right up until he passed himself."

I scrutinized her as I carefully framed what I wanted to say in my head. How could I present my view while still being delicate about treading on her childlike notions about what went on in someone else's relationship? "You don't think that you could be romanticizing their relationship? As you said, thirteen is awfully young..." I knew it came out patronizing even when I'd intended it not to.

Or, perhaps that's what I'd exactly intended. Whether her parents had actually had a magical marriage or not, she obviously believed that it was the ultimate goal. She didn't realize those relationships were not typical, and that she could love and dote and devote herself to the man of her dreams, and he would still shit all over her.

She needed saving from her fairy-tale notions.

But was I the hero for being the asshole who exposed the reality of her sweet memories?

She didn't fall for it for a minute.

"There he is!" She pointed at me while giving me a toothy grin. "There's the man I met last night. You've been almost likable all afternoon. I was beginning to wonder if your curmudgeon behavior had all been an act." She clapped her hands together suddenly. "You know what it is? I'm good for you! I bring out the best in you. How lucky you met me!"

How lucky I met her? "Humbug," I said. But it was impossible not to smile.

And as long as I was being authentic, as long as I was being honest, she did bring out the best in me. She reminded me of that pure passion I'd felt for life so long ago. It was nice to remember that man I'd once been, even if it wasn't a man I ever wanted to be again.

But she was wrong on one point—it wasn't *good* for me. *She* wasn't good for me. To believe she was would be an absolute lie.

EIGHT

AUDREY

> Are you still awake?

My pulse picked up at the message from Dylan when it arrived. It was half past midnight, and I'd texted him hours ago during the intermission of *Waitress*. I'd been antsy waiting for a response, afraid he was bailing on me, so obviously, I was relieved to see his name, to say the least.

Now was a better time to talk to him anyway. Sabrina was already asleep, and I wasn't as into my reading of *A Curator's Handbook* as I should have been.

But I *was* into Dylan Locke. *More* than I should have been.

> I was beginning to think u'd gotten cold feet.

> Ha ha. No. Not particularly. It was a lot of rigamarole to get the flat ready for habitation, even though it came furnished. Then Aaron and I had to battle through Latin homework. After that, we ordered pizza and played a rousing game of Risk.

I giggled. He was so formal and long-winded in his messages. No one spoke like that in text. No one used proper grammar. But *he* did. He texted like he talked. I'd probably make fun of him about it someday—I was known to tease—but secretly I loved it. It was old-fashioned and charming.

I curled my feet underneath me in Sabrina's guest room armchair and typed out a response.

> Risk, huh. He let u win, didn't he?

> Now that you mention it...I really think he did.

I could picture it—a baby teenage boy, awkward and gangly after a recent growth spurt, chocolate eyes like his father, a dry but still underdeveloped sense of humor. The two would crack witty wisecracks while forming armies and taking over the world, and Dylan would be so enamored with the idea of connecting with his son, he wouldn't see that the same son was throwing the game.

It was a sweet image, and even if it was inaccurate, I liked imagining it that way. It made me miss my dad who'd died ten years ago this holiday season. I had fond memories of nights when it was just the two of us. Years after my mother had died when Sabrina had gone off to school at Harvard. Nights playing Rummikub past midnight. After I'd win a handful of games, I'd start losing on purpose so my father would stay interested in playing.

Those were good times.

These were beautiful moments Dylan was creating, too. Did he know that? He had to assume they had some meaning. Why else be so engaged? Why else buy an apartment he only planned on using a handful of times a year? He was a very wealthy businessman, a man I suspected that could afford staff and "people" to look after all his needs. He probably lived quite a different life when he was back home in London, but here, where his son was concerned, he seemed very ordinary. He was just like most dads. He cared about his kid, and it showed.

It made me want to care too. It made me want to ask too many questions and get involved.

But that was always my problem—I cared too easily. And this wasn't a situation where caring helped me.

I blew the air from my lungs and shook my head free from sentimental thoughts. Yes, Dylan was a good dad. But I needed to focus on the kind of "daddy" he could be to me.

This was a conversation I decided would be best voice-to-voice.

I hit the phone icon next to his name and put the receiver up to my ear.

And then I waited.

And waited.

He made me wait four flipping rings before answering. Four long rings where I pictured him staring at my name on his screen and panicking, trying to decide what to do.

Answer it, you nincompoop! You were just texting me! I know you're there!

"Audrey," he said in a stern bass when he finally picked up. It made my stomach buzz deep and low, as though trying to match his pitch and resonance.

"Dylan," I said, in kind.

Then neither of us said anything and silence stretched out between us.

It wasn't awkward silence, really, but it was noticeable. Noticeable enough that my lips went dry, and my hands began to sweat. It seemed to me it was his turn to say something since I'd just spoken, whatever it was that I'd said. I'd already forgotten. I was too consumed with replaying the way he'd said my name. How beautiful it sounded when he said it in his very British dialect. It made me feel regal and classic and adored, which was crazy since we were practically strangers.

But I felt that way all the same.

And I sat there without speaking as I soaked it in. I didn't know what *his* reason was for not talking, but that was mine.

"*You* called *me*," he said eventually. "I believe you have the obligation to do the talking here, Audrey."

That answered that question. And he'd said my name again, and I felt heady.

But I got my act together, somehow. "Yes. Right! I wanted to tell you that I can be there in half an hour. Sooner if you don't mind getting me in my pajamas. What I wear shouldn't really matter since the clothes won't be on long anyway. Unless that's not how you do things. Do you keep your clothes on and just uncover the necessary part? That does sound hot, in a way. Maybe the secret to all my bad sex was getting naked?"

"Bad sex from getting naked? No. I don't think that's it. I've done both with the same results. I expect we'll see what...hold on. Hold on. What am I even saying?" He sounded flustered, like he always was when I threw myself at him. I found that part charming as well. "Audrey, it's nearly one in the morning. And Aaron is still here. He's sleeping right now, but I don't think it would be appropriate to have a late-night visitor of the female persuasion."

Yeah, probably not.

"Or any persuasion, for that matter. Ellen would have my hide, and the whole purpose of getting this flat was to make things easier between all of us, not more strained."

"Fine," I said, laying as much disappointment as possible into the single syllable.

He let out a slow breath, and I pictured him running a hand through his hair as he did. I'd seen him do it on more than one occasion, and now it had become A Very Dylan gesture in my mind.

"What's your day look like tomorrow?" he asked.

It was my turn to sigh. "Tomorrow's terrible. Well, not terrible, really. Terrible for the two of us getting together, though. Sabrina took the day off to take me around the city. And then we're seeing the Rockettes' Christmas show. It's going to be jam-packed with holiday fun. Woot! Oh, hey! Maybe you could come up with some project she needs to take care of at the office, and make her have to cancel her plans so she can come in and work."

"I can't possibly do that. I'm not in her direct chain of command. I don't even work in the same office. Not to mention the questionable judgement of ethics required to use my authority over her simply to arrange a booty call. And you can't tell me you don't want to spend time with your sister. You came here for Thanksgiving break to be with her, not with..." He paused and seemed to come to his senses. "I see now. You were winding me up."

I bit my lip to stifle a laugh. "I was totally 'winding you up.'" I was also keeping that phrase and using it forever and ever. "But I'm thoroughly impressed with your moral code. You're a good man, Dylan Locke."

"Or, at least, I'm a gullible one." He laughed softly. "Then if the daytime is off the table, that leaves the night. I'm meeting with some old friends for dinner so I won't have Aaron. I don't imagine we'll go too late, and I can cut it short if need be. Will you be too tired to make a trip over here after your show?"

"Uh, I'm a college student. All-nighters are kind of my gig. The question is—will it be a problem for you, old man?"

"You like to remind me of our age difference, I think." I could practically hear his scowl through the line.

"Only because it makes you so hot and bothered."

"Does it make *you* hot and bothered?" His voice had dropped and the words that came out were ragged.

"Yes, Professor Locke." My answer sounded just as raw as the question, and the buzz in my belly had spread out through my limbs. It made me hotter the more I thought I about it.

"Let me ask you then—as your professor, I should know what sort of prior education you've acquired."

Oh, geez. He was always incredibly sexy, but he was even hotter when he played the teacher part. Especially when he was also enthusiastic.

"Um." I stood up to pace the room, hoping to release some of the restlessness he stirred in me. "Let's see."

"If you're uncomfortable discussing this—"

"I'm not," I cut him off. "At all. I just know our time is limited, and I have a lot to learn."

"I find it hard to believe that you are truly that inexperienced. Why don't you just lay it all out, and I can decide what would be most useful for us to focus on?"

I got the sense that he wasn't so much feeling me out as he was feeling himself out. Trying to decide if he was really up for what I wanted of him.

It was probably a cue for me to proceed cautiously.

But cautious wasn't my nature. "Okay, then. I'm pretty sure I'm good on blowjobs. I can deepthroat and swallow and I know the tricks about humming and using a peppermint lifesaver at the same time. And I've never had any complaints in that area, but if you think you might have something to teach me... I'm terrible at receiving oral sex, on the other hand. I can't ever decide if it feels good or just weird, and that makes me tense, and I never come. And positions. I've done missionary practically every time. Oh, and cowgirl—or whatever it's called when the girl is on top. But I don't think I know how to do that right because I've heard that it should be easier to orgasm that way, and I never have. I've never orgasmed at all, actually. Not from a guy, anyway. I mean, I've come on my own, but isn't sex supposed to be better with someone else? I'd really like to figure out how to make it better with someone else."

I bit my bottom lip and waited, sure that what I'd said would wind him up.

That was part of the fun of Dylan, after all.

"That's. Hm." He cleared his throat. "That's quite a list of concerns."

"Told you." I flopped down on the bed and put my feet flat on the headboard. "Am I unhelpable? Is it humiliating that my education is so sparse that I can't even orgasm with a guy?"

"That's not a problem with your education—that's a problem with the men you've been with. *They* should be humiliated. Truly."

Maybe it was flattery, but he didn't have to try to get in my pants. And Dylan was generally earnest. He meant what he said, and his show of support made my insides feel warm and twisted. Not to mention wet.

Kind as it was, it also didn't fix my situation. "Thank you for that. I appreciate it, I do. But it's still a problem for me, even if it isn't my fault. So I'll teach the next guy. No big deal. Just...how can I teach a guy what to do if I don't know what I like myself?"

"Then we have to figure out what you like. And teach you how to ask for it."

Yes. That. "Mr. Locke, I think we're on the same page. Does this help you with your lesson plan?"

"I believe it does."

He was so solemn that I couldn't help poking at him. "You know, I'm grateful you're taking this project seriously, for my sake. But it's okay if you enjoy it, too."

He let out a gruff laugh that made goosebumps scatter down my arms. "I'll have you know that I'm enjoying this very much.

Now, you might not need much sleep, but I'd better get some if I'm expected to be at my best for you. I'll see you tomorrow night, sweet girl."

"Good night, Professor." I clicked the button to end the call and stretched my hands over my head in giddy victory.

Humming to myself, I set the phone on the nightstand, turned off the lamp, and climbed under the covers. I was all talk about all-nighters. In truth, I liked my sleep.

But I sat awake for a long time, smiling in the dark, as I thought about all the possible ways Dylan would *enjoy* me.

I GOT TRAPPED.

After a full day of sightseeing and holiday activities, I'd figured that Sabrina would want to call it a night as soon as the Rockettes' show was over. Especially since she was also exhausted from the emotional turbulence of her relationship with Donovan Kincaid.

Unfortunately, she'd gotten a second wind right as the curtains closed, and instead of going straight back to her apartment like I'd hoped, we ended up at a Don't Tell Mama's until almost two in the morning.

I might have tried to persuade her that I was tired, but she knew me better than that. And she needed to have a good time, a night where she could unload all her worry on me. I rarely got to be the comforter between the two of us. She was my sister, but in many ways she was also my mother. Even when I wanted to be there for her, she rarely allowed it.

This time it was Dylan who texted to check in on me. Not wanting to divert my attention away from Sabrina, I hadn't gotten a chance to reply until Sabrina and I were in our separate rooms back at her place.

> I just got home! I'm so sorry! Is it too late to come over?

I wasn't even sure he'd answer at this time of night, and if he did, I was certain he'd want to reschedule.

But I was wrong.

> No worries. I got a nap in this afternoon. But I don't want you taking an Uber at this time of night. I'll send my car for you. Text me when you're in my lobby so I know you've arrived safely.

He "got a nap." I chuckled out loud. Either he was taking this project ultra seriously, or he was winding *me* up for a change. I had a feeling both were likely.

And he was sending me his car—that was...nice. Really nice. Make-my-heart-flip-in-my-chest kind of nice. He was essentially a stranger and still he cared about my safety. I'd practically been engaged to my last boyfriend, Mateo, and he'd never been the slightest bit concerned about me walking around late at night after study sessions. Certainly a university campus was at least as dangerous as a sidewalk in Midtown for a girl like me.

Grateful and glad that our plans were still on, I threw Dylan a quick text back before slipping out of Sabrina's apartment.

> Thanks for looking out for me, Daddy. ;)

His reply came when I was in the elevator.

> I sense teasing in your last message.

And another followed right after, one that instantly made me feel the most taboo kind of sexy.

> Be careful. Daddy only rewards girls who show him respect.

Oh, boy. Dylan was good.

When I got to the lobby of Sabrina's building, I realized exactly how good he was—the car was already waiting for me. He must have had it on standby, ready for whenever I finally got back to him.

The ride to Dylan's apartment was quick with the late-night quiet—eh, quiet*er*—streets. I hummed Christmas songs from the show as we drove, and even though I still had the key Jeff Jones had given me, I texted Dylan as soon as I got there to let him know I'd arrived like he'd asked. The key got me in the front door without trouble and into the elevator, so I was bouncing down the hallway toward his unit in a matter of minutes.

All of it had happened so fast, in fact, that it wasn't until I was outside his door with the key in my hand, lifted toward the lock, that I thought to step back and take a moment. It wasn't that I had doubts about my plan—I didn't. Not a one. And I didn't have doubts about Dylan either. He was everything I wanted in a teacher. He was kind and protective and level-headed. Most importantly, he was out-of-this-world attractive. The apex of my thighs felt slippery just from the thought of being with him.

But there was me to think about. Who I was and what kind of reactions I usually had to men I was into. I fell for them, was what I did. Over and over. I'd only had two serious boyfriends in my life, but the number of guys I'd been smitten with was countless. I easily swooned over kind gestures. Butterflies resided in my stomach at all times. If a man looked too long in my eyes, laughed at my stupid jokes, or listened attentively to my rants about art, he was sure to win my heart.

The only reason I'd survived as long as I had in the world—if twenty-three was considered having survived long at all—was because I also had a level head. Because I knew not to run blindly into the arms of every guy who gave me goosebumps. Because I'd learned to tuck my feelings deep inside. I'd perfected the art of not being vulnerable, partly by making sure I didn't jump into bed with anyone until I was sure he loved me too.

Everything about this situation with Dylan was against the Audrey Lind Code of Conduct.

So how on earth did I expect to get through this without getting burned?

The same way you always do. That was how.

I'd remind myself of the facts—that Dylan wasn't emotionally available. That he lived across an ocean. That he wasn't interested in any relationship with me or anyone, for that matter. I'd repeat those facts over and over until they were seared into my brain, and when I started to feel—which was highly likely considering my past—I'd bury those feelings and never mention them out loud. Then, after a while, a new guy would cross my path, and I'd get all twitterpated again and the cycle would continue until eventually I found the *right* guy. And finally I wouldn't have to hide anymore.

It would happen. I believed it with all of me. And this thing with Dylan was preparing me for being ready for that guy, and it was important. And logical. And I would survive this way until that future arrived.

With my pep talk completed, I threw my shoulders back, inserted the key in the lock, and swung open the door.

Before I even had time to cross the threshold, I was grabbed by the wrist, pulled into the foyer, and pushed against the wall.

"You hesitated in the hall," Dylan said, his mouth at my ear, his voice husky. He'd shut the door with his foot, and now the length of his body was crushed against mine. "Are you having second thoughts?"

The light was off in the foyer, and except for the moonlight that shone in from the front room, it was dark. But I didn't need to see to be able to tell how much Dylan hoped that I wasn't reconsidering our arrangement. His eagerness was evident from the thick ridge pressing against my lower belly.

"No second thoughts," I assured him. "I was just pulling myself together."

His lips hovered along the curve of my jaw. "You can still back out of this. At any time. You just say the word, and everything stops."

The only word I wanted to say at this moment was "Don't." *Don't stop. Don't back out of this. Don't make me wait a second longer.*

But I was speechless. My heart was in my throat, hammering away at my vocal cords. A shiver ran through my body, despite the heavy coat I was wearing. I licked my lips, inviting his mouth to cover mine. I willed it with all my being. *Kiss me. Kiss me!*

"Tell me you understand," he insisted.

I dropped the key and my purse to the floor and swept the palms of my hands up his torso, over his shirt. "I get it. Please, don't stop. Please—"

He cut me off with a kiss, immediately deep and frantic. Without breaking his mouth from mine, he undid the buttons of my coat and pushed it off my shoulders, letting it join my other belongings on the ground. Then he shoved closer against me, inhabiting the space the bulky coat had previously owned.

My chest rose and fell rapidly, the bullet points of my nipples brushing against him with each breath. I threw my arms around his neck and silently begged for more—more contact, more kissing, more of all of this.

It was happening. Really happening, and already it was so thrilling and charged that I was absolutely sure I wouldn't retain anything that I learned. What's more, I didn't even care. Screw the lessons. I just wanted him to screw me.

Thankfully, Dylan still had his head about him. "Without speaking, tell me what you want."

"But I...I don't know, remember? I..."

He amended. "Show me where you need to be touched. I know you need it, you saucy girl. Show me where your body aches for my hands."

I couldn't think. I didn't know. But I closed my eyes, and I could feel the heaviness of my breasts and the aching of my nipples and the buzzing from below, between my thighs. I arched my back, pushing my chest toward him.

"You need my hands on your tits, don't you, sweet girl?"

He was already undoing the top buttons of my shirt dress, but I nodded anyway. "I do. I do!"

"Shh. I know." He kissed me quickly, then pulled back to watch as his hands drew my dress open. He hadn't removed my belt or undone any of the buttons below that, so the top only fell down to my elbows, trapping my arms from excessive movement and revealing my bra and the globes trapped beneath the white lace.

He stared hungrily as he brushed his knuckles across my decolletage, so close—but not close enough—to where he'd correctly identified I needed him. Such a good professor. I arched my back again, reminding him, and he chuckled. Then, with one swift movement, he tugged both bra cups down, exposing my breasts and my embarrassingly erect nipples.

And finally—*finally*—he touched them, scissoring my nipples with his fingers as he filled his palms with the fatty flesh. I let out a whimper, but leaned into him, asking for more. His pinch tightened, bringing me to the balls of my feet with a full moan.

Dylan kissed me and whispered praises. Praises that I couldn't quite make out over the increasing buzz between my legs. It was loud and urgent, demanding attention. I wriggled, rubbing my thighs together, seeking relief.

"Show me." Dylan's harsh command cut through the haze, prompting me once again to tell him where I needed to be touched.

I stepped a foot on either side of one of his and bucked my hips forward. He bent his knee, and now I could ride him the way I wanted, rubbing my pussy against him, showing him where I ached.

"Good girl," his voice rumbled, gathering my dress around my waist. "Good girl for showing me where you need me."

Instead of touching me there, though, he slid his hands down inside my leggings to palm my behind. It was torture, feeling the burn of his skin against mine while elsewhere I was on fire from the absence of his caress.

But then his hands were inching lower, down into the crease between my cheeks. "No knickers," he said in a hiss. "You are as much of a bad girl as you are a good one, aren't you, Audrey?"

Really, it had been about panty lines. Tight leggings show everything, and I wasn't fond of thongs.

But before I could respond, he dug his fingers into my flesh and pulled me forward, bringing his knee up tight against my pussy at the same time. The increase in friction took the buzz from mono to stereo. I put my hands flat against the wall behind me for support as my mouth parted in a desperate sigh.

There were more murmurs from Dylan, more sighs from me, and then he was pulling my leggings down to my thighs, exposing the recently trimmed (thank heavens) patch of hair above my naughty bits, to borrow the British term. I spread my legs farther, unabashedly. Showing him. Begging him.

And somehow he knew.

Because his fingers found his way between my pussy lips, and with expertise, he strummed my skin, he stoked the fire, until fireworks were going off in front of my eyes and my head was spinning in circles, and I was clutching onto him while the most beautiful, most tremulous climax wracked through my body.

Oh, my. Oh, wow. That was...it was *everything*. It was ecstasy and paradise and yes, oh, yes, sex was definitely better with another person. Dizzying and delicious and divine.

Slowly, I came to my senses again, and I realized Dylan was kissing my jaw and stroking the delicate skin above my clit, easing me back to reality.

I moved my hands up his arms and braced them on his shoulders, steadying me as I looked into his eyes. I had to tell him how good it had been, how perfect. How monumental.

But all that came out was, "I liked that."

He laughed lightly. "Which part?"

"All of it. Every single bit." I couldn't narrow it down if I'd tried. I'd been too captivated by feeling to even know what had happened.

Which was entirely beyond the point of this exercise. I needed to be able to recall every detail. "What did you do?"

He leaned back to study my face. "Can you stand through another one?"

"I think so." My legs were wobbly, but I had the wall at my back, and Dylan to help keep me up.

"Then this time I'll tell you. Try to pay attention." He moved his hands back to my breasts, plumping them. "I watched how your body leaned into me. I watched where. Those were the parts of you begging for attention."

He pinched my nipples now, light at first, then, when I moaned, harder.

He waited for me to quiet before going on, his voice so low it was almost a whisper. "I listened to your whimpers. If you'd backed away, I would have known it was too much. But you arched your back toward me. So I gave you more."

He continued this way, easing through each of the same

movements as before, showing me how he decided he'd touch me based on my reactions. Teaching me that I was the one who ran the show. All he had to do, he said, was observe. Observe how my breaths grew shallow the closer I got to orgasm. Observe how my grip got tighter on his shirt. Observe how my eyelids fluttered and my head fell back.

I heard him talking. I heard what he was saying, but also I didn't. I was whirling again in a second, more powerful climax. I exploded like a bomb, shaking and crying out with volatile pleasure. It was agony. It was rapture. It was fire and ice and everything in between.

And I knew—absolutely without a doubt knew—that I was in trouble.

Not only because I was bound to become very fond of this man—more likely, it had already happened, and I just hadn't admitted it—but also because I was one thousand percent certain that whatever it was that he'd done to me—twice now!—couldn't be taught to someone else. It was a skill. It was a talent. Something a person was born with or wasn't. Maybe it could be honed, but only if there was already a natural inclination and a desire to please, and I'd never dated a man like that before. Never dated a man with those gifts.

I couldn't teach this to a lover.

Dylan Locke was meant to make things better. Instead, he'd ruined me forever.

NINE
DYLAN

I was caught. Ensnared in her net. I'd taken the bait, and after one sweet taste, I was captured. There was nothing left for me to do but surrender, let her cut me open and skin me. Let her feast.

I'd never guessed that my end would be so inviting, yet here it was, so delicious and tempting.

After watching her beautifully fall apart—not once, but twice—I knew there would be no sleeping that night. I had to have her in every way. I'd devour her, let myself be devoured, until dawn, if she let me. We still hadn't made it past the foyer. There were so many places left in my flat to defile her, and I planned to take advantage of them all.

I pressed tightly against her, grinding the steel rod in my trousers into the softness of her belly while I kissed her with abandon. With one hand braced on her hip, another cupped under her chin, I anchored myself in the moment, ignoring the nagging worry about tomorrow and the late hour and the incessant vibration of my phone in my pocket, and kissed her so deeply I lost myself.

"What is that?" she asked, breaking away suddenly. "What is

that buzzing against me? Do you have a vibrator in there?" She moved her hands down to my trousers and reached, not for the aching rod of my cock, but into my pocket.

Then she withdrew my phone, still buzzing, the screen lit up brightly in the darkness with a single name—**Ellen**.

It should have been **Hell-en**. That would have been more fitting considering the moment she seemed desperate to destroy. She was, in every way, a devil.

The ringing ended and the screen showed I'd had six missed calls. A second past and it began buzzing again.

That's when I came to my wits.

Ellen calling, late at night, over and over—it had to be Aaron.

I snatched the phone from Audrey's hand and answered it as I brought it to my ear. "What's wrong?"

"Thank God you finally answered. I didn't remember you being such a sound sleeper." Ellen sounded both worked up and accusing.

I had no interest in addressing the latter. "Tell me what's wrong."

"It's Aaron. He's not in his room. I can't find him."

Cold panic washed over me replacing the heat that had blazed through my veins only minutes before. I stepped away from Audrey and ran a hand through the flop of my hair. "What do you mean you can't find him? It's—" I glanced at my watch. "Nearly three in the morning. Where the hell would he have gone?"

"I don't know, Dylan!" She was terrified. I could hear it in the shrill pitch of her voice. Ellen was never terrified. She was cool as a cucumber, that one. Her agitation fed mine, urging me to act.

"I'll be right there. Ring the police." I glanced at Audrey and found her already putting herself together, hiding away the soft silk of her luscious breasts, covering the damp curls of her stunning pussy.

"I already have. Please, hurry," Ellen said, and I hated her in this moment more than I'd hated her in years. Hated the reminder that we still shared our son, though we'd never share anything else again. Hated that she'd asked me nicely, as though she assumed I had a choice in my own child's safety. Hated the intrusion of harsh reality into my perfect lie of a fantasy.

I hung up on her in reply.

Without pause, I headed straight to the coat cupboard and pulled out the cashmere Ted Baker hanging inside. I put it on, then turned back to my guest. She was just slipping an arm through her own coat. I rushed to help her, brushing her long caramel hair off her shoulder before moving to button her up.

"I'm sorry," I said, wishing I had time for other words, sweeter words. She deserved better than this.

She shook her head adamantly. "No, you have to go. I get it." She brought her hand up to stroke her knuckles against my cheek.

I caught her hand as she dropped it and brought it to my mouth to kiss her palm. "I'm still sorry. There's so much more..." I closed my eyes, forcing away the thoughts of all the *more* I'd meant to address with her this night. When I opened them again, I couldn't look directly at her. "I'll walk down with you."

We were silent in the lift. I was too worried, too frantic, too furious at Ellen to make conversation. Whether Audrey was respectful of my situation or peeved about the interruption to our plans, I wasn't sure. I didn't allow myself to think about it. I could only think about Aaron.

Halfway across the lobby, I stopped suddenly. "What am I thinking? You need a ride." I pulled out my phone and dialed my driver.

Audrey put a hand up as though to stop me. "I can Uber. You take the car."

"It will be faster if I walk. It's only a couple of blocks. I'd prefer if—" I cut off when the driver answered the line. "Yes, she's ready to be picked up now. Same address as earlier." He gave me an estimated time of arrival, and I hung up.

"He'll be here in seven minutes." I looked out the front doors to the snowy street beyond then back at my companion, longingly. "I wish I could stay."

"No, please don't. Go. Text me when you find him safe." A thought seemed to occur to her. "Oh, and Dylan. When you find him...listen to what he has to say. Kids don't usually do crazy things like this without a reason, as silly as their reasons might seem."

My brow furrowed as I endured her advice. I didn't generally like counsel without invitation, particularly from someone without any kids of her own.

She sensed she'd overstepped. "I'm sorry. It's not my place. Just...it wasn't that long ago that I was sneaking out of my house, and I thought I could help."

She was genuine and utterly enchanting, and I realized, I wasn't bothered after all by her intrusion. I was *grateful*.

I wanted to kiss her for it. Because she had perfect plump lips. Because she tasted like honey. Because she was warm and the night was cold, and I'd been in the dark for so long.

But casual kissing wasn't what we were about, and I was in a rush, so I nodded my goodbye, and dashed out the door.

It took less than ten minutes to walk from my building to Ellen's. The doorman let me through, having been alerted that both I and the police would be arriving. When I got to her unit, I rapped quietly on the door, aware of the wee hour of the night.

She answered right away, ushering me in quickly.

"Tell me what happened," I ordered, already heading to Aaron's room to see for myself that he was indeed not there.

She followed after me, tripping over herself to keep up with my wide gait. "He went to his room right after dinner, around seven, saying he had homework he wanted to get done ahead of the weekend. I did some work, changed into my pajamas, then curled up with a glass of wine in the living room to watch a holiday thing on Netflix. I meant to check on him when I went to bed, but I guess I fell asleep, and when I woke up, I looked then, and he was gone."

"So you have no idea how long he'd been missing?"

"No. But I couldn't have fallen asleep before nine-thirty or ten. It was probably after that when he..."

Unless he'd snuck out before then, while she wasn't paying attention.

New York flats being what they were, it only took a second to verify Aaron's absence. I turned to my ex-wife, looking at her for the first time since I'd arrived. She was wearing a long sheer nightgown with a silk robe that nearly reached her feet.

She'd never worn anything that fancy to bed when we'd been married.

I took a step toward her. "You were alone all evening?" I meant to sound as accusatory as I did.

"What are you asking?" She clutched the lapels of her robe like she did to her defenses.

"You're sure you weren't entertaining a male gentleman and that's why you didn't realize our son had disappeared before three in the goddamned morning?"

"As though it couldn't happen on your watch."

"I find it hard to believe I wouldn't notice a thirteen-year-old boy sneaking out of a flat this size. It's not like this is Grand Central Station, for Christ's sake. It's not even two thousand square feet."

She stuck her chin out. "Really? You'd notice? Like how you noticed your wife had been having affairs for nearly a year before you confronted her about it?"

Splice. Right through the skin, straight to the heart. She knew where to hit me, how to strike with her words. I *hadn't* noticed her affairs. I hadn't wanted to.

And maybe she was showing me something of herself too—that she'd *wanted* me to notice, and I hadn't. She'd wanted me to save her, and I couldn't. Another reminder of how I'd failed her. How I'd failed all of us.

See that, Audrey? Love doesn't win. It just disappoints. Over and over again.

"Mom? Dad? What's going on?" The thin voice in the doorway pulled our focus immediately.

There he was, still bundled in his coat and a beanie cap that said *Excelsior!* in bold red letters across the front.

God, we were both shitty parents—Ellen and I. So wrapped up in ourselves and the same old argument that we couldn't even notice the kid we were looking for when he came home.

"Aaron!" Ellen ran to him, enveloping him in her arms. "You're here! You're all right! We were so worried! We called the police and your dad came over and I was out of my mind..."

Her relief at his appearance quickly faded and the anxiety of the night crept in to take its place. She pulled out of her embrace and gripped him tightly by the upper arms. "Where the hell have you been, young man? How dare you frighten us like that!"

"I went out!" he answered defiantly.

"To that damn YouTube meetup with your friends, didn't you? The one I said absolutely not to when you asked if you could go?"

His guilty expression told the answer as much as his silence.

I hung back and watched, my own relief seeping in slowly and heavily, trapping me like quicksand. What could have happened? What might have been? This late on the streets of a busy city. Barely a teenager.

It was easier not to think about. Easier to just watch and sink.

They made an odd tableau, the two of them. Ellen, who stood

on the upper side of average, barraging Aaron, who nearly stood as tall as she did these days, with her verbal onslaught. How long before she lost all control over him? Soon, if she wasn't careful. Soon if she hadn't already.

But could I even judge her parenting? Was I any better of a father, absent as I was? And, truth be told, I would have been yelling myself hoarse if she hadn't taken the lead. If I weren't drowning in my emotions. If I weren't remembering Audrey's last words to me—*Listen to what he has to say.*

So far, he hadn't much to say at all. Or, rather, Ellen hadn't given him much chance for a defense. She didn't let up, in fact, until she seemed to remember the police were on the case. She stormed out of the room to retrieve her phone and make the call.

Left alone together, Aaron chanced a glance in my direction. I could feel the frown on my face. Could imagine the disappointment he saw on my features. It was no surprise that he hung his head sullenly in response.

I took a breath and forced the tension from my body. "Aaron..." I began carefully.

"I know already," he snapped, throwing his beanie on his desk. He unzipped his coat and threw it over the back of the chair. "Mom said everything, okay. You don't need to be involved. Why are you even here?"

Because I'm your father. Because I love you, you idiot.

I forgot, sometimes, that the teenager method of communication was very often brutal and unforgiving.

Another breath. Another careful start. "You went to a YouTube thing? What sort of event was this?"

"Just a thing that the guys from the AV club were going to." His back was to me, but I felt his eagerness to share as well as his reluctance to do so.

"Was it a concert? A seminar?"

With a sigh that resembled so many of my own, Aaron turned

to me. "Just a YouTube personality. Two of them, actually. Jacksepticeye and Markiplier. They're friends so sometimes they do their meetups together."

"And you get their autographs? Is it like those comic conventions?" I was so out of touch with today's culture.

He gave me a frustrated glare. "No, Dad. It's like...they're YouTubers. They do shows. They're famous."

"Oh." I didn't have any better understanding now than before. "Are they inappropriate? Was that why your mother didn't want you to go?"

"Not really. They're just...normal. They comment on video games while they play. Mom didn't want me to go because she said I needed to get my homework done tonight since I wouldn't get any done tomorrow because of Thanksgiving and then after that you and I are doing that ski trip." He paused as he toed off his shoes. "I would have rather skipped Connecticut, but nobody asked me."

Again, that cruelty. I wondered how much of his ability to hurt me had been learned from his mother. How much he'd inherited from me. How two broken people could raise a boy to become a whole man.

Ellen had defeated me that way. She'd destroyed parts of me that I'd never have back. She'd made me bitter and cruel in return.

I vowed not to be that man to my son.

"You could have told me. I would have canceled my dinner plans tonight to take you to the event."

His eyes lifted to meet mine, surprised and curious.

"And we can cut Connecticut short. Come back Saturday night instead. If you'd like. So you can get caught up on your homework on Sunday."

"Really?" He grinned. "Thanks, Dad. That would help."

"No worries." I stepped forward to tousle his hair. It was as much physical affection as he allowed these days, and even that he often pulled away from. This time he tolerated it, and it made up for the disappointment at losing an entire day of his company.

And I couldn't say I'd been completely selfless in giving up the day with him, anyway. I had other ideas of how I wanted to spend that time.

I SHUT the door to the den behind me and slumped against it. "Well, that was terrible."

"Tell me about it," said Donovan, who had led me to his father's office with the promise of *"fucking escape."* He surely needed it more than I did—this was *his* parent's house, not mine. The Thanksgiving meal we'd suffered through with all its pomp and circumstance had to be more of an affront to him, and I had been quite offended.

"Are all people this terrible?" I asked, crossing over to the bar to scour for a decent alcohol.

Donovan finished cutting the cap off a cigar and stuck it between his teeth. "Rich people are."

"Thank God we aren't them," I said cheekily. "Looks like we have the option of bourbon or bourbon." I held up both overpriced bottles so he could choose.

He looked up. "The Michter. It's more expensive. We've earned it." He toasted his cigar, drew in a puff, and rotated it until the heat was evenly distributed. "You'll like this though. Illusione Epernay. It's mild the way you Europeans tend to like things."

He handed me a cut cigar in exchange for one of the glasses I'd poured. I sniffed the foot. It smelled like coffee and cedar and, when I drew off it myself a few moments later, I detected floral and honey notes as well.

"Very nice." I sank into the oversized leather armchair and

crossed my ankle over the opposite knee, letting the tension in my shoulders uncoil with the pleasant body of the tobacco. "Are all holidays with your family as awful as this one?" With more than two dozen high-class guests, the day had been filled with pageantry and performance. Much like this office with its overabundance of wood paneling and the gold-plated details. What a nightmare of a life.

"I couldn't tell you." He plopped into the rolling chair and leaned back to prop his feet on the massive desk in front of him. "I don't spend time with them for a reason."

"But now you're in the States. For good?" He hadn't given any indication that he was returning to the Japan office anytime soon, but with Donovan, you could never be too sure what his plans were.

He hesitated, either uncertain of the answer or uncertain he wanted to share it. Finally, he said, "For good."

"I'm guessing Sabrina Lind has something to do with that." I was fishing, and it was obvious. Hopefully it wasn't as evident that the person I was really curious about was Sabrina's sister, and he'd unwittingly tell me something useful.

Donovan had never been one to show his cards, though. Even years ago when I'd first met him. When he'd practically been engaged to my stepdaughter.

He wasn't eager to show them now, either. "We'll see. We'll see."

"I'm somewhat surprised she isn't here today, after that scene you made the other night. Declaring you were her boyfriend right there on the streets of Manhattan."

He gave me a sharp glare. "It wasn't a scene. It was a necessary declaration." Then, after a beat, "She's spending the day with her sister. I didn't want to interrupt."

Neither did I, which was why I was poking around for information. As she'd asked, I'd sent Audrey a text the night before when I'd gotten back to my apartment after Aaron had been found. It had been short and factual.

> He's home. I'll talk to you tomorrow.

> I'm so glad.<3

She'd responded right away, and I'd wondered if I'd woken her or if she'd waited up for my news. Probably the former. And still the possibility that it could have been the latter intrigued me. As did the symbols that followed. A heart, according to Urban Dictionary. Or a ballsack, depending on which definition I wanted to rely on. Either could be considered appropriate.

And yet I longed for the meaning of the heart.

I was stupid. I was raving mad. Letting my thoughts drift to her as often as they did. It was all the buildup. All the wrought-up tension between us. I needed to get laid. Obviously. It would be the only possible way to cut through the bullshit and get down to the meaning of our companionship, the pure sexuality that was the only true connection we shared.

I took another draw on my cigar as I pulled out my mobile from my jacket pocket and was surprised to find another message waiting from her. I'd forgotten I'd put it on silent for dinner.

> Our T-Day reservations aren't until five, btw.
> You can call or text anytime before that.

I looked at my watch. It was a quarter to four. *Really?* That early, and I already needed a drink this badly?

The good news was I had time to catch her.

I set my drink down and stood up. "I, uh. Need to ring someone. Can I step out there?" I nodded toward the single French door that led to a balcony, so small it could only fit one person comfortably.

Donovan shrugged. "Doesn't bother me any. Aaron?"

I puzzled for half a second before realizing he was asking if I was calling my son. "Yes. Yes, Aaron. You understand."

Pushing open the door, I stepped quickly out into the biting cold before I could feel too guilty about the lie. Then I clicked on Audrey's name, put the mobile to my ear, and puffed on my cigar until she answered.

"You called me!" she exclaimed.

"You said I should." Had I misread her message?

"I know I did. I just didn't think you'd actually call. I expected a text, at the most."

"I've felt you come around my finger—I think we're beyond texting, don't you?"

She was silent for a moment, and I watched my breath curl with the smoke of my Epernay, anxiously wondering if I'd gone too far. Said too much. My head was filled with her was the only reason I had for my behavior. I needed to be inside her. Needed to fully have her before I could get over the distraction she imposed.

Whatever the excuse, I was preparing to deliver an apology when she said, "Ohhhh. I liked that. Is that dirty talk?"

"It's a rather lame attempt, I'm afraid. Fortunately, I was going for frankness."

She giggled, and despite the godawful temperature, I felt my cock jump at the tinkle of a sound. "So we've discovered I like frankness for sure, and possibly I like dirty talk as well. Should we try more of that to see?"

Oh, how I wanted to. Right then and there. There were a slew of filthy things I wanted to whisper to her. I wanted to tell her all the ways I meant to touch her sweet little pussy, how I would pet it and lick it and fill it up with my cum. Wanted to tell her how good her skin tasted, how drunk the scent of her made me, how the slick clench of her cunt while I'd fingered her made me ache with the need to bury my cock inside her to the hilt and fuck her until she saw stars.

But after a glance behind me at the door with its thin panels of glass separating me and my friend, I thought the dirty talk should probably wait.

"I'm hoping this call will lead to the chance for just that. Our night was cut short. I owe you a raincheck." No, that wasn't how I wanted to present that. As if she were an obligation. That was a far cry from the truth. "I'm *looking forward* to the opportunity," I amended.

She sighed wistfully. "I want to. So badly. But you have Aaron tonight through the weekend, and I leave Sunday."

"True, true. But my plans with my son have changed a bit, and I had a thought—would you be able to change your train ticket back to Delaware to something later in the day? I'm more than willing to pay for the change fee."

"Yes!" she squealed. "In fact—I didn't say anything because I didn't want to be presumptuous—but I already looked into it, and there's a train leaving at four-fifteen, and there's no charge for changing with twenty-four hours' notice. I can be at your apartment by ten-thirty in the morning."

She was fantastic. Truly.

"Then everything's settled. Sunday at my place." I glanced once more behind me and found Donovan had his eyes closed, likely sleeping off the tryptophan and dreary dinner company. I braved another comment. "I'm warning you, little girl—our lessons won't be over until my face is wet with your juices and your pussy is sore from my cock, so be prepared to learn."

She let out a noise that sounded like a shiver. "Wow, yes. I definitely like dirty talk. And now I need to go spend some alone time with my hand before I have to leave for dinner. 'Kay, thanks."

I hung up and took another draw from my cigar before

opening the door, thankful that the cold prevented me having to walk in with a tent in my trousers.

"Aaron's doing good?" Donovan asked, not bothering to open his eyes at my return.

"Yes. Quite good. Excited for...for our plans this weekend." I headed back to the warm burn of the bourbon and the comfort of the armchair.

"Great to hear. I guess I won't worry about how sore your cock is going to make his pussy then."

Donovan was listening, that bugger.

Talking to Audrey had put me in such a good mood, however, I didn't have the heart to respond with anything other than a sly grin.

TEN
AUDREY

I don't know exactly why I didn't tell Sabrina about Dylan beyond that kiss.

There were a few reasons not to, sure. After she'd rode off that night with Donovan Kincaid, they'd put their relationship on hold until they could talk, which was to happen immediately after I left town. Even with the pause, I knew she was still completely consumed with him. She didn't need to hear details of my affair. She'd fuss too much over me and neglect her own emotions like she always did. And my affair was silly compared to hers.

Or I was afraid she'd think it was silly.

Or maybe I was afraid she'd realize it really wasn't—afraid she'd realize that this thing with Dylan was really important to me in ways I couldn't explain, even to myself. Maybe I did have some daddy issues, but it was nothing I planned to discuss with my sister.

Mostly, I was afraid she'd demand those explanations. Sure, I'd tell her what I told him—that I wanted the experience, that I needed a teacher. But would I also tell her that I wanted the experience exclusively *with Dylan*? That I was attracted to him from the first words that slipped across his tongue in that to-die-for British dialect? Attracted to his tall frame and his dark eyes and that frown that rested permanently on his lips.

Would she have lectured me more about his cynicism, warning me that it was a situation that could only lead to heartache? She would have presumed I believed I could transform him.

And, no matter how much I protested, she probably wouldn't be convinced otherwise.

Most scary of all, I was afraid she would have been right. Because deep inside me there was a flicker of hope, that eternal flame that burns in hearts like mine, the same kind of light that allows zealots to proclaim tirelessly about their god. I believed, *I believed* that love fixed all. I believed in sharing that faith. Of course I wanted to convert everyone around me.

Of course I hoped I could convert Dylan, too. And that *was* silly. I didn't need Sabrina to tell me just how silly it was.

So I didn't say a word after telling her about that first kiss, and I didn't tell her I'd changed my train ticket. I worried about it silently over our last breakfast together at a cute cafe down the street. She was planning to take me to Grand Central Station to see me off, and how was that going to work? What if she saw me to security, and they didn't let me through because I was so early? What if they *did* let me through, but I couldn't sneak back out to meet up with Dylan?

"You seem distracted," she said, as we rode the elevator to her apartment to get my luggage after breakfast. "Do you have a lot of homework waiting for you?"

I did. But that wasn't on my mind. "Yeah. Homework. Finals are coming up now too."

"I should have insisted you studied more."

I threw her a glare. "No. You shouldn't have. Because you're not my mom."

She twisted her lips as though trying not to say what she wanted to say. Then she lost the battle. "Feels like it sometimes."

My immediate instinct was to take her comment personally, but I didn't want to argue with her when we were close to saying goodbye, and when I let myself think about her position, I totally understood why she'd feel she had to mother me.

"I'm sure it's a hard habit to break," I said stepping out of the elevator ahead of her. I'd meant to let it go at that, but I turned back to her instead of walking on to her door. "I'm ready to have you just be my sister. I need you to be that more than my parent these days."

She wrapped her arms around her body and frowned a moment. But then the lines around her mouth relaxed and her lips turned into a small smile. "As long as you still need me."

"I'll always need you, you psychopath."

We walked silently toward her apartment, both of us in our thoughts. Then, when she opened her door and held it open for me to go inside, she said, "I might be crazy, actually."

"Because you're going to give Donovan a chance to win back your heart?"

She kept holding it while I tugged my suitcase into the hall. I'd left it just inside the apartment so we could just grab it and go.

"Maybe." But I could tell it was more than a maybe. That she was already back in his arms in her mind. That their impending talk was just a matter of procedure.

She was agonizing over it, though. And that's when I realized my opportunity. "Hey, you don't really need to go with me to the train station. I'll be okay getting there by myself."

"But, I want to come!"

"That's stupid and out of your way. We can say goodbye here just as easily, and then you can get to Donovan sooner."

She finished locking up and then, out of character, she pulled me into a tight hug. "I love you," she whispered, and I knew it wasn't just her way of saying thank you for letting her get to her man, but that she really meant for me to hear it.

"I love you, too." I did. More than I could ever say. She was the reason I'd made it as far as I had. She was why I hadn't turned out grim and grumpy. I'd been an orphan, and she'd upended her whole life to take care of me. She made fun of me at times, but she'd been the one who'd taught me that love wins. She'd never let me know any other way.

Downstairs, we each summoned an Uber and after another hug, we drove our separate ways. My eyes got teary, but I didn't cry like I usually did when we parted. I'd see her again in a month for Christmas, and I had a date with Dylan to distract me from how much I'd miss her.

Because I didn't have to deal with Sabrina at the train station like I'd thought I'd have to, I ended up at Dylan's building earlier than I'd planned to. I bustled into the lobby, humming "Carol of the Bells" and pulling my suitcase behind me with one hand while I wrestled with my phone's screen lock with the other. I'd just send him a text, let him know I was there already.

Obviously, I was preoccupied, which was why I wasn't paying attention and smacked right into an older guy who was coming off of the elevator. He had a solid body. Toned muscles were definitely hidden under the brick-red pullover sweater. His smelled of cinnamon and aftershave, and my belly began fluttering with butterflies before I even looked up and confirmed that the body belonged to Dylan.

His hands came up to steady me, grasping my elbows firmly. Sparks shot through my veins, and though we were about to go upstairs and get busy touching in so many other ways, I didn't want him to let me go long enough to move at all.

"Hi." I sounded shy and awkward. Not my usual self at all,

which I blamed mostly on the collision, but the way he was looking at me with those liquid brown eyes didn't help.

"Hi." He gave the slightest of smiles.

Then quickly it disappeared. "Pardon me. I wasn't watching where I was going. Are you okay now? Steady enough? You aren't hurt?"

"Dad, she's fine," a thin voice grumbled.

My eyes flew to Dylan's side and collided with a teenage boy who could only be Aaron Locke. Even if he hadn't just referred to him as Dad, it was apparent the two were related. The boy had his father's height, his dimpled chin, his puppy dog eyes, his floppy brown hair.

Immediately, I stepped back, not sure how to act or what to say. I stammered through some version of, "I'm fine, thank you." Then stood, jaw slack, as I tried to figure out what to do next. Should I zoom away without another word? Pretend we'd never met before?

Yes. That was exactly what I should do.

Instead, I stood there frozen.

Dylan wore the same panicked expression, but fortunately he seemed able to string together coherent thoughts. "Audrey, this is my son, Aaron. Aaron, this is Audrey, my...my..."

Okay, so maybe he was just as flustered as I was.

I pulled myself together and stepped in. "Your dad is my sister's boss," I explained directly to Aaron. "We somehow all ended up at dinner together the other night, and we met then."

"Weston was there as well," Dylan hurried to add, as though that might legitimize the innocence of it all.

"Right. And Donovan too," I said. Just because Donovan had shown up *after* the meal didn't make it a lie.

Of course, none of that explained what I was doing in Dylan's apartment building at the moment. I pasted on a grin and prayed silently that the kid didn't ask.

He didn't. All he said was, "Oh," barely glancing at me before throwing his gaze to the top of his shoes.

"I was just walking Aaron home," Dylan said.

His son looked up and rolled his eyes. "For the seventy-billionth time, you don't need to. It's two blocks. I walk this street alone all the time."

Dylan's jaw tensed. "Well. We're still negotiating the walking, I suppose."

"I see," I said with a chuckle. It was the perfect opportunity to say goodbye, let them go on their way while I slipped upstairs to the apartment. I still had a key. I didn't need to be let in.

But I felt caught. Not like I'd been found out doing something I shouldn't be—though, that too—but like caught in the moment. Engaged. Drawn in.

I'd known Dylan was a father from pretty much the moment I met him. We'd talked about his son. I'd understood completely that he was a parent.

But it was totally different actually seeing him in the role.

It was the kind of thing that was hard to look away from. It felt private, but I was nosy. Like, I would see this man naked later today—if everything went as it should—and seeing him with his son seemed even more personal. Even more intimate.

I wasn't ready to walk away from it. I wanted to look a little longer. Watching the man I knew from my fantasies in his real life, as a father, was the sweetest thing I could imagine.

"I'm glad to see you made it back safely from your adventure the other night," I said, knowing I was walking a tightrope.

"You told people about that?" He threw his head back with a sigh and ran a hand through his hair, very much looking like his father.

Dylan's eyes widened, but he kept his composure. "Forgive me if stories about my son come up during small talk."

Again, Aaron rolled his eyes. "It wasn't a big deal. We just went to see a show, is all."

Dylan hadn't told me where Aaron had been. I hadn't thought it was my place to pry. Now, I asked, "A Broadway show?"

"Jacksepticeye and Markiplier had a meetup. They're YouTubers. Like, they..." Aaron trailed off, as though trying to think of how to explain them.

I helped him out. "I know who they are."

"You watch Jacksepticeye and Markiplier?" His eyes lit up for the first time since meeting him.

"Oh, no. No," I said too quickly. "I know who they are, but I don't watch them." I wasn't about to admit that I'd been at many a party hosted by someone in the art department where everyone got high and watched video-game commentators and funny things pets did.

Even not saying it, my cheeks went red. How immature was my life that I related so closely to Dylan's son? Proof that he was a grown-up, and I was just a kid myself.

"Anyway," I said, regretting the conversation. "I hope it was a good time."

"It was amazing! Had to miss a day of my ski trip with Dad, and I'm stuck doing homework all the rest of tonight, but it's not too bad."

Dylan's expression softened. "If you get done early, we'll play another game of Risk tonight."

My stomach dropped. "You're...*staying with* Aaron when you walk him home?"

He rushed to answer. "No. I'm going over later. His mother's going out, and I didn't want him to be alone."

I let out a small sigh of relief. He wasn't canceling on me, then.

"I'm alone all the time when she goes out. It's not like I'm five."

Dylan didn't respond to his son's sass. "Ellen does go out a lot. She's quite good at...*entertaining*."

Entertaining. There was so much weight in that one word. So much history and bitterness. I'd been right when I'd guessed that she was the one to poison him, but the wound ran both deeper and closer to the surface than I'd originally thought.

"And you never entertain at all," Aaron sputtered. "A happy middle between you would be nice."

Dylan smirked. "I do too entertain. Just not when you're around. I have morals."

Aaron's cheeks pinked as he realized what his dad meant. "I mean, you could go out on a date every once in a while. You're never going to get married again if you don't."

Dylan pulled his neck back in horror. "Whoever told you I'd want to get married again?"

The disgust in his tone, the pure shock in his expression, it reminded me what the situation was between us. The reality wasn't him as a father. The reality was him as a bachelor. He was jaded. He was a cynic. He was hard-hearted, and I was soft. So very soft, because somehow the truth that I'd known all along hit me with a heavy, cruel punch to the gut.

I didn't pay much attention to the rest of the conversation. I'm sure I was polite and present, then I excused myself at the next opportunity and scurried away to the elevator. As I waited for the doors to shut, I watched them continue outside, talking animatedly. Dylan never looked back once.

I bit my lip and concentrated on taking deep even breaths until I was safely in the apartment, alone. Inside, I leaned against the back of the closed door and let out a slow, deep sigh. This was why I hadn't told Sabrina about this thing with Dylan—because I really had thought I could change him. That this little speck of an affair might make him feel something again. Something warm and wonderful.

Something warm and wonderful *for me.*

Ugh, I was such a girl. Such a romantic, pathetic, stupid girl child. My head knew better. Why couldn't my heart?

For the first time since I'd suggested this whole arrangement to Dylan, I had second thoughts. I needed to back out. I couldn't go through with this without becoming invested. He'd understand. If he didn't, he'd at least pretend like he did. He was polite like that.

And I'd learn what I liked the normal way—in a relationship with a guy who had feelings for me. The same kind of feelings I'd have for him.

My sister would have already been out the door. I felt it, firm and hard and solid behind me. It would be so easy to turn around and walk back through it, and I would—just as soon as I was sure I wouldn't start crying.

I blinked back the threatening tears, took a sniffling breath in, and tried to pull myself together. If I didn't, Dylan was going to return to find me a hot mess, and wouldn't that be the most embarrassing moment of my life?

I parked my suitcase where it was and headed further into the apartment to search for Kleenex or toilet paper. I couldn't remember where the bathroom was, though, and once I was in the living room, the glass windows called to me with their dizzy, terrifying view. I approached them cautiously, drawn to them like a tugboat being pulled at sea. I couldn't stop if I tried, even as I felt the thud thud of my heartbeat against my chest as I got closer. It was high up—so high—and looking down felt like being clutched in the fist of a giant, a fist that squeezed my torso until my lungs could no longer inflate.

I closed my eyes and the panic didn't ease, and still I felt like I was walking the edge. I was so far from it when all of this with

Dylan started. I'd wanted a man who would indulge me with a no-strings sexual education. He was a man who didn't believe in strings. It had been a perfect match. We'd been fated to meet.

But I'd expected banging and dirty talk, sneaking away to meet up for something sordid and naughty. That wasn't what this had turned out to be at all. This was heartfelt conversations and seeing a magnificent man trying his best with his son. This was human and sweet and real, and I'd be lying to myself to say it didn't change everything.

So here I was now. Walking the edge. Trying with all my might not to panic and look down. Knowing there was only one sure way to stay safe.

Knowing if I didn't turn and walk away, I'd fall.

ELEVEN
DYLAN

My heart pounded for long minutes after she left us in the lobby. My hands were sweaty, and I hadn't even put on my gloves yet. The encounter had been unexpected, and I was free-falling in the aftermath.

"She's pretty," Aaron admitted as we walked outside.

"Is she?" As if I'd been fooling anyone. As if I hadn't been simultaneously trying to tamp down my erection while she'd made casual conversation with my teenage son.

God, she was closer to his age than mine!

Did that make me a sick man to want her as much as I did?

Possibly. Probably. Definitely when I considered the kind of poison that I would be to a guileless innocent like she was, in her fashionably ripped jeans and pink-glossed lips. Colliding into her had been like crashing into sunshine. She made me feel warm in places that had been cold for oh, so long.

What did that mean that I did for her? Did she absorb the pervasive chill from my bones? Did I leave her feeling bitter, bleak, and barren?

What kind of person could take so freely from a light like her? I'd beat anyone who attempted to do the same to Aaron.

I didn't want to be that callous of a human. I refused to be.

I stopped short on the pavement and turned to my son. "I've reconsidered. You can walk as long as you go straight home. No dallying."

Aaron beamed with gratitude then scooted on his way.

And, with a sigh, I retreated back inside to do what must be done. If I was going to put a stop to this farce of a situation with Audrey, it was best to do it quick and fast. Best not to leave her waiting.

She was at the window when I stepped in. I knew she'd heard me arrive. Her head had shifted toward the sound of my footsteps, though she didn't completely turn to face me.

That made this easier.

"I think we need to reevaluate," I began.

But she spoke at the same time. "I didn't mean to come so early. I..." She pivoted in my direction. "I'm sorry. Go ahead."

"You first," I prodded, determined to remain the gentleman.

"I...just..." She pushed a lock of hair back from her face. "I got here earlier than I meant to, for which I truly apologize. I didn't think for a second I'd end up seeing you with your son." Her tone of voice suggested her line of thinking matched mine.

Why was that so disappointing?

I cleared my throat. "It does put things into perspective, doesn't it?"

She nodded ever so carefully.

"It's best, I suppose, that we figured this out now." I attempted a smile.

"It is. Definitely best." She couldn't meet my eyes. "I'll go." She lifted her chin and started toward me, toward the door.

Cold washed down the back of my neck. She couldn't stay,

but I didn't want her to leave. "That's not necessary, is it? Your train doesn't depart for hours. Surely you could…"

She could…what?

"I don't think that's a good idea," she said quietly, only a meter from me now.

"No. I suppose not." I could feel the heat radiating off her body. I wanted to bathe in her sun. I wanted to bask and burn, and when she went on her way, I'd settle back into the familiarity of the gloom. Was that so wrong?

I took a step toward her, against every instinct in my body. "It was fun, though, wasn't it? As brief as it was."

"It was. It really was."

Did she just inch closer? Likely wishful thinking on my part.

"It was silly, too," she said now, and this time she definitely moved nearer. Or I did. "Thinking I could learn anything in such a short amount of time."

"I'm still convinced you didn't need to learn a single thing." We were so close I could breathe her in now. She smelled fresh and crisp, an unusual combination of baby powder and apples. She smelled young. She smelled *too* young.

"Maybe it was just an excuse to have a new experience." She slid her tongue across her lower lip. Her gaze flicked from my eyes to my mouth.

"A new experience," I repeated.

"An amazing new experience." Her chin tilted upward. "An experience that would stay with me for a lifetime."

Someone shifted, both of us maybe, because she was in my arms suddenly, our mouths moving against each other with unbridled longing. Her hands worked eagerly at her coat, shirking it to the ground when she'd gotten it open.

I ran my nose along the slope of her neck, down the line of the shoulder that peeked from her wide cowl neck, goosebumps peppering in the wake of my journey. All thought left me. I was consumed with only her—the scent of her, the taste of her. The reality of her. I no longer cared about our age difference or the ill effect I could have on her or that I was undeserving of even a small piece of her.

I simply let the wind blow, and I let myself get carried away with it.

Never breaking our kiss, I walked her to the back of the couch, then spun her around so she could brace herself there while I enjoyed the full of her body. My hands snaked around and found their way under her gray jumper. My fingers danced over her silky, supple skin. She was soft where I was hard, inside and out, and the need to feel her everywhere, with every part of me, was desperate and unyielding.

"I feel very conflicted about these windows." I tugged her pullover off then pinched her nipples through her bra, thrilling when she let out a delicious squeak. "I can't decide if I need to shelter you, or if I should show you off."

"Do that!" Her voice was breathless and thin, as though she were on a razor's edge the same way I was. "Show me off. Show me off!"

I lowered my hands to undo the button of her jeans, then knelt as I pulled them down as far as they'd go before becoming trapped by her boots. "Show you off it is. Everyone can watch while I eat you out."

The sound she made this time—a high-pitched, need-filled yelp—made my cock expand to its full size. I scorned the ache of it, pressing brutally against the fly of my trousers.

It distracted me, called for my attention, and the only thing I wanted to pay attention to at the moment was her, standing between me and the couch, her lace-covered ass at eye level. She'd curved her body just so, spread her legs just wide enough, that the crotch panel of her panties was front and center in my field of vision. The material clung to her shape, outlining the lips of her pussy.

She shivered as I traced the path with a solid swipe of my tongue. She was wet, and even through the cotton lining, I could taste her. She tasted sweet like pineapple and musky like bourbon, and before I'd even had my lips on her flesh, I knew she was the most delicious thing I'd ever had my mouth on.

Moving the panel aside, I tried to focus on doing some good with my lust. She'd wanted to be taught so I endeavored to show her what she liked.

"Pay attention to what I do now," I instructed her. I brushed my tongue vertically over the nub of her clit. "That was up and down." I tilted my head and lapped horizontally. "That's side to side. And this—" I flattened my tongue and drew small circles. "Is circular. Hopefully that helps you figure out what you enjoy."

"I'm not sure. All of them," she said. "Just don't stop."

I swallowed back a laugh. There was no way I was stopping now. Burying my face in her pussy, I went down on her in earnest. I stroked and teased. I went fast, and I went slow. I sucked and nibbled, and when her legs quivered and her knees buckled, I wrapped my hands around her thighs and renewed my vigor.

She was easy to learn—her hips bucked when she wanted more, her muscles tensed when she was close. When I hit the right spot, she growled. When she was mad with desire and frustration, she begged.

She bloody begged.

"There, please, please right there," she pled like a spoiled girl. "Make it good, right there. Please, don't stop. Please, oh, please."

She was greedy, and I enjoyed gratifying her. Fucking delighted in it. Twice, I made her come. Once with only my mouth, the second time with my fingers plunging inside her as well. I could have spent all day with my face between her legs, with my tongue buried inside her cunt. If she hadn't rode through her last orgasm crying for my cock, I might have stayed on my knees long after my lower limbs had gone to sleep.

I stood, and she turned eagerly toward me, kissing me with urgency, as though she thought I might end everything right there if she didn't.

If that was truly what she thought, she was incorrect about my ability to restrain myself. I was a beast without a leash. I had no will but to devour her.

I lifted her into my arms, carrying her like a child to the bedroom.

"You aren't going to take me all the way in front of the windows? I think I'd like that," she murmured as she kissed along my jaw.

"I'm sure you would, you naughty thing. But I'm quite sure I would not." My confliction had a line, it appeared. New York City did not deserve the pleasure of her naked form.

I set her on the bed, still rumpled from the last night's restless sleep, and tugged off first one boot, then the other. She watched me, rapt, as I followed with the removal of her jeans.

"I like being undressed by you," she said, when she was only in her bra and panties. "I like how you're completely focused on me."

I couldn't not be. It was impossible to look anywhere but at her. She was exquisite and engaging. Irresistible perfection.

The wonder in her comment made me guess that no one had ever given her the attention she'd craved. What stupidity existed in her world? Boys pretending to be men, unsuitable and unworthy of such a gift as her.

I wasn't worthy either. I was a selfish vampire, feeding off her vibrant life. Even if I was damned to hell, I no longer cared.

Grabbing her bra at the space between her breasts, I tugged her forward, urging her to her knees and kissed her. Devoured her, really. It was sloppy and bruising. I wanted her lips swollen and bee-stung. I wanted her cheeks flushed and her lungs filled with my breath.

She crawled closer, her hands reaching for my belt, her mouth never breaking from mine. When she had my buckle and zip undone, she reached inside my trousers to stroke her hands up and down my bloated cock.

She pulled back and flashed me a grin. "You're big. I already know I like big."

"You're not experienced enough to know big." *Shut up*, my brain told my mouth. *You like hearing it.*

"I've only slept with two guys," she reminded me. "It doesn't mean I've only seen two cocks. And this cock..." She pulled my pants down low enough to expose the rod of flesh, red and pulsing under her gaze. "This cock is a good cock."

Fuck...this girl. She was going to be the death of me.

A bead of cum gathered at the crown, and her tongue flicked out across her lower lip.

"No," I scolded with a stern finger. "This is not for your mouth." If she were to take me that way, I wasn't sure how long I'd last. Certainly not long enough, and while I was pretty sure she made me hot enough to recover quickly, I wasn't going to make an ass of myself and prove otherwise.

Her lips turned down into an exaggerated pout. "But I've been such a good girl."

"Patience. You'll get it where you need it." I reached around to her back to undo her bra while she stroked the length of me, causing my spine to tingle and my balls to draw up. "Take my jumper off," I commanded, attempting to distract her.

"Okay, Daddy."

If she'd still been holding me when she'd said that, I definitely would have exploded. How long had it been since I'd been with a woman? I tried to recall as she lifted my pullover up and over my head. Not too long. A matter of months. Six maybe. Not so long that I should be so near out of control.

Except that the last time I'd been with a woman, it hadn't been *this* woman. This woman hit my buttons, wound me up, got me hot like no one I could remember in a long time. Possibly ever, though that was likely an exaggeration. There was no way I was thinking rationally in a moment like this, after all.

With my torso bare, Audrey found something else to steal her attention. "Dylan...you've been hiding some seriously toned pecs." She traced the planes of my chest with the tips of her fingers, then bent forward to swirl her tongue around one very lucky nipple. When she moved to the other, she peered up at me, her eyes dark and dilated under long lashes.

Breathtaking.

That was the word for her. She stole the air from my lungs. She smothered me with her beauty, with her bewitching character. She made me heady and delirious, and if this was what it felt like to die of suffocation, I'd gladly choose this method of death anyday. Every day.

I wound my hand in the length of her hair and sharply pulled her up to face me. "Take the bra the rest of the way off. Panties too," I whispered against her lips. I kissed her, quickly. "I'm getting the condom."

I pulled open the nightstand drawer where I'd tucked a new box of condoms I'd purchased earlier in the week and retrieved a single black and gold packet. We hadn't discussed protection, but if she wanted to learn, this was something I insisted be taught—protection. Always. Without exception.

And thank God for a rubber sheath. It was the only chance I had at lasting more than a minute inside her.

When I turned back to her, she was completely naked, and I had to blink several times in order to take her in without combusting. Everything about her was pink and supple. Her puffy, well-kissed lips, the bloom of her cheeks that extended down her neck to the dusky tips of her breasts, the flush of her pussy, wet and swollen between her spread thighs.

Wet and swollen and waiting for me to fill her up.

I stripped my clothes the rest of the way off at lightning speed, and ripped open the condom packet. I was seconds from rolling it over the throbbing steel jutting from my pelvis when she spoke up.

"Can I put it on?"

The few remaining pints of blood that hadn't yet made it there, surged to my cock in a rush. "Have you ever put one on before?"

She bit her lip and shook her head.

"Then it seems this is the perfect opportunity to learn, doesn't it?"

She perched herself on the side of the bed, and I handed her the unwrapped condom. She studied it for a moment, working out which direction was up, then set it on my crown.

"I don't want it to break," she explained as she delicately smoothed it over the length of me.

She looked so innocent and naïve with her small hands wrapped around the circumference of my erection, her brows knit together in concentration. I was a dirty old man in contrast. A man old enough to be experienced at fucking by the time she was born. A man with scars worn on my aging skin and wounds that ran deeper, unseen by the naked eye. A man who knew better than to believe that sex with a woman like Audrey could ever be casual.

A man who could still crawl to shore if he tried, but didn't have the willpower to do anything except sink.

With a burst of outrage—outrage at myself for being so foolish, outrage at her for being so potently irresistible—I flipped her so she was bent over the bed, lined myself at her entrance, and drove all the way into her cunt with one blunt thrust. She cried out at the force, her body trying to jolt forward, but I dug my fingers into her hips and kept her steady and in place, ready for me to pound into her again and again. She squeaked and wriggled and grew wetter until she adjusted. Then she moaned and leaned back into the slap, slap, slap of my thighs against hers.

I wished I could watch her, wished I could scrutinize each wrinkle in her face while I stretched her and filled her and punished her pussy for being so perfect, so tight, so inexperienced. But I couldn't face her right now, couldn't look into her guileless expression while I fucked her like a well-used whore.

Because that was exactly how I fucked her—like I'd paid for the hour. Apropos since I had a feeling, when this was all said and done, there would be a price to pay. I just hoped I could afford the cost.

She was a good girl for me. She told me what she wanted with her sounds, with the rhythm of her breathing, with the way her cunt clutched at my violent stabs. She obeyed me when I demanded that she played with herself, and she stayed with the effort even as she shattered around my cock, her body convulsing with the force of her orgasm.

And I wasn't yet finished with her.

I sat on the edge of the bed and pulled her to sit on my lap. I let her ride me reverse-cowgirl style while I licked the back of her neck and pulled at her nipples. When she tired, I spanked her upper thigh then gripped her hips and moved her body for her. She came again, stuttering my name, a sound that made me wild with lust.

I couldn't resist anymore—I had to watch her face.

Again, I shifted her, laying her back onto the bed. I knelt in front of her, my knees driven wide. With my hands gripping her ankles, I spread her legs apart. She was completely on display now—the twist of her facial features, her tits as they bounced to my unrelenting tempo, her pussy as it swallowed each and every one of my cock's thrusts. This time I didn't have to tell her to touch herself, she just did, her eyes locked on me as she stroked horizontally across her clit—she was a quick learner. The best of students.

"This," she said, her gaze glossy. "I really like this. Watching you like this."

"You've had sex face-to-face before." I was always quick to anchor things in reality.

"I have. But never like this." Her thighs tightened with her oncoming climax. "I've never watched anyone watch me like you're watching me now." Her words strangled as she threw her head back and surrendered to the pleasure, but I understood them well enough.

Well enough to undo me.

I shoved in, slipping past the grip of her pussy until I was planted as deep as possible, and with a rumble of curse words, I let my orgasm wash over me, bathing me like the cold immersion of baptism, leaving me drenched and soul-stirred and new and convinced that nothing, nothing would ever be the same.

But hormones have that effect.

When I was calm and thinking straight, after we'd stroked each other's skin and bantered back and forth, after we'd each showered and washed up, I recognized the folly of the notion. Of course everything would be the same again. She was just a pretty girl—sweet and too young and sinfully wicked with her naivety. She was one of a million girls of the same mold. Maybe she was one of only a handful that would look twice at a forty-plus-year-old man, but she wasn't unique in any way.

I'd put her on a train, she'd ride off, and in a week she'd be nothing but a sordid memory to pull out when I jerked off in the shower.

"I do hope this was somewhat educational," I said when we'd

reached the top of the escalators at Grand Central Station. It was as far as I intended to go. Watching her train take off from the platform was entirely too romantic for a curmudgeon like me.

"So educational." Her cheeks pinked, and I wondered exactly what it was she was remembering. "You're a very thorough teacher."

She was being kind with her flattery. Yet, I smiled and accepted the compliment all the same.

"Is anyone meeting you at the station?"

"My roommate."

She had a roommate. She had friends. She had a whole life that I knew nothing about. Didn't it feel like she knew every important thing about me? Every dull detail of my lame existence. Anything I hadn't said out loud in our brief time together could be guessed at and pieced together while she was an enigma. A puzzle I was never meant to solve.

I stopped trying. I let the cloud of mystery settle back around her and didn't ask her anything else. And when it was time for us to part, I resisted the gut-deep instinct to pull her into my arms and kiss the hell out of her, and instead, pulled her in for a polite hug.

"I suppose I have to believe in kismet now," I said, because she deserved the sentiment.

"Isn't it wonderful?"

Wonderful. Yes. It *was* some kind of wonderful.

Then I walked away, refusing to look back, even once. Refusing to do anything but move on.

I FLEW home to London the following day despite Weston's emphatic request that I stay for his upcoming nuptials.

"Lose another week in the States to attend your fake wedding?" I chortled. "I think not."

"What if it's not so fake?"

"Even more reason not to stay." I sounded as bitter as usual. Things did return to normal, then. As I knew they would.

A week passed. Ten days. A fortnight. Every day my thoughts turned to Audrey. Her smile haunted my dreams. Her cute quips replayed unbidden at the oddest of times. The light soprano of her voice sounded in the chorus of every Christmas carol.

I missed her. I ached for her presence. I was...

Oh, fuck.

I was *pining*.

I'd most likely never see her again, and that was best. For both of us.

But if our paths did cross in the future, if fortune deemed that we'd once more come face to face, I'd have to believe in kismet, wouldn't I? Would I believe in more, too?

Would I be ready to believe again in love?

Only fate alone could know.

SWEET FATE

TWELVE
DYLAN

I noticed her the minute she came outside.

She hadn't been in the house when Aaron and I had arrived, almost half an hour earlier. We'd been greeted by Susan and Raymond Kincaid, Donovan's parents, who had cordially shown us to the grounds behind the house where the rest of the guests were waiting. I'd scanned the crowd for her. There were many faces I recognized—mostly employees from Reach, the company I co-owned, but a few were people from the long-ago past when Donovan had been engaged to my stepdaughter. So many familiar acquaintances, but not her.

And she was the only one I cared to see.

I'd spent the next thirty minutes milling about, nursing a too-sweet glass of champagne while pretending to be interested in the small talk of associates and friends. Petty subjects received great attention—the weather, the stock exchange, the latest hit Broadway show, what designer the bride would wear.

I'd perked up when I'd heard that last one. Though I cared not a fig about couture, any mention of Sabrina was of interest. It would be in conjunction with her name that someone might address the whereabouts of her sister, the bride's only family. She had to be here, hadn't she? Would there be anything at all that would keep her away?

Perhaps it wouldn't seem too obvious if I asked Weston. We'd all shared dinner the last time I'd been in the States, rode home in the same car. Surely it would be natural to inquire about that lovely girl...*what was her name?*

I'd considered the best way to broach the subject while Weston's old assistant poked at him.

"Don't talk to me, don't even look at me without that little boy in your arms," Roxie scolded her former boss in her husky Hungarian accent. "I barely got time to be in his life before you take him away."

Weston had responded with a laugh. "He's here, he's here. Calm down. Elizabeth is showing him off to—"

I never did get to hear where Weston's wife had absconded with Weston's son because that's when the woman I'd been waiting for arrived—all rosy-cheeked and glossed lips, her hair knotted loosely at the back of her neck, her eyes twinkling with excitement—and all sound rushed past me like white noise. My vision tunneled to only see her. Audrey Lind. The most beautiful woman in existence.

She was bustling out of the house, the skirt of her dress gathered in one hand so as not to trip. The red wine of her outfit matched the color on her lips and fit her like she'd been sewn into it. Her curves were accentuated with a twisted tie around the waistline and sheer material at her neckline. She must have been locked away inside getting ready all this time. She was a lone ruby in an array of plain stones. It was impossible to miss her presence.

I pinned my eyes to her, watching as she pushed past guests, making her way to the band. She whispered something to the guitar player, who then gave a signal to the singer. The current song was wrapped up, and Audrey stepped up to the microphone.

"Hello, everyone, if I could have your attention..." She waited for the rest of the crowd to catch up to me.

"That's Sabrina's sister, Aubrey," Weston informed Roxie.

"Audrey," I corrected without moving my gaze from the woman in question.

"Right. Audrey. Wasn't that what I said?" It most certainly wasn't what he'd said, but I refrained from arguing. "Real sweet girl."

Sweet, yes. Girl? She was a woman in so many ways that mattered.

And a girl too, I supposed, in ways that mattered more.

With the guests, for the most part, quieted, Audrey continued with her address. "I've just gotten word from the driver that Donovan and Sabrina are about ten minutes away—seven minutes-ish now—and I wanted to tell you all what to expect from here."

"Is there a plan in place for if she says no?" a male voice shouted from the audience.

I knew that voice—Nate Sinclair, another of the men who owned the advertising company with me, Donovan, and Weston. I cringed internally on Audrey's behalf. My eyes left her briefly to find him in the crowd.

A tall brunette clapped her hand over Nate's mouth. His girlfriend, Trish, I assumed. I had yet to meet her. "Don't listen to him!" she cried apologetically. "He thinks he's funny."

"Yes, ignore him, please!" Audrey exclaimed in horror, as I knew she would. "There is no way Sabrina won't say yes, but that's just bad luck to even think such a thing!"

Nate backed down. "Sorry, sorry. Tasteless joke."

"It *is* unusual," Roxie remarked critically at my side. "You think a surprise wedding is okay for the guests, but for the bride?"

I couldn't agree more. Weddings, on the whole, were much ado about nothing. The biggest marketing ploy since the invention of Valentine's Day, if anyone asked me. And I would know. Advertising was my job.

Today, though, I was less impatient with the jollification. Enduring the hoopla was scarcely a hardship when Audrey was the reward.

"As soon as they arrive," she said, picking up where she'd left off. "Sabrina will be whisked to a private room to get ready, and guys, I'm telling you, she is seriously low maintenance. She'll be prettied up in thirty minutes, forty minutes tops. We'll have another announcement to gather everyone in their seats when it's showtime. Until then, feel free to munch on hors d'oeuvre, drink champagne, and dance! Isn't this day amazing?"

A burst of applause followed her speech. Conversations resumed and the band started up once again. Audrey casually made her way back to the house, stopping to greet people on the way. Nearby, a waiter opened a champagne bottle, popping off the cork with a loud crack. She jumped then fell into a fit of laughter as she clutched her hand to her heart.

God, she was enchanting. I couldn't look away. She could light up an already brilliant day. She was incandescent. She absolutely glowed.

"... Dylan, for a toast."

"Hm?" I'd missed the beginning of whatever it was that Weston had said, only tuning in at the sound of my name.

He clapped a hand on my back. "I was just saying we should go up and have a drink with Donovan when they get here."

The only place I wanted to be was alone with Audrey.

But I wasn't counting on having the opportunity, and I'd lost sight of her now, so I turned my full attention to my friend. "Sure. Let me find Aaron so I can tell him where I am."

My son was exactly where I'd left him, curled up with his earbuds and his mobile in the shade on the side of the house. He was a shy thirteen—er, fourteen-year-old; he'd recently had a birthday. I hadn't expected him to want to mingle. He'd only accompanied me, in fact, so that we could continue on to Hartford afterward to stay for a few days. I planned to take him to the Mark Twain House & Museum and the Harriet Beecher Stowe Center. Whether he appreciated it or not, I meant to culture the boy.

Of course I'd also had to agree I'd take him to a video game competition being held over the weekend, but I felt comfortable with the compromise.

I stooped down in front of Aaron. At the sight of me, he pulled a bud from one of his ears. "Is the wedding starting?"

"No, you have another half hour or so."

He gave a fist-bumping motion and picked up the bud as if to return it to his ear, apparently done with the conversation, but I halted him.

"I might be MIA for a bit. I'm going to see if Donovan needs help getting ready. I'll come and get you when it's time."

"Yeah, yeah," he said impatiently, his eyes already back on the screen of his phone.

Well, then. No need to worry about him.

I stood up again, just as another round of applause came from the crowd behind the house. Imagining that signalled Donovan and Sabrina's arrival, I headed inside through the side door to meet up with Weston instead of returning to the backyard.

The Kincaid's country home was large enough to be called an estate. I'd been there before, but not enough times and not recently enough to know my way around the place, especially coming in from an entrance I didn't normally use. I ambled through the halls, my ears perked, listening for sounds to direct me to the lounge.

I was also conscientious of Audrey. If Sabrina was in the house now, her sister surely was as well. When I'd reached the front hall, I froze. Was that her giggle coming faintly from above? I looked up the stairs, hoping to catch her.

"There you are," Nate said, making me jump. He grinned. "Sorry for startling you. I tracked down Donovan. Weston just stepped out to his car to get—"

Just then the front door opened and Weston walked in, carrying a box of Macallan.

"—the Scotch," Nate finished. "And here we all are."

"Shall we?" I asked, still half listening for the beautiful melody of Audrey's laugh.

Nate nodded. "I'll lead the way."

A few minutes later, after swiping four tumblers and a corkscrew from Raymond Kincaid's bar, we were gathered in a downstairs guest room with the groom. Donovan was already mostly dressed in black tuxedo bottoms and a crisp white dress shirt when we'd arrived. Now he was leaning against the windowsill, seemingly relaxed except for the constant twirl of his pocket watch.

A drink would do him well.

Weston handed him a tumbler and broke open the Scotch, then poured two fingers into his glass before turning to fill mine and Nate's.

"A toast!" Weston exclaimed, raising his own drink when he'd finished serving the rest of us. "To Donovan—may all your days be filled with rich love."

"Hear, hear," Nate agreed, and everyone took a sip.

"Look at you—a proper best man," I said to Weston. He was the only groomsman at all, actually, Donovan having figured it was too much of an ordeal to have more with the casual nature of the ceremony.

It was a reasonable decision, and an expected choice, though Weston wasn't generally considered the most responsible of our bunch, and my tone hinted at the fact.

"Shut up. You didn't even bother to come to my wedding," he scoffed.

I shrugged, unwilling to feel any remorse for not attending. "It wasn't a real wedding at the time."

"It was always a real wedding," he insisted. "It wasn't a real marriage."

"Both sound terrible." This remark earned a short laugh from Nate.

Weston wasn't amused. "You're such a grouch. Is this really fair to Donovan on his big day?"

"Donovan knows who I am, and he still thought to invite me." I looked to the man in question and felt validated when he nodded in agreement. "Nate isn't big on these affairs either. Why aren't you poking at him?"

"Because *he* came to my wedding." Weston would never let that go, I was beginning to realize.

"Came *at* your wedding too, from what I heard," Donovan said pointedly.

And now Weston's attention was somewhere besides me. "Nate? Something you'd like to share?"

"Only that I *heard the same* about Donovan." The two exchanged a look, some recognition of an inside joke that was apparently filthy in nature. "But I will say, to your point, Dylan—though it's true I could take or leave the whole marriage tradition, it doesn't mean I'm down on love all together."

The comment was directed toward me, the last single man in the room.

"You're really smitten with this girl you're dating, aren't

you?" It wasn't the comment I wanted to make, but I was being polite. For now.

"Trish?" Nate thought a moment. "I love her. I'm in love with her. I basically live with her. We're as married as we're ever going to get, but that doesn't mean we aren't solid."

"Christ, you too? You're daft as a brush, the whole lot of you." Apparently, my civility had expired.

"You must be looking in the mirror, Locke."

"Original, King."

Weston ignored my retort. "You know who's really the dick-hole—Cade. He should be here. It's bad enough that he's gone on leave of absence for an eternity. It's another to miss one of your only friend's weddings."

It wasn't the first time today I'd heard him griping about the fifth owner of Reach. "Why are you so cross with him? He came to *your* wedding."

"Eh, not really." He looked to Donovan, as though seeking permission.

Curious, I turned my attention to the groom as well.

Donovan grabbed his vest from the bed where it was draped and turned toward the mirror. "He was in town for other reasons. Attending Weston's wedding was incidental."

There was no doubt that Donovan was watching what he said. I didn't mind people having their own secrets for the most part, but Cade's disappearance from the business had been abrupt. He'd been gone now for almost seven months. It was beginning to be an elephant that no one wanted to address.

"What did he have to do in New York?" It wasn't the day to pry, but I could certainly tiptoe around the subject. Cade rarely ever came to the States. He'd been managing the Tokyo office since Donovan had returned to New York, which meant, at present, there was only an acting manager running the place.

Donovan shrugged as he buttoned his vest.

"You don't know or you're not at liberty to discuss?" I pressed.

"Something like that."

"Uh-huh. Then I'm guessing the reason for his extended leave is also something you aren't at liberty to discuss."

He shifted his eyes toward mine in the reflection and smiled slyly. "Something like that."

Obviously this was going nowhere.

Giving up, I turned to look out the window into the backyard. The guests who had, for the most part, been standing and chatting earlier were now starting to take their seats. I scanned the sea of faces, searching for the one I most wanted to see.

I hadn't yet found her when Weston came to peer over my shoulder. "Looks like people are starting to gather. I'm going to go down now so I can make sure Elizabeth is good with Sebastian before it's time to line up."

Nate finished off his glass. "I'll go with you. Trish gets antsy at these things. I shouldn't leave her alone for too long."

I listened halfheartedly to Weston and Nate bestow congratulations and well-wishes as I continued to study the crowd, looking always for her. She'd said it was kismet when we'd met before. I didn't believe in that nonsense, not anymore.

But if she were outside right now...if she looked up and our eyes met...

"She's helping Sabrina get ready," Donovan said.

I looked back and was startled to find we were now the only two in the room. Meaning Donovan had been addressing me. But he couldn't have guessed who I'd been looking for. Could he?

"Who?" I asked innocently.

"Audrey."

As I'd assumed, and yet, still I'd searched.

"That is why you're here, isn't it? I can't imagine any other reason you'd attend a wedding, let alone fly across an ocean for one. Had to be to see her."

I threw him a scowl. "Poppycock. I was coming to the States anyway to see Aaron." And yes, also to see Audrey. Not to start anything or have some glorious reunion, but after seven months of pining, I'd hoped seeing her might knock the want of her out of my system.

I wasn't about to tell any of that to Donovan though.

Too late, I realized my defensiveness had caused me to respond incorrectly. "But if I hadn't already planned to be here to see Aaron, I'd have come anyway. For you. I'd never miss *your* nuptials."

"Uh-huh." He smirked like he was in on a joke. "She's graduated now, you know. Looking for work."

"Who?" I could play this game all day.

He threw me a glare that reminded me he could play all day too, then went about tucking his tie into his vest. "There are ways to influence where she ends up. I'd be happy to help if..."

"'Influence where she ends up?' Whatever is that supposed to mean?"

"That if you want her close to you, it's possible to make that happen."

I wanted to ask more about those possibilities, wanted to pursue them sincerely. While I couldn't know what Donovan had in mind, I did trust that he could do what he said. He was a man who made things happen, and wasn't it tempting to pounce on his offer? To live a life where I saw Audrey Lind every day? I couldn't imagine anything more miraculous.

But I was a pragmatic man. Even if a woman like her would want a man nearly twenty years older than she was, we were on different paths. Especially now that she'd finished school. She had her entire future ahead of her. Who was I, with those days long in my past, to step in and hold her back?

"I'm not moving back to New York," I said, my jaw set. "And if you're offering something else, I'm definitely not interested in that."

"Are you sure about that?"

Yes. As miserable as that made me, I was sure.

But why was Donovan pushing us together anyway? I'd assumed he didn't know anything about me and Audrey.

Did he?

I turned my full attention on him and narrowed my eyes. "What exactly are you suggesting is between she and I, might I ask?"

"I'm suggesting nothing."

"It sure sounds like you're suggesting something," I grumbled.

He picked up his tuxedo jacket from the bed and paused. "Such as?"

"Such as some imagined relationship between me and your soon-to-be sister-in-law."

"Nope. Not suggesting anything of the sort." He slid one arm through the sleeve of the jacket, followed by the other.

"I'd appreciate it if you continued that way." What on earth had provoked this conversation in the first place? Had I given any indication that I was interested in the girl or had he simply been fishing?

More importantly, had I confirmed anything if he had been? I quickly replayed everything that had been said in my head. A frown sunk on my lips. "No one needs to know about this conversation, either. Including Sabrina."

Donovan stood in front of the mirror again, fidgeting with his collar, but stopped to consider me. "Are you asking me to keep something from my wife?"

That had been what I'd implied, hadn't it? Perhaps that wasn't fair. Especially since my own marriage had been destroyed with secrets and lies.

A thought suddenly occurred to me. "Has Audrey ever...has she mentioned...me? To you or Sabrina?"

"A shared kiss. Nothing else."

That shouldn't have been as disappointing as it was. I hadn't told anyone about Audrey, after all. Not even about the kiss.

But I was a different beast than she. I wasn't prone to gushing and prattling on about such things, whereas she was. If there was anything to gush and prattle on about, it was hard to believe she'd be able to bottle it in.

"Good," I said, trying for nonchalant. "Because there's nothing besides that for her to mention. Which is why there's nothing to mention to Sabrina either. It's not asking you to keep something from your wife if she already knows all there is to begin with."

He turned to face me, again with that knowing smirk. "Sure. Whatever you say."

Worried that wasn't the end of it, I changed the subject myself. "Enough about me. This is your day." I stood back to size him up. "You look good! Are you nervous?"

"Not since the Scotch kicked in."

"Sounds about right." Though it didn't need it, I reached out to straighten his tie. It was an excuse for an intimate moment. "You took a long time to get here. You deserve this, my friend."

"Misery and woe?"

I really had been a shithead, spreading my doom and gloom all over his big event.

With a sigh, I attempted to steer a new course. "That's how it worked out for me, but perhaps I'm not a man who knows how to hold onto happiness."

"Never too late to learn."

Maybe that was true. Maybe I could find joy with a woman once again. Maybe this time I could keep it in my grasp, protect it, never let it go.

I didn't believe that rubbish, however. I didn't subscribe to the fancies of fairy tales or the notion that happily ever after could exist.

But despite my skepticism, I said, "Then show me how it's done, will you?" Because on Donovan's wedding day, I was a good enough friend to pretend it was possible.

THIRTEEN

It was a beautiful wedding, considering that it was, in fact, a wedding.

Sabrina had chosen a tailored gown with sleek lines and a plunging neckline. An oversized bow trailed to the floor behind her, adding just a hint of drama. Her eyes glistened throughout the ceremony, and her face wore a smile that reached from ear to ear.

It was difficult not to remember that Amanda had once been slated to stand where she was, and it added a bittersweet flavor to an event that already tasted tart in my mouth.

Donovan remained stoic as always, but he gave his own hints at emotion. The shallow rise and fall of his chest, the tightening of his throat while reciting his vows. His gaze never left hers, as though he were chained to her through their eyes. It was obvious he loved her, that he worshipped the ground she walked on, and I imagined for those reasons that he considered this the best day of his life.

I hoped, for both their sakes, more best days would follow.

I watched them intently, paying attention to every exchange

between them, to every soft word whispered, every slight touch. Focusing completely on them was the only way to keep from sneaking glances at the bride's sister. The only look at her I'd allowed myself had been when she'd walked down the aisle ahead of Sabrina, when *everyone*'s eyes were on her.

But even without giving her my direct focus, I saw her. She stood to the side of Sabrina the entire wedding. She was there in my periphery, her presence pulling at me like she was an industrial strength magnet and I, an iron rod. She kept herself together, neither fidgeting nor breaking down in happy tears, but I could sense the joy inside her, wanting to burst. I could feel it as if it were an emotion coming from inside myself. I could feel her as though she were in my arms and not five meters away.

After the kiss between the bride and groom and the proclamation of man and wife, Donovan and Sabrina were pulled aside by the photographer while Audrey resumed the spot behind the microphone. She directed everyone to the tent where dinner was soon to be served, informing guests how to find their assigned seats. Then she was swept away with the fluster of activity, and I lost sight of her again.

For the best.

I didn't want to know who she was with, who might have come as her date. I didn't want to hear the laughs she shared with others and not with me. I didn't want to see her *not* looking for me. So instead I looked for Aaron.

I managed for a good part of the evening to stay occupied with my son. Through dinner and the cutting of the cake and most of the toasts. Then it was her turn to raise her champagne glass and deliver her blessings, and then I had to look again.

"For those who don't know, Sabrina is as much a mother to me as she is a sister," she said. "Our dad died when I was thirteen, and mom had been gone a while by then. And this woman—this wonderful, beautiful woman—changed her entire life to look out for me."

She choked up and had to pause, dabbing at her eyes, until she could talk again. "I've been so very lucky to have her devotion. So lucky to be loved by her. She deserves every bit of happiness and affection that she spent on me to be returned to her with interest, and I know Donovan is the man who can deliver. I wish you everything your heart desires, sis. You deserve it. And no more worrying about me. You've been the best example, and I only hope that if or when I find a love as amazing as you've found with Donovan, that I have the ability to recognize it."

She mouthed some form of I love you and blew a kiss, and I closed my eyes and tried to figure out why her gorgeous speech left a pit in my stomach. Certainly I worried that Donovan and Sabrina wouldn't last, that years later they'd look back on today as a bitter memory and despise every shallow sentiment that had been spoken.

But concern wasn't the feeling twisting in my gut. This burned more like jealousy. Yes, yes, I was jealous—of Donovan and Sabrina who were at the beginning of their happy days, for their love, still pure and untainted. Jealous of Audrey and her ability to be so genuinely candid. But most of all, jealous of whomever it was that she was waiting to find, the man who would get to love her and feel her love in return.

I took a deep breath in and let it out. This was ridiculous. *I* was ridiculous. If I wanted the girl so badly, why didn't I just go talk to her? What was keeping me from her?

Only myself, that was who.

After the toasts had finished, I left Aaron in a passionate discussion with Weston about some animated show called Voltron and went to find her. I discovered her at the punch bowl, patiently listening while Donovan's mother rattled on about the disappointments of the day. That wasn't a conversation I wanted to be in the middle of, so I stood nearby, waiting for them to wrap up.

I saw when she noticed me.

Her forehead, which had just a moment before been creased, relaxed and her brows rose. Did I imagine that her eyes sparked? That her entire face lit up?

"Dylan!" she exclaimed when she was finally free of Susan Kincaid.

Without reservation, she moved in to wrap me in her embrace, and my entire being sighed with relief. She smelled just as I'd remembered—like apples and bourbon, like spring and vibrancy. Her touch sent warmth shooting through my limbs. And the feel of her, the weight of her in my arms, was like finding gravity. Like discovering the best ballast. Like being firmly anchored after too long adrift at sea.

It was a brief harbor.

Too soon she was stepping back, putting an acceptable distance between us.

"I saw you earlier," she said, and I clung to every syllable she uttered. "I confess—I'd been looking, and I meant to come over, but then I'd get distracted or you'd be with your son, and I worried about intruding."

Then she had looked for me. I could feel the span of my chest increasing with that knowledge.

"It never seemed like the proper time," I agreed.

"I'm glad you're here now. It's so good to see you."

"You as well." Silence stretched between us, a comfortable quiet that kept our gazes locked while all the words I couldn't say effervesced inside me like champagne bubbles pressing at the cork. She smiled as though she understood what I hadn't spoken. Her cheeks pinked, and finally she broke our gaze with a quick glance at her feet.

"How are you?" she said when she looked back up.

At the same time, I asked, "You've been well?"

She laughed, that angelic tinkle that always made me heady.

"Go on," I offered. I would have said nothing at all for the rest of our interaction, content to simply listen to every one of her precious sounds.

She swept a stray piece of hair behind her ear. "Things are good with you? And Aaron?"

"Yes, we're good. He's grown more than three inches since Thanksgiving, at least two since I saw him in the spring. He curses more than a child should probably curse in front of his father, and he is glued to his phone..." *Shut it, will you? She doesn't want to hear about your parenting woes.* "But we're both good."

"Except you're at a wedding—are you completely miserable?"

"Not completely." Far from at this particular moment. "And you? You're finished with your master's, I presume. How goes the art conversation?"

She smiled at my purposeful switch of the word *conversation* for *conservation*. "I am done. Walked the stage three weeks ago. Now I'm doing the find-a-job thing, which is almost as dreadful as school was. I started applying months ago, and well, you know art conservation is a real specialized career. Entry-level work isn't spectacular. I'm still building a portfolio and all." She twisted her bottom lip between her teeth. "But! I do have a second interview at the Boston Museum of Fine Arts. Jax and I are driving out there tomorrow." She glanced toward a young man sitting at a table, drawing with a stylus onto a digital pad.

I didn't want to ask. I didn't want to know.

"Boston Museum of Fine Arts? That's fantastic!"

She blushed again. "It's only an interview."

"It's still fantastic." I couldn't help myself—I asked. "And Jax is...?"

She nodded toward the man. "We went to school together.

Jax is a digital artist. We're thinking of maybe getting a place together if I end up somewhere 'cool.' His words."

The burn of jealousy returned, acidic in my stomach. "He's a boyfriend, then?"

"No, no," she said quickly. "A friend."

As if sensing he was being talked about, Jax looked up from his iPad and gave Audrey a smile. It was the same kind of smile that I imagined I gave her—adoring and full of want.

"He likes you more than a friend," I said, my throat scalding with the words.

"Ah, no. Well..." Her eyes darted down again. "Maybe. We'll see."

The floor felt like it was plummeting beneath my feet. Of course she'd have a beau. Who could know her and let her get away?

"But I am excited about the possibility," she said eagerly, apparently unaware that I was sinking into despair. "Boston isn't that far away from New York, and especially if Sabrina starts having babies, I'm going to want to be close. I need to live vicariously through her until I get some of my own."

"You want children?" This shouldn't have been a surprise.

"Definitely. I'm one of those greedy women who want it all—a fulfilling career, an adoring husband, *and* a brood. I'm thinking five is a good number. But maybe I'll squeeze out six."

"Six?"

"Like I said, a brood."

A brood. She wanted a brood.

I spent my days dreaming of retirement and putting my teenager through college. At my age, perhaps, one baby could be considered. Two, if I worked fast. Certainly not five. Not six. Not *a brood*.

This was what was keeping me from her—this vast chasm that stood between her future trajectory and mine. She was at the start of her life, when girls wanted marriage and family and white picket fences. And why shouldn't she want those things? She had many years ahead of her to want it all. Many years to *have* it all.

I would be nothing but an obstacle for her dreams.

If she were even to want me.

So though I yearned to ask her to dance, to press my face into the curve of her neck and hold her tight against me, I didn't extend the offer.

"Of course, I have to find the right guy first," she said, twisting her hands in front of her. "Who knows? Maybe I already know him."

"Maybe it's Jax."

"Yeah. Maybe."

She opened her mouth to say something else when Sabrina's voice cut through the noise of the crowd. "All right, ladies. I'm throwing the bouquet!"

Audrey clasped her hands at her heart. "The bouquet! That's my cue." She stepped forward and placed a soft kiss on my cheek, a kiss that I was sure I'd feel for the rest of my life. "This wasn't so terribly awkward, after all," she said when she pulled away.

"No, not terribly awkward, after all."

My eyes didn't leave her as she walked away. Inside, a vice gripped my ribs, squeezing all the air from my lungs, splitting my chest in two, and still I watched her with a smile pasted on my lips.

It wasn't entirely fake. It *did* make me happy to see her, even while seeing her taught me the most wretched lesson—though I could never have her, though we were fated to be two ships that passed in the night, Audrey Lind was not a woman I was getting over anytime soon.

FOURTEEN

"Thank fuck it's finally stopped raining. I'd forgotten what the sun looked like." Amy threw back the last of her Diet Coke and stepped away from the window to toss the can in my recycling bin. Then she perched on the corner of my desk, a habit she was wont to do when she intruded on my lunch hour as she was doing now.

Honestly, I didn't mind all that much. Though I was the head of the London office, I mainly took care of the finances, a rather isolated job. Amelia Rahim—Amy—managed our sales division. She was bullheaded, cold-hearted, and churlish. We got along splendidly.

"I didn't take you as one who complained about dreary weather. Isn't grey your favorite color? You sure wear it often enough." I grabbed the stack of month-end reports that were stacked precariously near her bottom and moved them to a safer location on my desk before returning my focus to my screen.

"Grey, charcoal, nickel, jet—all shades of black, really. I like my outside to match my in." She picked up the Granny Smith sitting next to my computer and bounced it up and down in the palm of her hand. "And I do love it when the sky takes on my moods, but I'd prefer to do without the wet. My hair frizzes." She caught the apple, brought it to her mouth, and took a crisp bite.

"I was planning on eating that," I grumbled.

"You were taking too long to get to it."

"I suppose you need to eat healthy more than I do, at your age." Amy was the one employee on the management team older than me. Though it was only by three days, I didn't often let her forget it.

"You're a real barrel of laughs today, Locke. Considering you've been moody as all get out for the past several months, I have to ask what's up. Has the sun gotten to you too?"

I looked up from my work to gaze out the window at the clear sky. Frankly, I hadn't noticed the weather was any different today from any other day. Since I'd returned from the States this summer, it had seemed that it didn't matter if the sun was shining or not. Every day of the past three and a half months had been dreary and bland.

I was well aware of the problem. It was Audrey. She'd ruined me when I'd seen her again. I'd been reminded that she was the brightest light in existence. Everything else was dull in comparison.

Amy's remark was the first indication that anyone else had picked up on my sullenness, though. I'd been too self-absorbed to think about my mood's effect on others.

And *was* I feeling less solemn today?

I did a quick body scan, and yes, indeed, my chest felt less tight. The corners of my mouth were relaxed instead of turned down. My shoulders didn't feel weighed down with an unbearable heaviness.

Why I was feeling better, I had no idea. Maybe the sun actually had made a difference.

I turned my attention back to my computer. "It's our

numbers," I said, an answer that sounded as good as any other. "As of right now, this quarter is up twenty-two percent from last."

"We are? Damn. I had no idea. And here you were so certain that the new French location would put a dent in business."

"It was a reasonable assumption," I said defensively. We'd had three rather large international clients that had taken their business to Weston's Paris office since it was more central to their headquarters. But after I'd complained about it thoroughly a number of times, Amy had decided to do something about it and found us a number of good-paying clients to take their place. "It's all your doing, really. You deserve the congratulations."

"Not just my doing. If you hadn't moaned so loudly about the situation, I would have continued the method that has worked well for me so far in life—doing as little as possible."

I looked up to see if she was serious before breaking into laughter. Amy was a workaholic like no other. She ate, slept, and breathed Reach, Inc. She had practically no social life or hobbies, unless crushing the competition counted. She often claimed she'd never married because she believed in monogamy, and she was already married to her job.

"See what I mean? A couple of days ago, I don't think you would have caught the joke."

"What a shame that would have been." I finished entering the numbers on the report. The totals wouldn't be accurate until we got confirmation that the deposits had gone through, but I liked to have an estimate as soon as the quarter was finished. "There we are. Twenty-two point three percent growth, to be more specific."

"We're a good team, Dylan. We should celebrate. It's been awhile since we've done that—just you and I." Her meaning was clear, but she crossed one leg over the other to enunciate her point.

I couldn't help watching. The woman had long limbs that she

kept well-toned. I'd had them wrapped around me on more than one occasion. Apparently, she was offering to wrap them around me again.

While I didn't generally like the idea of sex with coworkers, Amy's commitment to no-commitment was as steadfast as mine. We were the perfect pair, only in it for the benefits. Often, it was easier to turn to her than go to a pub and try to hit on a stranger.

It *had* been awhile since I'd last hooked up with anyone. Not since before Audrey. I hadn't been interested, and it hadn't crossed my mind to think that maybe sleeping with another woman would be helpful. Perhaps it would help get me over my fixation on the girl.

And yet...

I paused too long with a response. "Think about it," Amy said, jumping down from my desk. "I'm here all afternoon. You can tell me if you're interested at the end of the day."

"I'll do that." Was I stupid for not jumping on her offer right away? We'd always had an uncomplicated arrangement in the past. Finish up in the office, leave together, and then... "Oh, Amy!" I called before she'd made it out of my office. "I just remembered. I'm meeting with that Lieber guy this afternoon. So you may be here all afternoon, but I won't."

"The car manufacturer? You've already met with him twice. He's not coming to the office?" Amy's tone said she was as annoyed with Hans Lieber as I was. The man brought prospects of a huge addition to the firm's accounts—which was fantastic. But his insistence on continuing to meet with an owner of Reach was beyond irritating. I was not the person who closed the sales. That was Amy's job.

That didn't mean I couldn't do it. It meant I didn't want to.

But I would. "He only has a limited time in his schedule to meet so he asked if I could come to his hotel. He's staying at the Corinthia."

Amy cringed. "How pompous."

"Yes. Very."

"But also, seems the man has money he wants to spend. Want me to come with? I could rearrange my afternoon."

I considered. "No, not this time. I think he's right on the verge of signing on, and I don't want to give him any reason to change his mind."

"Because meeting me might just be the best reason to run," she said. I rushed to amend what I'd said, but she put up a hand to halt me. "No worries. I'm joking. I get it. Take the meeting, and then text me and let me know if you'd like that celebratory dinner. My house. I'll even order takeout."

I laughed and agreed to text her later. I'd even think more about actually saying yes to her offer. After all, it would probably be good for me to have a little fun, reason to celebrate or not.

FOUR HOURS LATER, I walked out of the Corinthia Hotel with another reason to celebrate—Hans Lieber had only wanted to meet to tell me he officially wanted to hire Reach for his international campaigns. The contracts had to be written up and there would be more negotiating of fine details, but the deal felt solid. Irritating as the man might be, he had a reputation of integrity, and a handshake was as reliable as any signed paper.

It was definitely a win that made me feel good. There was practically a spring in my step as I walked toward Whitehall to hail a cab. At the corner, something came over me—a strange sense of whimsy that made me change my mind about the car. The weather was so nice, the temperature unusually warm for the first of October, that I decided to walk through the park instead. Then I could jump on the underground at St. James's Park Station.

The detour was the perfect choice. The trees were beautifully clothed in autumn colors. Red, yellow, and orange leaves dressed the walkways as well. I listened for them to crunch under my feet, but they were still too rain-soaked from the previous week's weather. Instead the air was filled with the sound of birds and kids. Most of the deck chairs were occupied. The sunshine had obviously called more than just me to the outdoors. And why wouldn't it? St. James's Park was magnificent. I'd forgotten how much so. How long had it been since I'd strolled through its gardens? How long since I'd strolled through any gardens at all?

I couldn't remember.

I lingered on my way, breathing the fresh air, and wished there was someone to share the experience with.

No, that was a lie. I didn't wish for someone—I wished for Audrey, as I'd wished for her so often over the last several months, and even before the wedding, since the week we spent together in New York. Nothing had changed in my philosophies because of her. I still believed love was miserable and ended in arguments with overpriced solicitors. I still held that I'd rather live alone than mess with that bullshit again.

But I also yearned for her. I wished for her companionship. I wanted her to talk to, to hold at night. I dreamed her everywhere around me. I thought I saw her every time there was a crowd—on the underground, at the market. Over there, watching the mallards at the edge of the lake.

I stopped short and stared.

My imagination was getting the best of me because the profile of that woman really did look like Audrey. From the high cheekbones to the point of her chin to the amber color of her hair. Even the boots she wore looked identical to the ones Audrey had worn in New York. I needed to get closer to really tell. I took a step toward her. Then another tentative step.

Suddenly, the woman turned in my direction, and I quickly

looked away, not wanting to be caught staring. I hadn't just been staring, either—I'd been creeping up on her. What the bloody hell was that about? My obsession was going too far, stalking strangers in the park. Audrey was not in Westminster. She was somewhere far away. Boston, maybe. Definitely not here.

I resumed my walk, leaving behind the stupid fantasies of my deluded mind.

But then a familiar voice called after me. "Dylan? Dylan *Locke*? Is that you?"

I turned slowly, cautiously.

And there she was—*my* angel, my light, my Audrey.

"It *is* you!" she exclaimed with a clap before bounding toward me. She wrapped me up in a ferocious hug. "I can't believe it! I mean, I *can* because that's the way it is between us. But I didn't know when it would happen, and I'm so happy that it's happened today, of all days!"

My heart was pounding like a bass drum, and though I hated it when she let go of me, I was relieved she wouldn't hear it trying to escape from my chest. I had so many questions, and I meant to ask every single one of them as soon as the air returned to my lungs.

"Audrey—what are you doing here? Are you on vacation?" I tried to ignore what it meant that she hadn't contacted me about her visit.

"No, I live here! Isn't it crazy? I thought about calling you, but I was an idiot and lost my phone right when I got here and when I got the new one, a bunch of the contacts didn't transfer over, including yours, and then I thought maybe that was best because I didn't want to be weird, reaching out uninvited, and I figured if we were meant to see each other we would, and look! We did!" She was excited, her words bubbling out of her so rapidly I had a hard time keeping up.

In fact, I was still stuck on the first part of her monologue. "Did you say you *live* here?"

"I did! I got a job! Today was my first day, which was an experience that I can't even begin to describe, and then it's the first day it's been sunny since I moved here, so I came to the park on a whim, and here you are! It's kismet!"

I felt lightheaded.

And happy. Really fucking happy.

"Yes, kismet." I almost believed it myself.

"Then it's settled. We'll have dinner." There she was with that fierce confidence I adored so much. "Are you free tonight?"

I already had my phone out of my pocket so I could shoot a quick text to Amy.

> I'm going to have to pass on your offer. Something else has come up.

I hit SEND and looked up to Audrey with a smile. "I'm completely free. Let's do it."

FIFTEEN

I didn't believe this changed things.

Audrey was in town—living here—and I was elated, but I didn't think that I'd suddenly become the right man for her. I didn't instantaneously believe that love was the answer or that I should give a committed relationship another try. I wasn't that naïve.

I simply wanted right then to spend time with her, in whatever way possible. It was selfish and greedy, one of those live-in-the-moment moments. There wasn't thought of repercussions or what happens next or what living near her might mean. Nothing mattered but being in her presence *now*.

"Where shall we go?" she asked, her eyes wide and sparkling as though I might suggest we dine at the palace. "You know the area better than I do."

I really didn't. As most who lived in London, I didn't make it out to the touristy spots all that often.

But I wasn't completely ignorant of the area. "There are a lot of nice restaurants around here because of the museum and

Buckingham. The Blue Boar is nice. Or the Roux at Parliament Square." I'd taken clients to both on an occasion or two.

She frowned and looked down at her denim dress and striped tights. "I'm not fit for fancy. Is eating at St. James's Café a cliché?"

I tilted my head, giving serious thought to the question. "I wouldn't say it's cliché to eat at the park café when you're already in the park, but I wouldn't recommend that particular park café. Not anymore. It used to be rather nice. Now it's cafeteria style."

"Ew. No, thanks."

I was out of alternatives. "We could walk and find something?"

She agreed, and we headed toward my initial destination—the park underground stop. I wanted to stare at her as we walked, to catalog every feature and compare it to what I had stored in memory. Somehow I kept my wits about me and focused on the brilliant streaks of pink and orange as the sun set instead, but I listened intently to the melody of her voice as it swirled around me like a crisp autumn leaf caught on the wind.

"I really didn't think this day could get any more beautiful or surreal. It was already mindblowing to get to go into areas of the museum that were for authorized personnel only. I got to look at a Bellini under a microscope. An actual Bellini! I really have to learn to stop putting limits on what the universe has in store for me."

She was like a missionary for the romantics. She proclaimed her gospel every chance she got, and her enthusiasm for her religion was nearly contagious.

I bet she made lots of converts.

I almost wished I could be one of them.

"So you said you worked your first day today? Where are you employed? What happened to Boston?" Not that I wanted her to be in Boston. I didn't want her anywhere else but here.

"Boston turned out to be a bust." She rolled her eyes indicating how dreadful she considered the situation. "They were interested in me, but it was basically an unpaid internship. There was a daily stipend, but it was so small it wouldn't have even covered my coffee requirements. So it worked out when they didn't offer. I was pretty bummed about it at first. I didn't have any real attachments to the city, it's just...Sabrina had left the Boston area to come home and take care of me when Dad died and I had this idea that, if I lived there as an adult, it would somehow bring everything full-circle. It would make her feel like everything was worth it."

That made me frown. "Do you worry she doesn't think her life has been worth it?" I'd only met Sabrina a handful of times now, but she had always struck me as someone quite content with the road she'd taken.

She slowed her stride to think about it. "I guess sometimes I do, but I know she'd never say that. She's only ever said she would have done anything for me, and I believe her. Maybe I wanted it for me. So that I could stop feeling guilty about everything she's sacrificed. But c'est la vie. And like I said, I had no idea there were better opportunities in store."

I glanced over at her and our eyes caught. There was still a very real pull between us. There was no denying it. Her body gravitated toward mine as we walked. Her fingers brushed against mine more than once, each time shocking me with an intensity that sent my heart racing. The tension trapped in our gaze alone was nearly unbearable.

I couldn't stand it. I looked away.

"The job you have now is a good one, then?" I asked, trying to find more solid ground.

"Well...it *can* be." She stuck her hands into the front pockets of her dress, making her look even younger than she was. "It's another internship, but this time it's paid, and when it's over, if they like me, I'll get to stay. I haven't even told you where the job is—The National Gallery! Can you believe it? I can barely believe it myself and I was there all day! The freaking National Gallery in London. Oh, and the project they have me working on is amazing. It's called Christmas through Art. I'm supposed to catalog and put in chronological order all of the pieces the museum has that might fit into that display. It's quite a task. It will go up the beginning of December, and they'll want me until it goes back down. Beginning of January at least."

The beginning of January, was that all? Not even four months away.

It felt entirely too soon.

I stopped in front of a pub that called itself The Feathers. It seemed as good as any. "Is this okay?"

She looked up at the restaurant as though she'd forgotten we were even looking for one. "It's perfect. I love pub food."

We went inside and got a seat. After a few minutes looking over the menu, I went up to the counter to place our order. I came back with two glasses of red wine.

"Wine. Good idea," she said, raising her glass up in the air. "What shall we toast to?"

"Your new job? Your new living situation?" I'd toast to her, if it were appropriate. To her rich brown eyes that looked like tiger's eye in the right light and her mouth that curved up on one side while she spoke. To her constant smile and the hypnotic sound of her voice. To the way she lived life so fully, so genuinely. The way she let herself be vulnerable and soft yet never diminished her strength.

"How about a toast to us?" she asked as if there could be no other choice. "To finding each other in a city with millions of people."

She clinked her glass to mine, and for just a moment it felt like we really had found each other. Felt like, until she'd called my name in that damn park, I'd been lost.

And hadn't I been?

"To finding each other," I echoed, before bringing the wine to my lips. It was sweeter than I had expected, and heavy, slipping slowly down my throat like honey, leaving traces of itself as it went.

"It's good," Audrey said after taking her own first sip. She took another then set the glass down and laced her fingers together on the table in front of her. "So, Dylan, how did you happen to be st St. James? Do you live nearby? Do you go there a lot? I like the idea of imagining you walking through every day after work, though that's probably more in line with my personality than yours."

Years ago that would have been me as well. Back when I didn't measure time in dollars. When I still thought things would work out in the end.

And today it had been me again.

I scratched the back of my head trying to remember the exact circumstances of how that had come to be. "Actually, it was rather on a whim." I told her about my meeting with Hans Lieber and the weeks of rain and about how I'd decided spur of the moment to take the longer route home.

She slapped the table so hard that her wine sloshed. "I told you it was kismet! That was fate nudging you in the right direction. Did you realize it? I'm so glad you were open enough to hear it!"

"Or, well, it was a rather happy coincidence." It was almost cruel to disagree, but I did have a reputation to attend to.

She glowered at me, but didn't let my refute get her down. "And! And you had no plans! I'm sure your schedule keeps you very busy. How was it that you were available tonight of all nights?"

I didn't tell her that I had a tentative fuck date set with Amy, and that usually my nights were quiet and dull, spent at home logged into the office computer via the cloud. "Yes. That was fortunate indeed."

"Then if you were going to the St. James's Park stop, you must live... No, no!" she halted me when I attempted to tell her. "Let me look at the tube map and see if I can guess." She pulled out her phone and entered the passcode. A couple more swipes and she was puzzling over her screen. "Tower Hill? That's on the same line."

"Wrong direction. Sloane Square would have been my stop. I live between there and South Kensington."

"Ah, of course! Trust Fund Wankers."

"I beg your pardon?"

She laughed, so hard she snorted. "Oh my God, that's humiliating. I'm sorry. It was this internet meme I saw. It had all of London's neighborhoods broken into stereotypes. Most of them, the ones that had anything to do with money especially, had Wankers at the end. Like, this area we're in, I believe, was the Civil Servant Wankers or Political Wankers."

"I see. Quite appropriate."

"And the park is for Tourists and Corgis. Corgis!" She was still laughing.

"You really studied this meme."

"It was a very helpful resource to learning the town. Don't knock it. Where's your office? Let's see if it fits too."

She was too new to know locations by address. I tried to think of the closest landmark she might recognize. "You know where Tottenham Court is? Reach is near there "

"Yes, yes! That's the Media Wankers!"

"It is not."

"It is! Look it up if you don't believe me." Her smile went from ear to ear, and I wanted nothing more than to kiss it off of her and lick the taint of wine from her lips. "Do you want me to pull it up?"

She started to flip through her phone again, but I stopped her. "I believe you. I do. It's just so accurate." I took another sip of the wine before casually asking, "Where do you live? Not too far, I hope. For commute purposes." As though there were any other reason I'd be curious about where she resided, where she spent her evenings and weekends. Where she slept and showered and dreamed.

"Not too far. Lamberth. Between Elephant and Kennington. Basically the Recent Graduates with Poorly Paid Jobs section of town. That's from the meme too."

This time I couldn't help but join in with the laughter. "Oh bloody hell. It's too good."

"Isn't it?"

Our food arrived then, fish and chips for Audrey, meat pies for myself. We dug in, and our conversation transformed into commentary on the tastes and smells of British food.

She also thought everything was called by a ridiculous name. "Soldiers, mashers, Toad in a Hole," she said at one point. "Bubble and Squeak. Welsh Rarebit."

"Don't forget Spotted Dick."

She nearly lost it at that. "I can't handle it. It's so funny!" When she stopped her hooting, she wiped tears from her eyes and said, "All your food sounds like it was named in an attempt to get a stubborn child to eat, I swear."

"I think some of it might have been named to get grown men to eat it, unfortunately."

She shook her head at that, her face still lit in amusement.

God, she was beautiful. As beautiful as my country's food's names were ridiculous.

When our meal was half eaten and a comfortable lull had settled between us, my mind wandered back to something she'd said when we'd been walking, something that had niggled at me ever since.

"You said you'll have a chance to keep on at the Gallery. Is that what you want to do? Stay here in London?" I practically held my breath for her answer.

She took her time giving it, waiting until she'd finished the morsel she was chewing and taking a swig from her drink before saying, "I don't know. I mean, I just got here so I don't have a good sense of whether or not it's home for long. The work itself is incredible, of course. It will look good on my resume if they choose to keep me on or not."

"Wow," I said, unable to come up with another word for what I wanted to say. My breathing resumed, but it was unsteady. I'd never been comfortable with unknowns, and right now, it felt like I was sitting across from a big giant question mark. Would she stay, would she go? Would I miss her as terribly if she left again as I'd missed her before today?

Would I miss her more?

But this wasn't about me. Her being here was all about her.

"I should say congratulations," I realized suddenly. "I'm sorry I didn't say it earlier."

She twirled a chip between her fingers. "Thanks. You know the funny thing—I don't even remember applying for this job specifically. You would think I'd remember a notice from the Gallery. But I applied for so many positions. I'm not sure I even read half of them by the end."

Oh, God. Did I smell a whiff of Donovan Kincaid's hand in her being here? Maybe it wasn't all about her after all. It wasn't beyond him to interfere. He was a man who pulled strings. If he'd intervened when I'd asked him not to, he was truly crossing a line.

I didn't want to jump to conclusions, but I vowed to speak to him about it as soon as possible.

"It all worked out," Audrey said, happily, and I could feel any concern about the how of her being here slipping away. "Because I got one of the best opportunities available. And if things go how I hope…" Her face wrinkled up like she'd had a stray thought and was following it on an absurd journey. "I guess the answer to your question about whether or not I want to stay here has to do with everything else. Like, I don't really have a preference about where I live. Right now my life is about making the best choices possible to keep me on a good career path and about finding The Guy. I'm ready for him. Ready to settle down, get married. Start a family."

I nearly choked on my turkey pie. "Settle down? Already? You're twenty-three!"

She pointed a chip in my direction. "Hey, I'm twenty-four now." As though that made any difference. "And this can't be any sort of a surprise. I have to start early if I'm going to get all those babies in."

Oh, right. All those babies.

Which brought me to a question I'd been avoiding. "What happened to that guy from the wedding?" His name was Jax. I hadn't forgotten. I just refused to use his name if I didn't have to.

"Jax? He was just a friend. Nothing more ever came out of that."

I tried not to be happy about how blaise she sounded about it. But I failed.

"He's dating another friend of ours now. Greg."

"Oh. He's gay." This relieved me even more.

"Pansexual," she corrected.

I had to set my fork down for this. "Jax is transexual?"

She laughed, and I wasn't sure she wasn't making fun of me. "*Pan*sexual. Not trans. It means who he loves isn't limited to a specific gender or gender identity."

"I see. In my day they called that bisexual."

She shook her head at me. "My day still has bisexuals. That's a different thing. That's being attracted to people from two genders. Pansexuals are attracted to people of all genders."

"And here I thought there were only two genders." I was thoroughly confused now and about ready to look around for cameras. This had to be one of those prank shows, didn't it. Someone—Weston probably—had set this whole thing up. Her being here. This conversation about new versions of sexuality.

Again she laughed. "Gender's more complicated than that, it turns out."

And she dropped it. No one jumped out from a hiding spot in the sidelines. She just went back to dipping her fish into her tartar sauce.

So, not a prank. Just me being from a completely different generation. Completely out of her league.

I sighed. "I'll have you know, I feel very old right now."

"Nah. Don't. This is all really new stuff."

"Oh. Good to know." I suddenly wondered if Aaron was as up to date on all this "new stuff." Certainly his mother wasn't.

And what about Audrey? "Are you...do you consider yourself...one of those?"

"Pansexual? I'd like to say I am, in theory. Because I love that notion of being able to love anyone, regardless of what's between their legs. But I'm as straight as they come. A disappointment to my generation, I'm afraid."

It was my turn to laugh. "I'm sure you're not the only heterosexual human your age." I shook my head, and attempted to get us back to where this had initially been leading. "You're not seeing anyone right now?" I only asked out of curiosity. No other reason.

"Nope. I...this is kind of embarrassing, but after that week with you, I shut down on that front completely. Not in a bad way. It was just a really good week, you know? And I wanted to take some time to reflect on it and hold it so it didn't disappear into time the way things do. Then there was so much to do to get ready for graduation. My portfolio became my priority. Then finding a job. And then getting ready to move. And now...well, it dawned on me recently that there would always be something else to distract me if I let it. So I'm putting myself back on the market. Seriously. I'm not looking for casual. I'm not looking for a pass-the-time kind of fling. I want the next guy to be The One. The universe has always been really good at delivering what I need when I need it, so I'm putting my intention out there, and I'm not settling for anything less."

My body felt heavy. My feet felt nailed to the floor. I hadn't even realized until that moment that I'd been hoping to take her home with me. I'd even choreographed it in my mind, how I'd offer to share a cab. Then invite her to see where I live. Then lead her through my lonely spotless lounge and to my bed where I swear I dreamed about her every night. Then...

Well. That wasn't happening now. Nothing was happening between us.

I'd already known that deep down. Hadn't I?

"Of course waiting for The One also means I'm horny as hell." She tried to hide her blush behind a tilt of her wine glass, but I still saw it.

Oh. That meant..."You haven't had any sex at all since, since...?" I couldn't finish my sentence. I was too flattered, too dazed, too blown over.

"Nope. No one since you. Do you think my hymen has grown back? Is that a thing?" Another round of giggles. "You should see your face! I've never seen someone look so shocked and intrigued all at once."

Now I really wished for another night with her. One where I could spank her ass red for all her teasing.

"I'm sorry," she said, and I wondered what she would have said if she could read my thoughts? Would she have changed her mind about no flings? Would she jump in my lap and purr like the kitten I knew she was? "It's too fun to wind you up. Does that make me a bad person?"

"I don't think so," I said honestly. "Not when I enjoy it so much."

We lingered in the pub, chatting and laughing. We had a second glass of wine each, then coffee (for her) and tea (decaffeinated, for me). By the time we left it was almost nine o'clock. The temperature had dropped, and when we stepped outside, she shivered.

"Would you like to share a cab?" I still hoped for the possibility of ending up in her arms. The only enemy I had here was my own.

She shoved her hands in her pockets and looked down the street that was very much empty of taxis. "It's only a block to the tube. We could be there before a car comes by, I bet. Walk with me?"

I nodded as though I had any choice in the matter, but I didn't. I was a slave to her at this point. I would follow wherever she led as long as she let me.

We walked together, close enough that our arms brushed. I could feel the heat of her all along my right side. I wanted to tuck myself into it. I wanted to live there.

I tried to imagine a different life—one where I'd met her in my twenties, before I'd become jaded and cold. Would we have worked in that scenario?

I didn't know. I didn't have the imagination she did to comprehend such things.

At the station, we paused at the spot where we were meant to part. The energy between us felt thick and charged.

"Are you sure you don't want me to accompany you? It's really not that far out of my way." It was, but I didn't care.

And if she invited me in afterward? It would only make more of a mess of things.

She seemed to have come to the same conclusion. "It's a completely different direction, and I'm good on my own."

"You know the route to take? You only travel on this train until Embankment and then switch lines."

"Yes, Dad. I know."

Dad. For once I wasn't sure I liked the term. It put me in a box I didn't like being in, even if it was exactly where I belonged.

"Look," she said, drawing my eyes once more to hers. "I'm not going to pretend I don't want to sleep with you."

I could hear the blood woosh in my ears. I could feel the *but* at the end of her sentence. I held my breath and waited for her to say it.

"But..." There it was. "Since we both have different goals right now, I think it would just make things complicated."

She was so much smarter than I was. So much more mature.

"Very wise," I said.

"Friends?"

"Most definitely."

We shared phone numbers and then, once again, I watched her go.

Friends.

She wanted us to be friends.

Oh, how it pained me to face that, even when I already knew that was all we could ever be. What else did I have to offer her? A few months between the sheets while she worried about her life passing her by? A mostly grown son and a witch of an ex-wife to battle and criticize her?

I wasn't what she wanted. She'd said it clearly.

And even if I was on the same path she was, I couldn't deliver what she needed. She wanted a partner that would be by her side for a lifetime. She wanted a houseful of children. She wanted a picket fence and forever.

Not in my cards. Not anymore.

So we'd be friends.

At least this way I'd still get to have something of her, no matter how small. If it killed me, it would be worth it.

SIXTEEN

We didn't see each other for a while after that.

I expected her to reach out. She'd always been the aggressor in our relationship—whatever our relationship was. Every morning I checked my phone for texts, for missed calls. Every evening after work, the same. But there was nothing.

After a few days, I considered contacting her myself. I'd never been very good about messaging, though, and I'd only ever used the phone to ring people if I had a solid reason. While I was comfortable talking to people when I was around them, coming up with topics out of the blue was never my strong suit. Not that I didn't have things I wanted to say to her. There was so much, actually. The tiniest details of my day, especially. The strange man dressed like a sweet pepper at the underground station. The new advertisement Creative came up with to sell peanuts. The snippet of a song I caught on the cabbie's radio. The moments that meant nothing but still made me smile—these were the things that gave me the urge to pick up my phone and share with her.

But was that appropriate? Was that what friends did? There

wasn't anyone in my life that I did those things with. Did I have no friends?

By Thursday, I was willing to interfere with her so-called kismet. I left work early to walk the banks at St. James's Park, hoping to re-create our union. When I didn't see her, I tried again Friday. I came earlier, I stayed later. Still, no sign of her.

Saturday night crept upon me, and I had a rare gig with the cover band I sometimes played with. We were barely a band, really. We'd been playing together so long now, we didn't need to rehearse. Sometimes Ian would throw in a new song last minute, but it was never too hard to pick up. I played the electric bass. It was an easy instrument, and I could fake most numbers if I didn't know them.

Though we only had shows about once every three or four weeks, playing with Thrashheads was one of the more enjoyable aspects of my life. It was a chance to tune out and relax. A chance to forget about work and teenage sons and ex-wives while I got lost in the chord progressions of the greats—Judas Priest, Metallica, Slayer, Zeppelin.

Saturday's show was in South Belgravia, a section of town that I'm sure Audrey's meme map would call the Decent Pub Dead Zone. The food at the bar was lousy, the service was worse. The crowd, though, was engaged. They were gracious with their applause and sang along to some of the more popular Black Sabbath tunes. It was my kind of gig, my kind of audience. A bunch of old farts born prior to 1979 who still thought old metal was the best kind of rock. Wrinkles and grey hair decorated the faces of almost everyone in the pub, and still I looked for Audrey, as if she'd come to a bar like this. As if she'd stay for a band like ours.

When we were cleaning up, I watched my bandmates with new eyes. We'd played together for almost five years, yet we never went out together. We didn't "hang." I didn't even know where

Russell or Dennis lived. I didn't know Clancy's last name, or if Clancy *was* his last name. I didn't know these men at all.

"Are we friends?" I asked Ian, the lead singer and guitarist of the band. Ian wasn't his real name, I knew that. It was Johnny, but he had an eternal hard-on for Deep Purple, and had taken the name of the lead singer in honor.

"Yeah, mate." Ian stared at me as though I'd asked him if Ozzy Osbourne was the best. "What else would we be?"

I shrugged. "People who play together in a band?"

He tilted his head and studied me. "Is there a difference?"

I shook my head, because I didn't know, obviously.

The rest of the weekend passed. Monday arrived, and my phone was still silent. Again I went to the park, this time with an umbrella in hand since the rain had returned. I stood at the water's edge and watched the lake break up with each splash of water, watched the increase of activity as the rain quieted and the fish came up to the surface to eat the worms that had been uncovered in the storm.

I felt like one of those fish, a creature that dwelled in the deep dark, only coming out of my sanctuary when baited. And then, how vulnerable and exposed I was in the translucent shallow water. On exhibition and bare to the elements.

I went home, taking the first taxi I found. I didn't return to look for Audrey at the park again.

Were we friends?

On Tuesday, after the office was closed and almost everyone had gone home but me and Amy, I was still thinking about my social life, or lack thereof. "Do you have any friends?" I asked her.

"Besides you?" Her brow wrinkled and she tugged at a corkscrew curl while she thought about it. "I suppose there's Dante. We work out together. And by work out, I mean we run on the treadmill for five minutes then go back to his house and bang like bunnies."

I frowned. "I don't think that's the definition of friends." If it were, I would've accompanied Audrey home that night, and every night.

"Oh really?" Amy thought for another moment. "What's the point then?"

So I didn't text and I didn't ring because, as Amy said, what was the point? And I tried not to think about Audrey, tried not to let her infiltrate my every waking moment, but it was hopeless. She was a cataract covering the lens of the eye—it was impossible to see the world without seeing her.

Then, Friday came. I took a long time shutting down for the day, a futile attempt to make the workweek last longer. I'd begun to dread the weekends and their dreary monotony. Eventually, the cleaning crew arrived and there was nothing much for me to do.

I put on my suit jacket and checked my mobile phone for the first time since lunch. There was finally a voice message from her.

"Hey, it's Audrey. I'm sorry to call out of the blue like this, but I need you! It's an emergency. Can you call me right away?"

I'd never pressed the RETURN CALL button so fast in my life. "Audrey! Are you hurt? Are you ill?" I didn't even bother with the greeting, I was so anxious to discover her ailment, so eager to help. "Do you need me to come to you?"

"Dylan! It's you! Thank you for calling back." She didn't sound nearly as exasperated as she'd been in the message. "And I'm fine. It's not that kind of emergency. Sorry to panic you!"

"Then you don't need me after all." I didn't know whether to feel disappointed or relieved.

"No, I *do* need you. It's just not life or death—I have a tendency to be dramatic. But it *is* important. Very important. To me, anyway."

Relieved then. I'd feel relieved. And also, while she chattered on, I couldn't help but remember the last time I'd been on the phone with her, when the thing she needed was of a carnal nature. Would this call go in the same direction? Was I a monster for wishing it would?

"Let me hear it." I leaned back in my chair and loosened my tie.

"First, I'm dreadfully sorry I'm asking this so late, but see, the thing is, the museum is having a fundraiser tomorrow night. It's a big fundraiser, a really important one, and each of us is expected to bring at least one guest who might donate. And there really isn't very many people that I know besides you. There's Lawrence, but I'm afraid his tattoos won't go over so well with my boss, not since he got the ones covering his face, anyway, and Betty said she'd go, but she's homeless. And she looks it. There's no way anyone's going to believe that she could give a dollar to our cause. Er, a pound, I guess it is. And Percy has another obligation, so he doesn't think he'll make it. And I know it's really a big favor to ask, the kind that crosses the line—"

"I'll come," I said, cutting her off. Was there really any other choice?

"You will? You can't know what this means to me. Thank you. Thank you! It's tomorrow, though. Is that going to work? Can you get a tux? I really wouldn't bother with any of this if I didn't think I needed to make a good impression on my boss."

"Yes, I'm free tomorrow night. And I own a tux. I'll be there." Joyfully. With bells on.

She could tell me more about Lawrence and Percy then, though I wasn't sure I wanted to know. Facial tattoos? I shuddered. And who was this homeless Betty person she was milling about with?

"You're free! It's—"

"Don't say it," I warned. I didn't want to hear that K word again. Not after this last week and a half.

"Not saying it doesn't make it any less true," she said coyly.

"But fine. I'm glad you're available. It's *convenient*. And thank you again. I can't say it enough. I mean it. I'm overflowing with gratitude. And I don't expect you to donate anything. In fact, please don't. It would be utterly humiliating for me if you thought that I only wanted you as a friend for your cash resources. All I need is someone who *looks* like he'll donate, and you very much do."

Her concern for my pocketbook was adorable. "I can be charitable. Especially to a good cause, such as art."

"No, I mean it, Dylan. I will die. Please."

"All right then," I acquiesced. "I won't even bring my checkbook."

I BROUGHT MY CHECKBOOK.

It seemed rude to show up to such a thing without it, and if the museum needed funding, I was happy to oblige. Because I liked good art, of course. I was often philanthropic with my money. It didn't have to be about Audrey in the least.

We decided to meet at the Gallery, though that hadn't been my first choice. I'd offered to pick her up. I didn't regularly use a hired car when I was home in London, but I did own an automobile that I rarely used, and it wasn't difficult to obtain a driver, even on short notice. But Audrey insisted that I didn't go to the trouble.

So there I was, entering the familiar museum with the exhilaration of a first-timer, knowing soon I'd see the most beautiful works of art in the world.

"May I see your invitation, sir?"

I raised my eyebrows at the door attendant, thrown off by the expectation of something I did not have.

"I...hmm." I stalled as I scanned the room behind him,

searching for my "ticket" in. "I'm here as a guest of a member of staff?" I hadn't quite meant it to sound like a question, but I wasn't sure enough to let it be a statement.

"Ah," the gentleman said. He opened the binder in front of him. "Then you'll be on the list."

I opened my mouth to deliver my name, when all of a sudden, there she was, swooping in to my rescue.

"It's okay, Cameron," she said, slipping her arm through mine. "This is Dylan. He's with me."

My heart stuttered. How long had it been since I'd been *with* somebody? It wasn't as terribly awful as I remembered, hearing her say it now.

Cameron checked off some line in his binder and let us in. Though we walked together, Audrey was the one in the lead, directing me past the crowd of donors that always huddled at the front of these sorts of things into the emptier center of the room.

As always, she prattled as we walked. "It's really busy already. I had no idea there would be so many people here. I've been to a couple of these before—one at the last museum that I interned for in Delaware. That was really nothing like this at all. Half of the guests were in jeans. And there was another for a library museum in Pennsylvania that I happened to get an invitation to. Also not the same. Neither museum really had any art worth funding, for one thing, and even if there was, they weren't the kind of places to draw attention from donors with deep pockets. Here's a good spot to people-watch. Let me look at you."

She stopped suddenly and put her hands up as if to keep me in place while she took two steps backwards. Then she threw her hand over her heart and exclaimed, "Dylan! Swoon!" She actually said the word *swoon*. The lilt in her voice and the way she moved her body put emphasis on the word. "You are absolutely magnificent in a tux," she continued, then bit her bottom lip as if to contain herself from saying more. "I can barely stand it."

She was the magnificent one, dressed again in the deep red gown she'd worn at her sister's wedding.

I told her, too. "And you truly look stunning, Audrey." My tone was light as I said it, not because I didn't mean it, but because she took my breath away. Always. *Always.*

She waved her hand dismissively. "It's super tacky to wear a formal twice, but I figured you're the only one here who would know." She put a finger to her lips. "Shh. Don't tell a soul."

"Not a word."

And I winked. Me—winking. I'd truly lost my head now.

If she noticed, she didn't let on. She took my arm again and perused the crowd around us. "I'll tell you who I know. The list isn't long. That woman, over there, with the sharp features and the brocade top? That's Etta, our marketing consultant. And the man next to her is Silas. He's my supervisor. He's in charge of conserving all the Raphael works. Can you believe that? Raphael! He's personally worked on *St. John of the Baptist Preaching* and the *Mackintosh Madonna*. I was dying just to be in the same room with them, and he got to touch them and look at them under the magnifying glass. Dead, I tell you."

I barely had time to agree before she was drawing me deeper into the museum.

"Over there to the right, the short one with the ridiculously large bosom? That's Sasha. She's an art handler, which is basically a fancy way of saying assistant." She lowered her voice as if the next part was a secret. "She barely makes more than I do, and I'm at the bottom of the heap. Oh, and the guy over there, the one talking to that dorky little guy with the tan suit?"

I looked over at the men. "By 'dorky little guy' you mean the Speaker of the House of Commons?"

She giggled as she blushed. "I just called the Speaker of the House of Commons a dork? I'm so embarrassed."

"Don't be. It's rather accurate."

She stayed pink though. "Well, the Speaker of the House of Commons is talking to Mr. Cavendish. No one knows what Mr. Cavendish does, no one knows what his first name is. He *insists* on being called Mr. Cavendish. I reckon he's really important though, because how can you insist on being called anything otherwise?"

That did seem reasonable. "And also," I added, "he is speaking to one of the most prominent dorks in England."

"Yes," she giggled again at my joke, making my chest feel warm. "That too."

Instantly, she had me in tow again, her eyes searching frantically around the room. "Somewhere around here is Jana. She's my boss. We need her to see us—or you, at least. I think she thought I was making you up when I said I had someone to add to the guest list this morning. It was too late to tell her last night. I have to show her you're not a figment of my imagination. Just, where is she...?"

Audrey was running herself—both of us, actually—in circles. I guessed she was nervous, and why shouldn't she be? It was her first big job, her first big event, and certainly she wanted to make a good impression.

I presumed that would be easier if she were just a touch calmer.

"Excuse me, one second, would you Audrey?" I stepped away before she could stop me, and headed to the nearest waiter. I retrieved two glasses of champagne from his tray, then returned to the girl I had left waiting. "Drink this," I ordered. "You'll feel better. Trust me."

"I'm being a little much, aren't I?" She took a sip, though, as I'd asked.

"Never," I said. Because it was true—she was never much, as far as I was concerned. She was always much *more*.

She didn't look like she necessarily believed me, but she took another sip of the champagne, followed by a deep breath. Then another. And a third. Then she knocked the remainder of the glass back, and smiled brightly. "Better now."

I took a swallow from my own glass so that I wouldn't grin more than was appropriate, although I feared I was already failing.

Since I was already acting like an infatuated dolt, it seemed like the best time to continue making a fool of myself and expose my jealousy. "You've made other friends in London, according to what you said the other day. Good friends, I hope?"

She scrunched her face up as she tried to figure out what I was referring to.

"You mentioned a Percy and a Betty. And Leonard?" It was Lawrence. I hadn't forgotten. I just wanted her to think I had.

"Oh, yes! I've met so many awesome people since I'd gotten here, it's hard to keep them all straight. Betty is amazing. She's this woman who lives on the street between my house and the tube stop. I bring her a sandwich every day." She frowned suddenly. "Except not on the weekends. I didn't even think about the weekends! I have to bring her one tomorrow and apologize for forgetting about today. Maybe I'll bring extras next Friday."

It was both moving and adorable how she felt responsible for this woman, as if she'd adopted her like a stray cat. Her concern for this new friend was an admirable trait, one I definitely didn't possess at her age. I wasn't certain that I possessed it now.

"And Lawrence, not Leonard, is a bartender at the pub down the street from here. He makes the best mixed drinks. I never know the names. I always ask him to surprise me. I mean, I'm not a lush or anything. It's just fun to go out after work every once in a while, even by myself. I like to study the people while I'm unwinding."

I could imagine this. Could picture her, all this time, going to a pub after finishing her job. Times she could've texted me to join her. Times I could have offered to take her to the best pubs in the city. That was something friends did, wasn't it? Was she as awkward at this new relationship label as I was or did she simply never think of inviting me?

"And Percy," she looked away. Purposefully? "He's an artist who lives in my building. He...He likes me, I think. He's asked me out a couple of times, but it's just never happened." Finally, she met my eyes. "But maybe I should take him up on the offer. What do you think?"

I thought she should never be with anyone but me. Because I was selfish and obsessed.

It wasn't fair to her because I didn't want her. Not really. Not the way she wanted to be wanted.

I cleared my throat, and attempted not to be the greedy asshole that I was. "I don't know the man, but you did say you wanted to date. If he's someone that you think could possibly be that special guy..." It was really hard not to cringe as I spoke. "Then I say go for it."

She sighed, and when she spoke she almost sounded disappointed. "You're right. I did say that. I'll think about it."

And I'd think about it too. Much more than I should.

"Oh my word!" she exclaimed suddenly, peering over my shoulder. "Carefully, carefully, look behind you. Dena—she's another intern. She's as nervous about keeping her job as I am, so she told me she was going to hire an actor to play a rich donor since she doesn't know anybody in town. And oh my gosh, who she hired is fantastically ridiculous."

I turned to look behind me.

"Carefully!" she warned with a hiss. "Don't make it look like you're looking."

I took another swallow of my drink and turned as casually as possible. I saw who she meant immediately. The man wore a traditional tuxedo, complete with a top hat and cane. The mustache he sported was pure white, and if we could see under the hat, I suspected he was balding. He looked like a fraud, like a caricature, an exaggerated imitation of a rich man stereotype.

"He looks like that guy from the Monopoly game," Audrey whispered at my side. "He's only missing the monocle."

He did indeed, but... "Rich Uncle Pennybags does not have a monocle."

"He doesn't?"

"No. That's Mr. Peanut. And also Scrooge McDuck."

"Scrooge McDuck has spectacles," she said defiantly. "And your error about that makes me less likely to believe you about Rich Uncle Pennybags not having a monocle—is that really his name? On the other hand, you *are* very wise. Maybe I should trust you."

"I am wise," I agreed teasingly. "And I know my rich old men."

She put her hand up to straighten my bow tie. "Not so old. Not old at all, really." Her hand lingered on my chest, and I could feel the warmth of it through both the layers of my shirt and my undershirt, all the way to my skin, where it branded like a hot iron. She looked up at me, her gaze trapping mine. Her expression grew serious and intense, and if she kept looking at me like that, staring into me for even one more second, I was going to kiss her.

"You are not going to believe this!" Dena, the woman with the hired date, pulled at Audrey's arm for her attention. "Am I interrupting? I'm so sorry if I am. I just have to talk to Audrey."

Audrey glanced furtively between me and her coworker, apparently torn between the two of us.

"Go ahead. I can entertain myself for a few moments." A minute alone was probably a good idea right about now, anyway. I needed to regroup, gather the wits she always managed to scatter back about me.

She seemed soothed by my permission, her features relaxing. "I'll be right back." She stood on her tippy toes and gave me a peck on the cheek before rushing away with her friend.

I felt the place where her mouth had been for long moments after she walked away.

She hadn't been gone long when I was approached by a brunette with a silver streak in her hair. "Good evening, we haven't met yet. I'm Jana Spruce, the art director here at the Gallery. Are you enjoying yourself this evening?"

Jana—Audrey's boss.

"I am, thank you. It's a lovely event. I'm here at the request of one of your employees, I believe. Audrey Lind. I'm Dylan Locke."

Jana lifted one brow in surprise. "Nice to meet you, Mr. Locke." She shook my hand. Hers were cold and bony, especially compared to Audrey's warm ones.

Already I missed the heat of her.

"I hope you don't mind," Jana said, stepping in closer, "but it *is* my job to try to entice you into a donation. We could use your support, Mr. Locke."

I scanned the room to be sure Audrey wasn't watching—she wasn't—and pulled my checkbook from my inside pocket. "I'm very interested in making a donation. Could you tell me what the money is going for? Specifically?" I started to fill in the check with the details—the Pay To, the date.

"Certainly. We are always in need of funds, of course. Grants and endowments only go so far, I'm afraid. Donations cover daily operations and pay our staff. This particular fundraiser is meant to pay for the renovations we have set for January."

I'd read about these renovations in the paper. "I thought the renovation had already been paid for. Wasn't that part of the promise to the public before going on to the next phase?"

"Indeed, Mr. Locke. You know your facts. It's the details

surrounding the renovation that need to be paid for. In particular, we are looking for funding for an artist who will watch over the art while the work is being done. We need a specialist to be sure that there will be no damage done to any of the pieces. We're hoping to give that position to one of our current interns."

In other words, this money could secure Audrey's place at the Gallery.

Naturally, I would donate it. "How much do you need to fill the whole salary?"

"We aren't expecting any one person to donate the whole amount. Any sum you give will be gratefully accepted."

"How much for the full salary?" Was it wrong to want to keep her here? It might have been, but it was also one thing I could give her when I could give her nothing else.

Jana said an amount that made me blink—an increase to Audrey's current pay, no doubt—but it wasn't too much to put a dent in my checking account. I filled in the total for the entire salary, signed my name, and handed the check over.

"Mr. Locke, I don't know what to say. I'm very appreciative." The way she batted her lashes, it seemed she was interested in more than just the sum I'd given her. She was an attractive woman. And likely born in my generation. Another time, I would have paid more attention to her.

She handed me a business card from her jacket pocket. When she placed it in my hand she left hers there a little too long. "Here's my card, if you need anything."

From the husky texture in her voice, it was clear she meant *anything*.

I took the card and put it in my jacket along with the checkbook.

"Audrey did say that you would be generous," Jana continued, heavy with flirtation. "I had no idea *how* generous."

A memory suddenly occurred to me from deep in the past.

Ellen and I, on the verge of divorce. I'd finally noticed her cheating, finally confronted her. In one of our more heated arguments, I had asked, *"If you wanted to be with other men so badly, why did you stay with me?"*

She had looked me directly in the eye and said, *"Because staying with you paid better."*

Long after the love between us had dissipated, her attraction to my money had lived on.

Was this why Audrey had brought me here? She'd asked me not to make a donation, but had that been a ruse? Was the content of my pockets what she cared about most? Had she only kept our status as friends because it *paid better*?

My throat suddenly felt dry and my skin cold. I looked to where Audrey had disappeared, and found her there again, giggling with Dena. It felt like they were watching me. Had I just walked into the trap they'd set? Willingly, no less.

I swallowed past the desert in my mouth. "Jana—may I call you Jana?"

"Of course."

"I prefer that my donation remain anonymous, even to Audrey." *Especially* to Audrey. I didn't need to bear the humiliation of her knowing I was such a fool over her.

Jana agreed and excused herself to mingle with other guests.

I turned back to Audrey and found her eyes were now glued to something else, some*one* else—a man who had to be around her age, wearing a hideous tux and crossing the room toward her.

She ran up to hug him, exclaiming his name loud enough for me to hear from where I was standing. "Percy!"

I could see things clearly now. Percy, the artist, was the type of man she wanted. A man who saw the world in full color like she did, young enough to give her a gaggle of babies, bold enough to show up at highbrow events wearing a purple suede tux. He likely couldn't pay to take her to a concert or an opera, but he could give her art in the ways that mattered most to her, on paper, in clay. He was the kind of man she could pine for.

And where did I fit in?

Now that I'd paid for her living, I didn't fit anywhere at all. What other interest would a girl like her have in a guy like me?

In quick strides, I approached her, wishing I was a different kind of man—a man who made grand gestures and dreamed big dreams—but I could only be who I was. A middle-aged pessimist who longed for someone out of reach.

"Dylan, this is—" she began when she saw me, but I didn't let her speak.

"Audrey, something's come up. I have to go. I'm sorry." More sorry than she could ever know.

She frowned. "Are you sure? I can come with you!"

"No, you stay." I left before she could say more, before she could change my mind. Before I could once again be sucked into the fantasy of her.

I didn't belong in her world. She didn't belong in mine. Life after love was a desert. That was where I lived. That was my truth. Any vision I had of Audrey being there with me was a mirage.

SEVENTEEN

"But I don't get why I can't say it," Aaron said in that godawful whining tone that made me want to claw my eyes out of their sockets.

We were talking over FaceTime. I usually preferred to converse over the phone where he couldn't try to interpret every gesture of mine. I also preferred these calls to take place while I was at home, not at the office, but he'd wanted to show me the art piece he'd drawn for class before he took it to school. His drawing was phenomenal, far superior to anything I could have drawn (he'd definitely gotten his talent from his mother's side), but as often happened these days, our conversation had turned from a complimentary discussion on his shading techniques to a battle about how to speak to adults.

"Because it's disrespectful. You shouldn't call anyone a 'loser,' let alone your own father." I fought the urge to pinch the sides of my nose. This shouldn't be something I had to explain to a fourteen-year-old.

"But I was joking!" That blasted whine again. He threw

himself down on his mother's couch—where was she during all of this? She could be helping here. "You don't understand me."

"I do understand you," I said impatiently. "It makes you feel better about yourself to put other people down, but—"

"That's not why I said it! You don't get it. You don't understand my humor, you don't understand my taste in music, you don't understand anything about me. No one understands me."

It was hard to argue with him. I *didn't* understand him. But I *wanted* to. I wanted him to believe I had all the answers and that I knew everything he needed me to know, but I did not, in fact, know anything. I didn't know why calling someone a loser was a "cool" thing. I didn't know why he insisted on turning everything into an argument. I didn't know what it was he wanted from me or what would make him happy or how his mother and I fell apart. I didn't know if she'd ever loved me or if it had always been about my money or if Audrey had used me for the same reason or if I'd assumed the worst, and most infuriating, I didn't know why I couldn't stop thinking about her and the anguished look she'd given me when I'd told her I was leaving Saturday night.

And right now I didn't know what else to say to my son.

It had been so much easier when these disputes could be worked out with a cookie and a cuddle. Where had the time gone?

"Parents never understand. That's, like, a law written in the stars somewhere," Audrey said, and I nearly jumped out of my chair.

"What, how, what?" I stammered. I'd been facing my computer screen and the windows when she'd walked in behind me, so quietly I hadn't noticed. More importantly, she'd come in without anyone telling me.

I leaned back in my chair and peered out my office door, trying to see if Louise, my assistant, was at her desk.

"There was no one there, so I just walked in. I'm sorry I startled you." She was trying not to laugh. "And I shouldn't have interfered. Sorry! I'll talk to you when you're done here."

She started creeping backward, but Aaron stopped her. "Wait! What were you saying?" He was sitting up again, his face filling the screen.

She glanced at me, as if to ask permission.

"By all means." I wasn't doing any good here. Besides, I needed a minute to calm my heart down.

Now that she'd been invited, Audrey had no reservations. She stepped right up to the desk next to me and knelt so he could see her face. "Hi! I'm Audrey. We met once a long time ago, but no worries if you don't remember. I was just saying that you're right—parents don't understand, and they never will. They share your genes, but there's the generation gap, and frankly, adults are so busy stressing over life, they forget to stop and feel their feelings. They think they've felt it all before, so why bother?"

I had to bite my tongue not to defend myself as both an adult and a parent. Honestly, though, she was right, and I wanted to see where she was going.

"So all that sucks," she said empathetically. "But the good news is that there *are* people who understand you. Maybe you haven't met them yet, but your world is small now. Get through high school. Once you get in college or are out doing the things you want to do instead of *have* to do, you're going to find them. Just wait. It's totally going to blow your mind."

"That's what I thought," Aaron said, sounding more upbeat than he had a moment before. He still wore a scowl, but that was his usual look these days. "And I remember you."

She beamed. "I'm in London now! Cool, huh? Working with people who totally get me. It gets better, man. Totally better."

"Awesome. Thanks."

Right. Thanks. Thanks for saying something I should have

known to say myself. Thanks for reminding me how completely inadequate and out of touch I was.

"If this has been settled, can we say goodbye and talk later?" My irritation was apparent. I took a deep breath and tried again. "Your picture is fantastic, Aaron. If you don't get an award for it, I'll be very surprised."

"It's just an exhibition. Everyone's showing their work. There's no awards, Dad."

"Well, there should be." Like I said, completely inadequate.

"Can I see?"

I wanted to be annoyed at Audrey for extending the uncomfortable call, but it was also endearing that she'd asked. She didn't have to.

Aaron held up the drawing, a portrait of his mother done in pencil.

"Oh, my! That's incredible! You did that yourself? And you're only fourteen?"

My chest expanded with pride. "It's quite good, isn't it? She knows her stuff, too, Aaron. Audrey works at The National Gallery."

"My portraits were never this detailed," she said, dismissing the attention I'd brought to her. "You're really good. You have passion for it, and it shows. That's not something you can teach. Keep it up!"

I heard Ellen calling Aaron in the background, and I wasn't in the mood to explain who Audrey was to my ex. "Yes, keep it up. Best get on to school now. I love you, and I'll talk to you later."

He rolled his eyes at my declaration of affection but said it back, quickly, then ended the call. *Well, that turned out quite better than it could have.*

Thanks to Audrey.

I turned my head toward her. "How did you do that?" And could she teach me?

"Do what?"

"Talk to him without him transforming into a Gremlin."

She blew it off. "It's easier to listen to someone who isn't his parent."

That wasn't all of it. "I wouldn't have even known what to say. I mean, I *didn't* know. Everything I said was wrong."

She gave me a gentle smile. "I'm closer to his age, is all. I remember what I wished someone had said to me."

Pointing out our age difference didn't help with my mood.

"I shouldn't have interfered, though. So I understand if it wasn't appreciated."

God, she could read me. Not quite accurately, but she was close, and that was irritating, for some reason.

Also irritating was her presence in general. I had walked away from her. Why was she in my office? And why did I want her presence to mean something? There was nothing *for* it to mean.

I swiveled my chair sharply to face her. "Do you mind telling me what you're doing here?" I could feel my mouth curled down in the same frown my son had worn. Maybe he'd gotten that particular expression from me.

Still on her knees, she sat back on her feet. "I should have called first. That was rude on my part. I just didn't have the idea to come here until my lunch break was about to start, and I don't know. I got so consumed with getting here, I didn't think about it."

Her demeanor was genuinely apologetic, and with the addition of her permanently sunny disposition, I couldn't help but soften. "You came over here on your lunch break?"

"Yep. I'll have to leave to go back in about five minutes or so. Your office is deceivingly farther away from the museum than I'd guessed."

She'd used her lunch break to come see me. I didn't know whether to be suspicious or delighted.

"Was there a reason you came by?" Suspicious it was, then.

"Yeah. I wanted to see if you were okay after you left so quickly on Saturday."

And now I was delighted.

I sat straighter in my chair, leaned forward a little. I could feel the closeness of her. I was the cat and she the fire. I wanted to stretch my paws out in her warmth.

She seemed to sit up taller as well, stretching toward me. "I didn't even get to thank you for coming."

"You did. I'm sure of it."

"Not properly."

The heaviness of her tone and the innocent way she looked up at me through her lashes had the unfortunate effect of making me think dirty thoughts. Very dirty thoughts. She was on her bloody knees, for Christ's sake. (*Don't get hard. Don't get hard.*)

As always, she was oblivious to my struggle. "Jana said she spoke to you, too," she said, "so I got points for your being there—and may I say good job not letting her talk you into a donation. She's very persuasive. Anyway, thank you. For coming. You didn't have to, and it really meant a lot."

I bobbed my head in a nod, not quite sure how else to respond. Had she really not wanted me there for my money? Had I jumped to conclusions? I could ask, but I was chicken.

"It was nothing. Really." *Bawk bawk.* Such a coward. "I must admit, I did give a small donation. Nothing to boast about."

"Your heart's too soft," she said, then we both laughed because it was me we were talking about. "You're okay, though? What drew you away wasn't too serious?"

"Not too serious at all." She wanted to know, and I felt bad lying to her, but what else could I say? I certainly couldn't tell her I'd run off because I'd felt used, not when she'd never asked for the money. When she'd specifically asked me not to give anything at all.

"Glad to hear it." She stood up and pulled her phone from her pocket. "I've got to be getting back now. Oh, I almost forgot the other reason I came over—want to join me and a few friends for a drink later? We're meeting at a pub down by the park at six."

The pub that Lawrence works at? I had no right to wonder.

"I don't know..." I shouldn't say yes to her invitation. It would only encourage the strange obsession I had for the girl.

"Nope. You can't say no. You left me early on Saturday, and now you owe me a night."

"You're saying I owe you for leaving early when I'd only come as a favor in the first place?" I shouldn't tease her. It wasn't good for my head.

"Yep. That's exactly what I'm saying." She reached out and pulled on my tie. That wasn't good for my head either. Nor the situation in my trousers.

She had to get out of here. She had to leave, before I did something foolish like pull her into my lap.

"I'll go," I said, anything to get her out of my office before she looked down at my growing problem.

"Yay! I can't wait!" She bent down to press a quick peck on my cheek—a habit that was surely meant to drive me mad. "I'll text you the address. Gotta go. See you then!"

I called after her. "Audrey, Jana doesn't hold a candle to you. You're the one, it seems, who's very persuasive."

She shrugged innocently. "Why do you think I had to come in person? I knew you'd have a harder time turning me down." She waved, opening her hand and closing it the way Aaron had when he was little. Then she disappeared down the hall.

My sigh was audible in the now quiet room.

Maybe she didn't mean to have me wrapped around her little finger, but I was. I so very much was.

IT ONLY TOOK HALF an hour to decide that twenty-somethings were too loud.

The pub was full of them, baby-faced Millennials with more energy at dinnertime than I had at six in the morning. The most raucous sat at our table. I couldn't name them all, even after being introduced. Dena, I remembered, from meeting her at Saturday's event. The rest I gave descriptors to in my head like they were Stieg Larsson novels in order to keep them straight. The Boy with the Nose Ring. The Girl with the Hyena Laugh. The Girl with the Cat Hair. The Girl without a Uterus—I'd learned that within moments of meeting her. Twenty-somethings were also very open, it appeared.

Then there was me—The Man Who Didn't Fit In.

It didn't take a genius to see that I was out of place and sinking quickly. I didn't share their exuberance, I didn't like their music, I definitely didn't know their lingo. In many ways it felt like the conversation with my son, except worse, because I didn't have authority over any of them and because I loved my son.

The only one I cared for at this gathering was Audrey.

At first, I tried to connect—I really did. I inquired about their jobs—they all worked together at the museum. I asked about their hobbies. I answered every question about the advertising business and squashed every ridiculous notion they had about PR people. I didn't know how to keep any conversation going, though. Every one crashed and burned after only a handful of volleys.

After one particular exchange that ended with The Girl with the Cat Hair telling me to "check my privilege," I resolved to keep my mouth shut except to give short, polite answers when addressed and to drink my wine.

Audrey attempted to make the whole thing bearable. "You

aren't having any fun," she said with a pout, while the others argued about the ending to the latest comic book turned movie.

"I'm fine," I reassured her. "I never have fun."

She smiled, keeping her gaze steady on me. "That's not true. We've had fun together."

Yes. Yes, we had.

Dena pulled at Audrey's arm, demanding her attention. "Remember when Trevor told Jana that he couldn't get it up? When he was talking about mounting the Manet? Did you see Jana's face?"

Trevor. That was The Boy with the Nose Ring's name.

Audrey broke into laughter with the others. "She went five shades of red, didn't she?" With her focus still on the others, she rested her hand on my lower thigh as though it would have no effect on me. As though I wasn't a functional man made of flesh and blood and sexual desire.

Or maybe as though I was exactly that.

I remembered her words when we'd parted that first night—*I'm not going to pretend I don't want to sleep with you...* Did she still mean that? It was pathetic how much I wanted her to mean it, even if it could never go anywhere. At least, then, she'd be as miserable as I was fighting my lust in her company.

As miserable as I was right now, trying to ignore the casual sweep of her thumb back and forth over my leg. My cock twitched, wondering if it should get involved.

The answer was no, it shouldn't.

I went to the bar to order another glass of wine.

"At least the fundraiser went well," The Girl without a Uterus was saying when I returned. "I heard Mr. Cavendish say they raised enough to hire two employees full-time after Christmas. Trevor's guaranteed one of them. Must be nice having a set of balls."

Trevor glared at her. "It's based on seniority. You know that."

"It should be based on talent," someone else said, I didn't pay attention who. I was too consumed with wanting to be sure that Audrey had the other job, the job I'd paid for her to have.

"Who's getting the other position?" After so long remaining silent, it felt like all eyes were on me.

Dena answered first. "Don't know yet. Audrey and I are the only other two interns. We were hired at the same time, so it's up in the air, for now. Me and my girl are going to have to duke it out, and by duke it out I mean sit back quietly with our hands tied while someone else decides our fate."

Fan-fucking-tastic. I'd given over a check, felt used in the process, and the money might not even go to the woman I meant it for.

I looked over at her, at Audrey, and found her staring into her beer mug. The pressure to perform must feel overwhelming.

"I'm sure you'll get it," I said quietly when the others had moved on to a new topic. She would, too, even if I had to contact that Jana and threaten to cancel my check.

"Thank you for the vote of confidence." She gave me a smile that quickly vanished. "I'm still not sure I want to stay in London, though."

It felt like I'd been socked in the gut. Like all the air inside me had been knocked out of my lungs, like I couldn't get a breath in. I'd assumed a job offer would be all she'd need after stating she was mainly focused on her career at this time in her life.

But she'd also said she wanted to settle down. With The One.

It was impossible to know what to wish for now. I wanted her here, because I was obviously enjoying being tortured with her presence. But was I so much of a sadist that I wanted to watch her fall into the arms of another man?

Thinking about it made me uncomfortable. Being near her made me antsy. I excused myself and took my wine to wander around the pub. When I found an unused billiards table, I took off my jacket, racked up, and practiced sinking shots.

This was better than being with Audrey and her friends. Reading the table, calculating sides, these things took logic and focus and skill. I didn't have to think about what I wanted or what she wanted. There were no feelings in pool.

I wished there were no feelings in my life.

Blue stripe to the left side pocket.

But I really didn't, did I? Because I liked the feeling I'd had when Audrey showed up at my office. I liked the feeling I'd had when she encouraged my son. I especially liked the feeling I had when she kissed my cheek or placed her hand on my thigh.

She made me feel good in so many ways.

Yellow stripe to the left side pocket.

But she'd also made me feel bad. She had the power to do it again, and I knew it. Which was why I'd decided to stay away from her.

So why was it I'd agreed to come out with her tonight?

Green to the corner.

The ball sank cleanly in the pocket.

"That was crazy! How did you do that?"

I didn't need to look up to know the praise came from Audrey, but I did anyway. Because I liked looking at her. "How did I do what?"

"Shoot the ball like that. So it would swerve to go into the pocket."

A complicated question, trying to reduce years of skill into a simple instructional paragraph. I doubted my usual "geometry" explanation would work on an artist. I ran my hand through my hair before I made the attempt.

"It's all in how you hit the cue ball. If you give it spin on the left, it's going to move right. And vice versa. Then add speed and pressure, and of course, the distance between the cue ball and the other ball has to be taken into consideration." I lined up my next shot. "Red, corner pocket," I announced before squirting the ball and sinking it in.

"That! How did you do that? And how did you make sure the cue ball didn't follow it in?"

I chalked up while I studied her. "Have you never played pool?"

"A bit. It didn't look exactly like this. The balls were bigger." She giggled at the word *balls*. "Sorry. I have the maturity level of a middle-schooler."

The maturity level of my son. This was why she got on with him so well.

Speaking of low maturity levels... "Where are the others?"

"They all left. It's just you and me now."

Time for me to be leaving too, in other words. If I knew what was good for me.

"So you going to teach me how to hit the ball like that?"

Or I could do that.

I cleared my throat. "We can do this another time. If you'd rather be going." God, I was obvious. Practically begging her to validate my being here.

"Nope. I wouldn't rather." She stepped closer and pulled on the knot in my tie, loosening it from my neck. "I'm sorry they're so obnoxious. I like them. I mean, they're my only friends here, really. Besides you. But they're kind of shallow."

"No, no. I wouldn't say that." Only because I was polite.

"They are. You don't have to defend them. I'm saying it because I want you to know that I hope you don't see me as that shallow. The gossip and unwinding is fun on occasion, but it gets old. And I want more from my personal relationships than that."

I wanted more details. I wanted to know exactly what she wanted from her relationships, and then I wanted to be the one to give her those things.

But she was standing too near to me, and I couldn't think right. So all I said was, "Okay."

She smiled softly. A beat passed, where we just stared at each other. The air crackled around us.

"Like pool!" she exclaimed suddenly, pulling my tie from my neck and breaking the tension with her exuberance. She wadded up my tie and dropped it in my hand. "Teach me how to do that shot."

It was a terrible idea, and I knew it. I didn't have to play through the possibilities of what might occur if I stayed to know that all of them would end in me kissing the fuck out of her, if I had my way. Friends. Sure, we could be friends, but I wanted to be a certain kind of friend. The kind allowed to touch her and caress her and make her come.

I think it would just make things complicated.

That's what she'd said that first night in London. It played over and over in my head, a taunting reminder why I couldn't have the things I wanted. Because I was a decent man. Because I'd lived long enough to know those complications weren't simply excused.

I was wiser and more experienced, and I *knew*. That was why I should go.

And yet I couldn't help myself where Audrey was concerned.

I stuffed the tie in my trouser pocket and picked up the white cue ball, memorizing approximately where it sat on the current table. "Here's what you see when you're aiming. Pretend there are eight points around the circle and one in the middle." I pointed at the top point and then circled clockwise as I named the positions. "Straight follow-through, follow-through with squirt to the left, squirt to the left where the ball stops, squirt to the left and the ball drops back." I repeated the positions on the other side. "Hit straight in the center for no sidespin and no follow."

Her eyes glazed over. "I didn't get a single word you just said."

I chuckled. I'd never been the best of teachers. "It will be easier if I show you." I placed the cue ball back where it had been. "Come here," I said, tugging her in front of me. "What shot would you take?"

I could smell her, the faint whiff of apple in her hair, the sweet natural musk of her body. While she studied the table, I closed my eyes and breathed her in.

"I'd probably go for the orange, because that's close to a straight shot. But I wouldn't know how to hit it so that the white ball wouldn't follow."

I opened my eyes and surveyed her options. It was a solid choice. I handed her the stick. "Let's line it up."

She bent over the table. I wrapped my arms around her so I could help guide the tip.

Or maybe I simply wanted the excuse to touch her. Certainly if Trevor, The Boy with the Nose Ring, had asked me to teach him, I wouldn't have used this hands-on technique.

"You want it to swerve to the right, and you don't want the cue to follow." My mouth was at her ear. I could feel her breaths become shallow, matching up with mine. Was her heart racing like mine was too? "To get the squirt right, we're going to hit the left side of the cue. Because we want it to draw back when it hits the orange, we're going to aim down."

"So I'm going to hit the tip on the lower, left side of the white ball." Her tongue swept over her lower lip, and my dick went stiff.

"That's correct." I closed my eyes again, and a memory overtook me. Not a memory, actually, but I suddenly remembered what it felt like to believe in wishes. Remembered what it felt like to put my intentions out into the universe and believe there was a possibility they would come true.

I wished right then that this moment would never end, that I could hold Audrey in my arms indefinitely.

When I opened my eyes, she was looking, not at the ball, but back at me. Her face was within centimeters from mine. Her lips were right there, begging to be plumped and bruised with my kiss. I just had to lean forward. She just had to stretch back.

I didn't breathe.

"Why did you leave on Saturday?" she whispered, her gaze never leaving my mouth.

"Why did you invite me tonight?"

"I asked first."

Her tiger eyes were heavy and dilated, her body soft in mine. She wore her desire openly. Blatantly. I would only have to close my pelvis against her ass, and she'd know how much I wanted her as well. I didn't even have to answer the question. I could just kiss her, and I was certain she'd be mine with no resistance.

But mine for how long?

Mine for a night, and then what? At what point would she remember the things she planned for her life were incongruent with the things ahead in mine? If I was this attached to her now, how attached would I be to her then?

I'd lived through heartache before. I wasn't subjecting either of us to that pain.

I stood back, letting go of her, the pool shot long forgotten. "I left so that I wouldn't be a third wheel," I lied, and yet, hadn't that been true too? "Your friend, Percy, had arrived. You've clearly indicated you're looking for a romantic relationship right now. I didn't want to stand in the way of an opportunity."

She straightened but didn't look at me. "Oh. That was very thoughtful."

I didn't imagine how disappointed she sounded. How hurt.

I hated myself in the moment. Not for what I'd done, because it was better to let her go like this. Better to encourage her on the road to whatever happiness existed on her path—hopefully there was more for her than there had been for me.

No, I hated myself for being the one who had to teach her this lesson, that life wasn't all roses and rainbows. That it was unwise to indulge every passing fancy. That sometimes it was better to be injured in the battle instead of killed in the war.

She dropped the cue stick and turned toward me, an overly bright grin on her face. "I really should go out with him. I've been procrastinating for no reason at all. In fact, I would like to call it a night, if that's okay with you. Maybe I can stop by his place and see him before it gets too late."

I already had second thoughts, already regretted sending her into the arms of a man who was most likely better suited to her than I ever could be. Already regretted not taking one more kiss.

She was good enough to hurry and be gone before I had a chance to do anything about it.

EIGHTEEN

AUDREY: **Percy is a terrible kisser.**

I was in my kitchen, heating up the casserole my housekeeper had left in the freezer for me when my phone buzzed with the text. After three days of not hearing from Audrey—three days of managing not to reach out myself—that was the last message I'd expected to receive.

I didn't want to know the details.

But I also did. Especially if they were terrible.

Except, what if there was more than just kissing? The thought of Audrey in any man's arms was near impossible to bear. I didn't want to know. I Did. Not. Want. To. Know.

> You kissed Percy?

I had no will, obviously. No restraint in the least.

> Yes, and it was the worst. I can't possibly go out with him.

I leaned against the counter and gave in. I would need to know everything about how Percy was not the right man for her after all.

> You had a date tonight, I presume. Was all of it a disaster? Or just the kissing?

My bets were on the whole thing being terrible. A woman would give a man a second chance after a bad kiss if the rest of the night had been pleasing.

As soon as my phone showed that the text had been received, it began to ring.

I answered just as fast.

"It wasn't actually a date," she said, skipping any formal greeting, as usual. "We bumped into each other in the apartment foyer. I had groceries, so he offered to carry them up."

He'd carried her groceries. That was commendable enough. Not that I was keeping a tally of his good and bad points.

"Then, after he helped me put them away—"

"He helped put the groceries away as well as carried them up?" More commendable than I'd credited him for.

"There weren't that many. A few bags worth. But, yes. And I thought I should offer to make him dinner for going to the trouble, except I didn't want him in my apartment that long. He might get the wrong idea."

A woman making him dinner, alone, in her apartment—yes, he would very much get the wrong idea, if I knew men. And I felt like I had a pretty good handle on the gender.

"So I said, 'Hey, want to grab something at the café?' It's this restaurant just down the street, and I go there all the time when I don't feel like cooking. Which is a lot."

"So you had dinner together. Or he tried to skip dinner all together and kissed you after the groceries?" These facts mattered, as far as I was concerned. Mattered very much.

"We went to dinner. The kiss came later."

"Hmm." I was done giving him points until I heard the whole story. "Go on."

"Dinner was fine enough. He sure likes to talk about himself, though. Every time I tried to bring up another subject, we somehow ended up back on his art. And get this—he wanted to know if I could hook him up with a gallery since I have 'connections.' His word, not mine."

That bastard. No points at all for him. He was negative points now. Minus fifty.

Also, what was Audrey thinking? "He said that to you and you still let him kiss you?"

"Well, you know. I hadn't *planned* it. Actually, when he walked me to my door, I think he thought I'd let him in for more."

"But you didn't, did you?" I felt like a father, waiting for an answer that might lead to punishment, and I was already revved up to dole it out.

"I didn't."

I practically sighed from relief. "Good girl," I said. The timer went off. I put the phone down on the counter and hit speaker so I could grab the mitts and pull the casserole dish out of the oven without missing a single word of Audrey's story.

"I specifically turned around to face him before opening my door. I thanked him for helping me with the groceries again, and then I said good night. That's when he kissed me."

I couldn't help picturing it—Audrey, with her back against her door, trying to be polite, the self-absorbed Percy leaning in to take her mouth. The image wound me up so tight I almost dropped the baking dish.

"Did you give him any indication you wanted to be kissed?"

"I didn't mean to if I did. How do you let a guy know you want to be kissed?"

"I don't know." I put the food on a hot plate and retrieved the phone. "You tilt your chin up. You lick your lips. You bat your lashes."

"I sort of just smiled. Is that an invitation?" She was wise beyond her years, yet every now and then, her naivety surprised me.

It was like she needed me. Needed me to guide her in these matters so that she didn't get taken advantage of. So that she didn't end up making a mistake she'd live to regret.

"That is most certainly not an invitation if you didn't mean it to be," I lectured.

"I didn't mean it to be, but it's for the best, really. Now I know I don't want to go out with him at all."

"Because the kiss was terrible." I wanted to hear her confirm this one more time.

"Because it was beyond terrible. It was like he thought he'd win a prize if his tongue made it to my tonsils. So he tried several times."

"Ew." How could anyone kiss her like that? Like they were playing tonsil hockey? She was sweet and delectable. She had to be tasted and savored. Her lips were meant to be adored.

"Total ew. Definitely not The One."

I felt good about the phone call, and even better about her conclusion about Percy. Still, I thought she needed a stern reminder about a woman's rights. "Next time a guy tries to kiss you, if you aren't into it, you can turn your head away. You should never be expected to give a kiss just because a man wants it."

"Got it."

"Promise me you'll respect yourself in the future." I was asking for a vow she didn't owe me. Hopefully she thought she owed it enough to herself to give it.

"Yes, Daddy," she said, causing my cock to stand at attention. "Don't let your dinner get cold."

She hung up then, but dinner was still lukewarm by the time

I got to it. Taking a moment to rub one out while thinking about Audrey calling me Daddy was definitely worth it.

I RECEIVED another concerning text from her the next night around the same time.

> Is this outfit 2 revealing for a 1st date?

An image of Audrey in a sexy, sequined, low-cut jumpsuit accompanied the text.
Yes. The answer was definitely yes.
I had to count to five before I responded. There were too many things I wanted to say, and if I rushed to say it all, I feared I'd say something I didn't mean.

> I suppose it depends on the sort of impression you want to give.

There. That was diplomatic.

> Never mind. I don't have a jacket that goes with it, and it's 2 cold 2 go without

It was mid-October now. I never thought I'd be so grateful for jumper weather.

> Perhaps you have a polo neck? You could pair it with jeans.

Too obvious?
Perhaps. Two minutes passed, and she hadn't responded. I sent another text.

> Are you giving Percy another shot after all?

I was suddenly a praying man. *Please, oh, please let her answer be no.*

No.

Thank God.
Another text followed right away.

Joshua.

Who the fuck is Joshua? I sent another text asking just that. Minus the cursing, of course. I didn't want to seem so invested in the conversation that I required expletives.

This time, her reply came through FaceTime.

Shit. I looked like shit. I'd hit the gym after work and hadn't yet made it to the shower. I'd just peeled off my shirt when she'd texted, and here I was, in gloriously sweaty flesh.

I carefully angled my phone to only see my head and answered the call.

Her face came through the screen, clear and beautiful and innocent. "I met him this morning at the Gallery shop. He asked me out for tonight, and I had no plans, so I said why not."

Now that we'd involved cameras, there was no way she couldn't see my distress. "You can't just go on a date with a stranger! You know nothing about this guy. What if he's planning to kidnap you and sell you into the sex trade business?"

"I'm meeting him in a public place, and I don't intend to go anywhere else with him," she said reassuringly. "And I've told you where I'm going. If I don't call you back by nine, you can send the police. Oh! Dylan muscles. How did I get so lucky?"

I'd inadvertently let the phone slip to show my bare torso. "I was just getting in the shower," I said defensively. But I liked the way she ogled me through the screen too much to correct the camera's view.

"Ooo. Can I join you?"

I blinked. "Pardon me?"

"Kidding!" Though it hadn't sounded like she'd been kidding. "I'll let you get to it. But first can you tell me if this outfit is better?" She turned the phone so I could see her entire image in a full-length mirror.

The new outfit was not at all revealing. Her pink jumper was indeed a polo neck. but it hugged her breasts and hips and flared out at her wrists in such a sweet feminine way, a way that made her appear as irresistible as she'd appeared in the low-cut jumpsuit. More so, even. I didn't want to encourage her to woo a man in what she was wearing. No man in his right mind would refuse.

But there was no valid reason to object.

"You're beautiful. Beautifully perfect," I said, somberly. "Call me when you're home. I'll need to know that you've arrived safely."

"Thank you. I will. Enjoy your shower." She blew a kiss and was gone.

I didn't enjoy it at all. I didn't enjoy a single moment of the next two and a half hours, waiting for her to ring and tell me she was all right. Not just that she was all right, but that her date had been meaningless and uneventful and that absolutely no kissing had taken place.

Then, when she did ring and tell me exactly that—that Joshua was a "snoozefest with Mommy issues"—I was so relieved that I couldn't let her go without hearing every detail. Then every detail of her day. Then every detail of the past week.

And thus began the new version of our friendship. Our FaceTime friendship.

At first, her calls were much of the same, asking advice about her upcoming date, but she'd always ring again afterward to tell me how awful the night had been before going into the rest of the day's events. Soon she began calling even when she didn't have a date. And when we'd run out of things to say, we didn't hang up, we just sat on the phone together, going on about our evening. Often, we'd even watch a show together.

"I think she used to like the other guy," she said one Tuesday, early in November. "The one who's not her husband. That's why he's acting so weird about it."

It was late, and I'd brought my laptop to bed. Audrey was also in her bed. I had a profile view of her painting her toenails while she watched her show in a separate window on her tablet.

I looked up from my computer, where I was simultaneously FaceTiming with Audrey and working up a spreadsheet for a new campaign, and stared at the telly. We were watching *Easy* on Netflix, and most of this particular episode was in subtitles. I hadn't been paying attention, so I was faking it when I pretended I knew what was going on. "She's going to cheat on her husband."

The show was an anthology type, vignettes from the lives of different characters in Chicago while they fumbled their way through love and other relationships. I'd predicted when we'd started the show that none of them would end up happy.

She scowled. "You say that every episode. Not a one has cheated so far."

"It might not happen in the show, but it would happen if it were real life. Love never ends well. I know you feel differently, but I'd be remiss if I neglected to remind you I've learned otherwise."

"This show makes you miserable, doesn't it? All the people surviving their relationships." She looked directly at me through the screen. "Would you rather we go back to watching *Gogglebox*?"

"No. Please, never again." That show's concept was by far the most dreadful—regular people were filmed in their own homes watching popular British TV. It was one of Audrey's favorites, though, and while I protested about watching it, I quite delighted in watching her laugh through every episode.

I quite delighted in watching Audrey do anything, it seemed. I certainly didn't participate in these calls for the television viewing.

I watched now as she stretched out her legs in front of her, her toenails displaying a bright orange hue. Though I'd thought I preferred lighter polish colors on women, I found I very much liked this shade on her, and I said so.

We settled into a comfortable silence while she watched more of the show, and I filled in more boxes on my spreadsheets.

"Oh my!" she suddenly exclaimed, out of nowhere.

I didn't bother to look up from my work. "What is it?"

"You were right. She *is* cheating on her husband." She let out a hiss of air. "And it's...wow."

That got my attention.

I looked up at the screen, and sure enough, the man who was not the woman's husband was seducing her. In her own apartment. While her husband slept in the next room.

I felt the familiar jumble of rage building in my chest, the righteous anger of a once scorned husband, ready to unleash in a spew of curse words and another rant on Why Love Fails.

Except, I was too caught up in the action on the screen to go there. Not just my telly screen, but my computer screen—Audrey was mesmerized.

She blinked several times, her hand stroking her skin at her throat. "This is really, super...wrong, of course, but also it's..."

The man had the woman pressed up against the window, going at her from behind. There were plenty of words that could easily be filled in where Audrey left off. *Dirty, filthy, nasty, arousing.*

I chose the simplest. "It's hot," I said clearly. Really hot. So hot, my boxers were starting to feel uncomfortable.

"I miss that," Audrey said in a raw tone. "I mean, I'm really happy with my decision to take this dating thing slowly, don't get me wrong. I have no intention of going to bed with any guy before I'm in a committed loving relationship. But..."

The words *don't get me wrong* were intriguing enough to draw me from the telly screen. No one says *don't get me wrong* without following with a controversial statement.

"But?" I was bracing now for whatever that controversial statement might be. Coming from Audrey, it could be anything.

"But I just have to say, I'm really missing the bedroom action. It's almost been a year since I...well, you know. You were there."

I was as dazzled about this confession as I was the first time she'd told me. I hadn't slept with anyone since then either, not that I intended to confess that to her.

"I think about it sometimes. I think about you and me and how good we were together and sometimes it seems a shame that we only have memories to replay."

"You think about us?" I asked cautiously. As though it didn't matter to me in the slightest what her answer was. As though I didn't bash the bishop nightly after we got off the phone.

"I do. Of course I do. And I know we can't actually do anything because we have completely different philosophies about how romance works, but... Do you know what a buddy booth is?" She was excellent at switching gears mid-topic. Sometimes it was a challenge to follow, but always a fascinating journey, and she generally made it back around to where she started. Eventually.

"I can't say that I do," I said, praying this was one of those times she circled back to the beginning.

"I've never been to one in person, but when I was still in Colorado getting my bachelor's, one of my friends told me about these booths they used to have at the porn shops on Colfax. You'd go in this booth, so small it just had a bench and a TV screen. You'd put your money in and then you could pick a porn movie to watch while you, you know. Did your thing."

I turned off the TELLY. Nothing in the show was as good as this conversation, and I didn't want to miss a single word.

"But there was also a window on the side of the booth, with a curtain. If you opened it, and if the person next to you opened their curtain, you could watch each other. I mean, maybe that's a little gross, depending on who the person is next to you, but if he was normal or if you knew him, it sounded like it could be kind of hot."

"I don't think there are any such booths in London." I didn't know where she was going with this, but if she intended for me to point her in such a direction, I was not about to comply.

"No, I don't want to go to one. They probably aren't even a thing now that the internet is the beautiful place that it is. But I thought maybe. You know. Maybe we could make our own buddy booth. Right here. Over FaceTime."

"Excuse me...what was that?"

"Porn. You and me. We could both turn on a show and—how do you Brits say it? Have a bit of a wank? Our computer screens can be the buddy window. You can watch me. I can watch you. What do you say?"

She was trying to kill me. The only reason we hadn't ended up in bed together already, as far as I was concerned, was because she'd taken it off the table.

And now she was dangling an opportunity to crack one off while watching her do the same?

I was stone hard at the thought.

She had to be pulling my leg, winding me up. Something. She couldn't be serious. So I didn't give an answer.

"Dylan? Dylan. We don't have to if you think it's a bad idea."

"I didn't say that." Most definitely didn't. "I was simply thinking through the possible repercussions."

"I really don't think there are any. We've already had sex. We're still both attracted to each other—I think—"

"We are."

"—and doing it this way will keep things from getting confused. Because it's obviously just a way to get off, and not about anything else. It's going to be fun. You'll see." The view of her changed as she picked up her tablet and set it on her lap. "I'm pulling up a video I have saved. One of my favorites. You should do the same."

The only thing I did on my computer was enable the image of her to fill the whole screen.

"Okay. I'm playing mine now. Are you ready?"

I wasn't even sure that I'd agreed to this game, but fuck if I wasn't going to play it out. There was no risk that I could see. This wasn't like kissing her—if I kissed her again, I was certain I'd never be able to stop.

Erotic moaning and sounds of kissing played in the background as her video began to play. She put the tablet back on the bed next to her, and the view of her changed again. In profile, I watched as she slid her hand under the waistband of her pajama shorts.

Ah, fuck.

I pushed down my sweats and my boxers, just far enough to release my cock from its imprisonment. There was already lube on my nightstand, and I grabbed it now and applied it liberally to the throbbing steel in my hand.

All the while, my eyes were on her. My ears were tuned to her.

She was breathing heavily while her hand moved inside her shorts. I couldn't see the pink flesh of her cunt, couldn't see if she was still bare or if her lips were glistening with her wetness.

"Are you wet?" I asked, desperate to know.

"I'm so wet."

The moans in the background increased. "What's happening in your video? Describe it to me. In detail."

She turned her head to look toward the screen, her eyes not quite looking at me. "He's going down on her. He's licking her clit, and she's really into it."

I could still taste Audrey's pussy on my lips. Stroking the length of myself, I imagined I was the one eating her out. That I was the one making her make those sounds. Those sweet, sweet cries as she played with herself, stroking herself toward climax.

I bloody needed her pants down. I needed to see her.

"Audrey, be a good girl. Pull down your shorts and let me watch." The words were out before I could decide if they might cross the line.

Fortunately, she didn't bat an eye. Just stripped off her shorts and knickers entirely, tossing them across the bed. Then she spread her legs and moved her screen so that I had a prime view of her gorgeous, pink cunt. Moisture dripped from her entrance. Her clit was swollen and red under her fingers. It was the most erotic thing I'd ever seen. Buddy booths couldn't possibly have been this titillating.

"Put your laptop where I can see you, too, Dylan," she said as she strummed across her sensitive bud, her voice thick.

I set my laptop down immediately, angling the screen so I could see her without turning my head too far.

"There's that monster cock," she said, and I grew even thicker. "What's going on in your video? Tell me what they're doing."

I'd never turned on a porn of my own. The only woman I wanted to watch was the one filling up my screen.

So that was the one I described, giving her directions in the guise of details. "She's alone. She's playing with herself. One hand is squeezing her clit, and with the other, she's pulling on her tit."

Audrey was such a good girl, such a good, good girl. She lifted the tank she was wearing, exposing her round, pert tits. With one hand, she tugged at the tight bead of one nipple, rolling it between her fingers. Lower, she pinched at her clit, harder until her hips were bucking.

The strokes of my hand quickened over my cock. "Now she's putting her fingers inside her. Two of them. She's so wet. She's drenched."

Again, Audrey followed the action of my imaginary porno. Two fingers disappeared inside her. When she pulled them out again, they were dripping with her juices.

"Fuck, that's beautiful." I sat up so I could really watch her when she did it again. And again. And again.

I matched my own rhythm to hers, pretended it was her warm hole I was plunging into instead of the palm of my own hand. I was getting close. I could feel my balls pulling up, could feel the tingling in the base of my spine.

"This isn't enough. I need—hold on." Abruptly, Audrey left the screen for a minute. When she returned, she had a purple dildo.

Jesus.

It wasn't even that big, but it was wider than her fingers. Longer, too. She turned the toy on to vibrate and lined it up to her entrance. If she put that in her tight hole, I was done for.

The truth was, I wanted to be done for.

"Shove it in, now, Audrey. Show me how good you take your fucking." My words were ragged and desperate. And when she shoved it in, I nearly exploded right then. "Ah, that's it. Take it. Put it all the way in. As far as it can go."

She pushed it in until it was deep inside her, then pulled it out halfway before driving it back in. Her tempo was fast, her breathing more shallow with each thrust. Her eyes moved back and forth from her pussy, to the screen—to me or the video, I wasn't sure—but each time I saw them they were more and more glazed over. She was close. As close as I was.

I increased my own speed as I neared the edge. I was out of control, out of my mind. "Does it fill you as good as I can?" I begged for her to answer. "Does it make you feel as good as I do?"

"No," she gasped. "Nothing fills me as good as you do. Nothing."

With those words, I erupted. Cum spilled over my hand as I jerked again and again, slower now, determined to pull every last bit of my orgasm from my cock.

She followed right after, her body spasming with the pleasure of the release. The utter beauty and carnality of the scene urged another wave of my own climax.

I fell back on the bed and tried to remember how to breathe. And figure out what to say. How did a person comment after such an incredibly erotic experience as this?

Audrey was the one who tried first. "That was...I mean...I don't...words." She sat up and reached for her tablet. "I'm trying to say that was good and thank you and all that, but I can't seem to remember how to speak right now, so how about we call it a night and I'll talk to you tomorrow?"

She'd done better conversing than I could have.

"Yeah. Yeah, that's good." The screen went dark when she hung up, but I stared at it for a long time wondering how it was possible that, after all that, I only wanted her more.

NINETEEN

"What are you doing? I need you!"

This was a common way for calls with Audrey to begin, as well as my favorite. Saturday when her image came through FaceTime she was dressed in another jumper-and-jeans outfit, half of her hair hidden inside a newsboy cap. She looked delectable. Good enough to eat.

I thought she looked good in everything, though. Especially since the night of the buddy booth. It had been four days since we'd played the game. We'd talked every day since without mentioning what we'd done, but I couldn't stop thinking about it. Couldn't stop thinking about her moan as she came and her erotic confession. *Nothing fills me as good as you do. Nothing.*

Words exchanged during sexual engagement are not to be trusted. I was old enough to have learned that lesson the hard way. Still, I liked the fantasy of it. Enjoyed the fancy of nothing being as good for Audrey as I could be.

At my age, it appeared, a man was still capable of dreaming.

"What's wrong? Is Jeffrey an asshole?" It was too early for her date to be over. I'd spoken to her while she was getting ready, and she didn't plan to be home until after ten. It was only six-fifteen. I was ready to be mad on her behalf.

"Yes, *Joffrey* is a bad dude. He stood me up."

Thank goodness for him that was all he'd done. I'd never been one to endorse violence, but I'd fight barehanded and without hesitation if it were to defend Audrey's honor in any way. In this case, he was an idiot, but hadn't sparked my fighting instinct.

"Another one bites the dust," I said, perhaps not as conciliatory as I should have. "Now you can cross him off the list and have your evening free to do as you please. A win-win as far as I'm concerned."

The corners of her mouth turned down into that pout that taunted me so. "Except I'm the one who bought the tickets to the Jack the Ripper tour, and they weren't cheap! Come and join me so they don't go to waste."

"I'm afraid I have other plans."

She rolled her eyes, as obviously as my son did every time we spoke these days. "No, you don't. You never have plans. You're as homebody as they get. The tour doesn't start for an hour, so you have time to throw some real clothes on and get out here."

Real clothes? I glanced down at the outfit I was wearing. They seemed fine to me, but I *was* wearing running pants and trainers. Guess I was changing before leaving the house.

And I *was* leaving the house. Soon, in fact. "I *do* have plans, thank you very much. Seems you don't know as much about me as you think." While I did feel disappointment at not being able to come to her rescue, there was also a sense of satisfaction at not being available. If she ever thought I was waiting around to rush to her aid, now she knew the truth was otherwise.

The truth was otherwise tonight, anyway. I really didn't usually get out for much that wasn't related to work.

She wasn't buying it. "What are they?"

"What are my plans? If you must know, I have a gig tonight."

One of the best things about playing with a band was how impressive it sounded to announce that I had a gig. More impressive than our actual music. We were not an original group in any way, shape, or form.

I could practically see her eyes go wide. "You do? You didn't tell me! Forget the Ripper. I'll come to you. Where are you playing?"

Oh dear. That was not at all where I'd planned for this to lead.

I backtracked quickly. "No, you don't want to come to this. It's not your type of music. Barely music at all."

"I don't care how good you are. It's you, and I've been dying to see you play! Thrashheads, right?"

I couldn't believe she remembered. The only time I'd mentioned it had been in passing. "You don't want to see us. I promise. It's going to be a terrible show. Don't ruin your night."

"What time do you go on? What's the address?"

"Audrey, I mean it. Go on the Ripper tour by yourself instead. That will be a much better use of your time."

Her pout had returned, I could hear it, and I prepared myself for another battle round, but she surprised me with her easy acquiescence. "Fine. If you don't want me there..."

I ran my thumb and first finger across my forehead in a pinching motion. "It's not that I *don't* want you there—"

"You just don't want me to see you play. I get it. Whatever. I'll talk to you later."

"Make sure you text me when you're home!" I shouted after her, but she'd already ended the call.

Fantastic.

I'd hurt her feelings. That hadn't been the goal. I considered for a moment, calling her back and inviting her after all, but there were reasons why that wasn't a wise idea. In the end, I deferred to an idiom I lived by—*the more you stir a turd, the more it stinks.*

I decided not to stir the pot.

IT WAS ALMOST two hours later when I heard from her again.

We had thirty minutes before our show started, and I was tuning my bass. The pub tonight near Regents Park was similar to most of the places we played—cheap, old, and empty. The owner of this particular venue was a cousin of a cousin or some equally far-off relation to the drummer, Russell, and the gig was more of a favor to us than to the pub. They didn't feature live music, as a rule, so rather than playing on a stage, the tables and benches in one area of the establishment had been stacked in the corner. We were to perform in front of this precarious tower.

I tuned my bass while Ian and Clancy, our keyboardist, set up their equipment and exchanged digs about the venue. I was doing my best to ignore them, but their sour mood was starting to get under my skin. Why was it we played together, again, if none of us found it any fun anymore? It had been an obligation for so long, I couldn't remember a time that it had been fun at all.

"Holy cow! This is fantastic!"

Oh, God. I knew that enthusiastic voice. It was the last sound I heard before going to bed most nights, the first sound I thought about when I woke up every morning.

With dread, I turned around to face the naughty little vixen. "Audrey," I huffed. "I told you not to come." I was already thinking up excuses to get her out of the place.

They don't allow women. They don't allow women under twenty-five. They don't allow women who know members of the band.

Lame excuses, yes. I'd never been very creative on the spot. And yet I was desperate to paint a picture that didn't include her.

"I'm glad I didn't listen," she said, stepping past the duct tape border on the floor that was meant to distinguish the "stage" from the rest of the pub. "This is, like, a real band, Dylan. With real instruments and real drums."

She used two fingers to do a roll on the cymbal. Russell was going to be livid. No one touched his drums but him.

But I was more concerned about what she'd just said.

"What do you mean this is like a real band? Of course we're a real band. What did you think I meant when I said I was in a band?"

"I don't know." She sat down on the drummer's stool and began thumping the bass drum pedal with her foot. "I guess I pictured more of a bunch of men with microphones and a karaoke machine. Especially when I saw on the map that this place was in the Drunk People Who Missed Camden part of town."

Ba dum da. She'd found the drumsticks now, and her rhythm wasn't that bad.

Russell's voice boomed across the pub. "Who's touching my drums?"

Good. Maybe he'd scare Audrey off.

"How did you find out where I was playing?" I asked, still more focused on the how and the why of her being there.

"Internet. Turns out Thrashheads has a website! A pretty good one, too."

I couldn't help puffing my chest a bit. The website was my doing. "It's more of a Wordpress account, really, but it does..." She was distracting me from the point. The point being I preferred she wasn't here. "Look, Audrey. I can't have you in the audience when I play."

"Will I be very distracting?"

Jesus, she was so adorable sitting behind those drums, her cap tilted on her head, her eyes twinkling with mischief.

Yes, she would be very distracting. She was very distracting already.

"Hey—who are you?" Russell peered down at the woman on his stool, and from his expression, I could tell he was fuming.

"Are you the drummer?" She stood up and handed him his drumsticks. "I've never met a real drummer before. Wow. Look at those biceps. Is that from playing?"

Russell seemed taken aback. "I don't know. A bit, I s'pose."

"That's hot." She gave him that glowing smile of hers, and between that and the compliment, he was won over.

"It *is* hot, isn't it?" He sat down and played through some of his riffs. *Show off.*

"Nice," she said.

Not nice at all. Particularly not nice was the way Russell was looking at her now, like she was the groupie he planned to take home after the set. But she wasn't.

Not on my watch.

"That's enough now, Audrey. Let's go outside and hail you a cab." I put my bass in its stand, but she was right there, ready to pick it back up again.

"Is this what you look like when you play?" she asked, striking a melodramatic pose. She strummed the strings, shifting to a new position with each sour note. "I bet you really get into it when you're onstage."

I didn't know what to say to that. It wasn't very flattering to tell her the truth—that I tended to stand in one place, playing through the chords with precision rather than passion. That I likely looked rather lame in the process. That I didn't remember how to enjoy any of it while it was happening. That I didn't want her to imagine a show that wasn't happening.

"Oh, yeah. Locke really puts on a show," Ian guffawed.

Audrey didn't seem to realize he was being sardonic, or she was protecting me with her response. "Awesome. I can't wait."

She pulled the bass strap over her head and handed me my instrument, her fingers brushing mine in the exchange.

I'd forgotten about the power she had over me in real life after only seeing her on screen for the last several weeks. I'd forgotten the way the air vibrated around her, forgotten how she made my skin tingle and my mouth feel dry.

I'd forgotten how much I utterly liked being in her presence.

"I'm so glad my date bailed on me so I could be here. It's kismet, you know."

There she was with that whole thing again. "I'm beginning to think that word doesn't mean what you think it means."

"Oh, I know what it means. Your hair needs mussing. It's too perfect." She reached out to run her hand through the brown flop on the top of my head. My pulse sped up at her touch. "There. Much better."

Our eyes locked. There was something familiar about this, about all of this. About her. About me. Something I couldn't quite put a finger on.

"Are you going to introduce us to your girl, mate?" Ian asked, bringing me back to the present moment.

Your girl. She most definitely wasn't my girl. She was...

"This is Audrey," I said simply. "Audrey, this is Thrashheads. Ian. Russell. Clancy. Bloke flirting with the waitress is Dennis. He plays second guitar."

A chorus of hellos sounded followed by a weighted silence where each of my bandmates looked from me to Audrey questioningly.

For Pete's sake. We knew practically nothing about each other, and now they wanted to know more?

"Audrey is...she's..." I didn't know how to explain Audrey.

"I'm his niece," she said, and everyone let out an audible, *Ah!* Because that made more sense, that she was a relative rather than a friend or a girlfriend. I got it, I truly did. "It's great to meet you all!"

She turned her focus back to me. "I'm going to grab a drink and get a seat before the show starts. Break a leg, and all that. Uncle Dylan." As she often did, she pressed her lips to my cheek.

I'd forgotten how much those kisses drove me out of my mind. Blissfully out of my mind.

"She's a looker," Russell said. "Mind if I—"

"No. Don't even think about it." There was no way in hell Russell was The One she was looking for.

"I thought your brother didn't have any kids," Ian said. Apparently he knew more about me than I remembered.

"She's Ellen's niece. She's living here for a while, working at a gallery. I said I'd show her around." As if I'd bring anyone to a Thrashheads show on purpose.

Which reminded me, I'd wanted her to leave.

I took a step to follow after her and stopped. I didn't actually want her to leave. Not really. I liked that she'd come. I'd only told her I hadn't wanted her to come because I was afraid of looking like a fool. And maybe I still would, but she'd been expecting karaoke, and she'd still bothered to show up. That seemed to indicate that she really didn't care if we were terrible.

So I let her stay.

Then, as the chords started to our first number, and my hand found its position over the frets, I was inspired with the most fascinating notion to let go. Just let go and play. Get my mind out of the way and let my body make the music that I'd loved since I was a teenager.

I got into it. I rocked that bassline. I rocked it on every song. I was brilliant. I was on fire.

I won the nonexistent competition.

It was because of Audrey, of course. She was in the audience, and I wanted to be brilliant for her, so that she wouldn't regret coming. But also, I played good because I *felt* good. Because *she* made me feel good.

She made me feel good the whole night long, the way she cheered and clapped, the way she called out for an encore when we'd reached our last number. The way she sang along to every song she knew. The way she never took her eyes off me.

It was more fun than I'd had in ages.

It wasn't until we were performing our encore piece that it hit me—why all of this seemed so familiar. I was struck with a memory from when I was about her age, playing with a different band in a similar pub back in Southampton. I'd been dating Ellen for a few months, and that night she'd come to one of my shows like she often did. I'd played my heart out trying to impress her, and when the set was done, she'd come with me back to my flat where she'd showered me with compliments and told me she'd "never felt this way about a man before."

I'd been over the moon, and it was that night I'd first known that I loved her. I'd loved how she made me feel and who she made me be and what I looked like through her eyes.

And that was what felt familiar with Audrey.

I loved how Audrey made me feel. I loved how she made me want to let loose and step out of my comfort zone and be engaged. I loved how she didn't seem to see me as an aging wanker, but as someone interesting. Someone worth spending time with. Someone with something to offer the world.

I loved all of it.

I loved *her*.

I was *in love* with Audrey.

What the bloody fuck was I supposed to do now?

TWENTY

I had to avoid her now, of course. What other option was there for me? It wasn't easy, by any means. By Monday I was in a foul temper, and I'd only been without her for the span of one day.

While everyone at the office was sure to notice my mood, Amy was the only one to mention it. "You're a might prickly today. Want to tell me what bug's crawled up your arse?"

"I've fallen in love with a woman I can't have," I said. There wasn't any reason to keep it secret. I'd always believed in sharing my misery with those closest to me when possible.

"Well, then." Needless to say, she was surprised. "It's not me, is it? Please tell me it's not."

Then we both broke into laughter because the idea was ludicrous. Leave it to Amy to coax out the last bit of cheer from my ornery soul.

"How sure are you that you can't have her?" she asked when we'd settled again.

I sighed and leaned back in my chair. "Very sure." I delivered a brief summary of my relationship with Audrey, skipping over the sexual details out of modesty. "So, you see, she's out to find a life partner, not engage in a torrid affair with a man twice her age."

"Ah. But..." Amy tapped her lip with a single finger. "Is there a specific reason why you couldn't be the life partner she's looking for?"

I chortled, but it ended short when I realized she hadn't meant it as a joke. "That's ridiculous. She's almost twenty years younger than I am. I'm planning my retirement. She's planning half a dozen babies. She's romantic and wide-eyed, and we both know I'm basically Scrooge reincarnated. She wants the fairy tale, and I don't even believe in the customs of matrimony or long-term monogamy. They're outdated and impractical notions."

A deep furrow appeared in Amy's brow. "If you really believe those are flawed traditions, why are you so supportive of her attempt to find a happily ever after? Why not step in, sweep her off her feet, and love her as long as it lasts?"

This was the tough question, the one I'd been grappling with myself for the past thirty-six hours. I was only just now able to confess the answer. "Honestly? Because I'm not sure if they really are terrible customs or if they're just terrible for me."

Amy, my hard-hearted friend, brought her hand to her chest as though she were wounded. "That's very sad," she said sincerely. "Whatever are you supposed to do with your love, then?"

My response was equally sincere. "Suffer in silence. Naturally."

It had been a long time since I'd endured the torment of unrequited affection, however, and the days that followed led to deeper and unbearable despair. Somehow I managed to refuse every one of her calls, replying after with a text saying I was unavailable for the night. Every evening I prayed that she'd get the hint and give up, but she was persistent. Relentless.

By the end of the week, my resolve was weakening. I yearned

to hear her voice. I ached to know the details of her life. So when she sent me a frantic text Saturday morning, saying once again that she "needed" me, I couldn't help but respond.

> What's wrong? What can I do?

> I need your help! Can you come over here ASAP?

I wasn't exactly a soft man, but I'd reached my limit of missing her, and I was vulnerable. Against my better judgement, I replied,

> I'm on my way.

I BEGAN to regret my decision as soon as she opened the front door. She wore only a gray sports bra and low-rise shorts, her hair was thrown up into a mess on top of her head, and all I could think about when I saw her was running my tongue along the rim of her exposed belly button. What did her skin taste like there? Would her voice quiver with excitement like it had when she'd played with herself on camera for me?

It was too late to leave, though, and before I could get my bearings, she'd taken my hand and pulled me inside the flat.

"I really thought I could do it myself, but I'm trying to be better about managing my expectations, and I think I definitely expected too much on this one. Therefore, you must be my hero and rescue me from defeat."

Oh, how I'd missed the sound of her babble. I had more than a little trepidation, however, about being anyone's hero.

She still had my hand in hers with the door shut behind us. "It's this way," she said, tugging me behind her.

While I was distracted by how natural her fingers felt laced through mine, I still managed to assess her living space. It was small and unremarkable. The place had obviously come furnished. They were all dull neutral colors, nothing she would have picked for herself. Her front room doubled as both lounge and dining room. Abstract flower art decorated the walls, but beyond that, it was dreary and drab. Not very Audrey-like at all. The galley kitchen, I noted as we passed, had barely enough room to fit one person, but it did have decent appliances. A multi-colored dish towel draped over the tap was the only injection of her personality. Another two steps and we were at the doorway of her bedroom.

She dropped my hand here, which was fortunate since it already felt too intimate to be so close to where she slept, and then swept her arm, introducing me to the space as though she were the hostess on a game show. "Here it is! My project!"

I stepped in cautiously. It was also tiny, barely big enough to fit a double bed, dresser, and nightstand, which was the extent of the furnishings. All three pieces had been gathered in the center of the room and covered with plastic tarps. Painters tape ran along the footboard, and half of one of the dull cream walls was freshly painted in robin's egg blue. More plastic drop cloths were spread over the wood floor, and a paint can of the same robin's egg blue shade sat next to the window with an assortment of brushes at its side.

I had one word for Audrey. "No."

I turned around, ready to walk out of the situation I should never have stepped into. But she grabbed my arm to stop me. "Please!"

"I did not rush over here to help you paint your flat. I thought you'd had an emergency. That you were ill or...or...that someone had hurt you."

"I'll be hurt if you walk out on me."

I scowled in her direction, but she was undeterred. "I *will* be hurt, Dylan! Emotionally hurt, but also physically. I can't reach to the top of the walls, and I don't have a step stool. Anything I try to come up with as a substitution could kill me."

"Hire a painter." I realized after I'd made the suggestion that she likely couldn't afford one. I amended. "I'll hire a painter for you."

"That's silly. It's too small of a space to hire someone. Two people could knock this out in no time." She was so charming, batting her brown eyes, giving me that luscious pout.

My resistance was waning, but for now, it still held. "There's no other poor sap you can rope into laboring on your behalf?"

She peered up at me like I had the power to give her the world. "I'm sure I *could* find someone else, but I don't want to. You've been avoiding me. And I need a man. This just works out, doesn't it?"

I hated that she thought that, true as it was. "I've been busy with a work thing," I lied, unable to give up the pretense.

"Do you have to work on your work thing today? Could you maybe take the day off and spend it with me? I miss you."

I missed her too. Insanely. But while I was happy enough to suffer through my own yearning, I didn't want to ever be the source of her suffering.

I ran a hand through my hair and surveyed the extent of the project again. It really *could* be tackled in one day with the two of us. Painting wasn't so hard. Deciding to do it was.

"It's just these three walls, really," she said, reading my thoughts too well. "I'm leaving the wall above the fireplace the color it is, and I'm doing a design on it with the blue."

I was that fish again, and she was baiting me the way she had when she'd first met me. Falling for the same lure, I had to wonder if I didn't enjoy being caught.

"I'm not wearing clothes fit to paint." I'd already decided to stay, but I wasn't quite done complaining about it.

She looked me up and down. "Do you like your outfit?"

"Should I not?" I couldn't see a thing wrong with what I was wearing.

"It's a fine outfit! I mean, it's a henley and blue jeans. Can't go wrong with the basics."

She was winding me up on purpose. I was sure of it.

"I like this shirt," I said, obstinate.

"Then take it off!"

Grumbling under my breath, I pulled the fleece-lined shirt over my head and tossed it into the hallway. I could feel her eyes on me—ogling, perhaps? I sucked in my stomach and threw my shoulders back, just in case.

She smiled coyly. "If you like your pants, you can take them off too. I won't mind."

I knew then what my gravestone would say—*death by winding*. There was already sexual tension between us before she started plucking at it, pulling it as taut as it could possibly be pulled. Added to that were my newly labeled feelings. I loved her, loved everything about her, and by God, if that didn't make her harder to resist. I wanted her lips, not just because I wanted them, but because I wanted to *love* them. I wanted to love her breasts. I wanted to love her skin and her toes and her cunt, and being trapped with her in a small space while she pranced around in a sports bra wasn't helping the situation.

But I was strong. If I wasn't going to leave like I should, I had to focus on the task.

With a sigh, I headed over to the supplies and selected a large, flat brush, then started on the wall already half done. Audrey poured some of the blue paint into an aluminum tray and chose a brush that seemed more suited for artistry than the task at hand, and went to work over the fireplace.

"Are you even allowed to paint your rental?" I asked after applying several long strokes.

"The landlord said yes, as long as I paint it again when I move out."

The skin at the back of my neck began to tingle. "Does this mean you've been offered the permanent position? Are you going to stay in London?" Why else would she bother with so much effort if she were only planning to move out in another month or so?

She made a noise that sounded like a vocal shrug. "Nothing's decided yet. But I can't live in this colorless apartment another day. There's no life to it. I can't be this boring."

I looked over at her—a look that was meant to be a glance, but turned into a full stare when I saw what she was doing to the wall she was working on. She'd painted winding strokes coming from the corner and extending across the bare wall. After a few minutes of watching, when she'd begun to outline the shape of a flower, I realized the strokes were stems, and that the abstract art I'd seen earlier had been her originals.

"Those were your pieces in the lounge," I said, wishing I'd studied them longer. "You're quite good."

She laughed and shook her head. "I'm *not*, but thank you for saying so."

"What do you mean? I couldn't even draw a stick figure and make it recognizable. This, on the other hand, is extraordinary."

She stood back to examine her work. "It's all right, I suppose. I spend so much time examining the art of the greats, it's hard to think of my own stuff as something that has value. But I like doing it. And that's pretty valuable regardless of the production quality."

As always, she was wise beyond her years. I had yet to learn the value of a hobby. Everything I did was practical and with reason. I'd only started playing with Thrashheads as a favor to

Ian when his bass player had dropped out, and I'd only stayed because I had nothing better to do with my Saturday nights. I'd only learned bass in the first place because my mother had thought that having an instrument on my transcript would look good when applying for uni. What did I ever do that I enjoyed? What did I find value in simply because I liked doing it?

I liked doing this together, actually. Painting, and playing, with Audrey. I could take or leave the actual labor, but being with her, helping her, standing in the same room while she created something that made her smile—*that*, I liked. I liked it a lot.

Enjoying the work made it pass quickly, as well as the small size of the room. By the time two hours had passed, I was applying the second coat of paint on the last wall. Audrey hummed as she painted. Her floral design had taken shape, curling up and around the fireplace like a living vine, and there we were now, at the corner where our walls met, standing entirely too close.

I could feel the heat radiating off her body. I could smell the crisp apple scent of her even through the overbearing fumes of paint. I could sense the tension between us stretching more and more taut. I could barely talk to her, could barely look at her anymore without being in danger of losing my restraint and pulling her into my arms.

Audrey, I surmised, felt none of it. She seemed as cool as a cucumber, even when her shoulder brushed against my arm.

"You've gotten quiet," she said, just when I thought the silence was so thick I'd choke on it. "Are you brooding over something?"

"Only your taste in music. This folk shit is putting me to sleep."

I didn't look at her, but I could feel her body turn in my direction. "This *folk shit* is quite popular, thank you very much. Excuse me for liking music that's actually musical."

I did turn then. Because, tension or not, I was not about to let her speak ill about the greats of my generation.

"Are you saying that Deep Purple isn't musical? That their guitar riffs aren't among the most recognizable in the world? 'Smoke on the Water' is all I have to say to that." I didn't care if it dated me, I wasn't wrong about rock.

She cocked one hip, and smirked. "I don't know what smoke on the water is. Is that some sort of British saying?"

"You don't—are you saying that you don't know the song 'Smoke on the Water'?" I was practically speechless. I had given her the benefit of the doubt, but this was asking too much. "It's one of the most famous songs of the seventies!"

She raised one shoulder and dropped it again. "I wasn't alive in the seventies. So..."

I drew my lips together in a tight line. "You know it. I promise you know it. We even played it the other night."

"They kind of all sounded the same. I mean, they were really good, but—"

I cut her off with an attempt of the famous guitar line. "Dun, dun, dunnnn. Dundun da dunnn. Dun, dun, dunnn, dundun." She *had* to know it.

She narrowed her eyes and grinned.

"You *do* know it. You're having your fun with me again. Poking at me." I tried, certain my instincts weren't wrong.

"Is that what I'm doing?" She stabbed the air in my direction with her paintbrush. "Poke. Poke."

The next stab was close to me, and I could see exactly where this was headed. "Don't you dare," I warned.

"Don't dare do what? This?" She waved the brush around threateningly. I leaned back reflexively, dodging her. She laughed and lowered her weapon. Apparently she hadn't meant to paint me with it after all.

Except, as soon as I relaxed, she reached out and swiped

across my nose and cheek. I could feel the gooey texture of paint against my skin.

I narrowed my eyes. "You'll pay for that."

"Really? How?"

I wanted to spank her, that's what I wanted to do, but I settled for stroking her across her waistline, that flat stomach that I so wanted to lick. My paintbrush was bigger than hers, so though she'd gone for my face, my hit felt like it had done the most damage.

I bit back a laugh of my own.

Her eyes grew wide. "I can't believe you did that!" She swiped her arm toward me again, striking out toward my chest this time.

Reflexively, I dropped my brush and grabbed her wrist before she could hit her target. The shock of my skin against hers was startling, like the whir of a car engine coming back to life after the battery's been jumped.

I felt resurrected like that in the moment, like I'd been dead and the touch of this woman had brought me back to life. And all I could think about was kissing her. All I could focus on were her lips.

I searched for a sign of permission even as I tugged her toward me.

There wasn't just one, but multiple invitations—the tilt of her chin, her tongue peeking out and dancing across her bottom lip, her eyes big and dilated under the bat of her lashes.

I stopped thinking, stopped holding back, stopped pretending I didn't want her, and pressed my mouth to hers.

TWENTY-ONE

The first time I kissed Ellen after I knew that I loved her, my world opened up. She'd said she loved me too, and I knew, *I just knew*, that we were headed somewhere together, that we were walking down this path hand in hand, and nothing but bright skies and the future lay before us.

It was a completely different experience kissing Audrey, after I'd accepted the gravity of the feelings I had for her.

I knew the kiss meant nothing, that it would lead nowhere, but it felt like being bathed in radiant light.

Like I was an imprisoned man in a dark prison cell who, for one brief moment, was allowed to step outside into the sunlight. I was completely present for it. Each brush of her lips, each touch of her tongue—I memorized it all, imprinted every second into my brain so that I'd have it forever. I might still have worn shackles with no hope of freedom, but this moment mattered. It was real and divine, and I would cherish every last second of the stolen sunshine until my dying day.

I would've been content with only kissing, with just the

shallow lifts and falls of her chest and frantic hands trying to caress and cling.

But Audrey had other ideas in mind, demonstrated by the quick work of her hands at my waist, unbuckling my belt, undoing my trousers, the slip of her hand inside the opening to stroke the outline of my very prominent erection.

"This," she said between kisses. She pulled at the elastic waistband of my boxers and dipped her hand in to touch me directly.

I hissed at the feel of her soft hand against my hot skin.

"I want this," she begged. "Can I have this?"

My cock jumped in her hand at the sweet timbre of her voice asking for pieces of me like she didn't already own the whole. Could she have this? Could she have *me*?

In this moment, yes. She had it all.

It was too erotic, and I was too close too soon. I grabbed her wrists and pushed her back against the wall, in an attempt to gain control.

"You want this?" I rubbed my erection against her belly. "You want my cock so I can fill your pussy like no one else does, don't you?"

She nodded her head vigorously. "Please. Give it to me, please?"

It was like dominoes, how things progressed from there, an event put into action that couldn't be stopped, building momentum in a frenzy of hands and lips and teeth and tongues. I dropped her wrists so I could push up her bra and descend with my mouth upon her sharply pointed nipple. My other hand ventured lower, into her knickers to find the sensitive bud hidden within her folds.

She was wet, so wet I could smell her. So wet that I couldn't resist sliding my hand down her slick crease to plunge inside of her.

"Look at what you have for me." I pulled my finger out and smeared her juices across her bottom lip. "Such a good girl you are, making your pussy all wet and warm for me."

She made a shuddering noise that could only be interpreted as pleasure. While my fingers thrust deeper inside her, I licked across her mouth, a low moan forming at the back of my throat as I rediscovered the wonderful flavor of her desire.

"You taste like a dirty girl. Are you a dirty girl?"

"I'm a dirty girl with *you*. Will you let me come so I can show you how dirty I can be?"

She'd learned well from our lessons of long ago, telling me exactly what she needed.

I leaned back to look at her. She was already tightening around my fingers, but I wanted to watch her face tell me exactly how to make her come, wanted to watch her gaze when she fell apart all over me. Her eyes were hooded and pleading. Her cheeks flushed pink. I bent my finger to rub against her inner wall, and her breath became choppy and unsteady.

I pressed my forehead against hers, letting the bridge of my nose rest against hers. "Show me, then. Show me how dirty you can be and come all over my fingers. If you want my cock, you have to show me how good you're going to treat it. Show me you deserve it."

Her pussy clamped down on my fingers, her body quivering as she let out a strangled cry. Tears spilled from the corners of her eyes. Her mouth froze in a wide O. I pressed my thumb against her clit, coaxing out every last bit of her orgasm.

As soon as it had made its way through her, she was ready for more.

"Need this now. Get it out. Need it." She spoke in short broken sentences while she wrestled with getting my boxers down my thighs. Once my cock was free, she stroked its length with both hands, drawing all the way up with one and following right after with the other. "Let me ride it, Dylan. I want to ride it."

I closed my eyes for a handful of seconds, letting the pleasure of her caress shoot through my body and light up every nerve ending. "Such an impatient girl," I teased.

But I was impatient too. I needed to be buried inside her, and if she kept tugging on my cock like she was, I was going to be finished before we'd truly gotten started.

"Get these off," I ordered, pointing to her shorts. She shoved them along with her knickers down her thighs, stepping out of them and kicking them aside when they reached the floor. She removed her bra when she was done.

Meanwhile, I stripped the rest of the way from my own clothes, then dug my wallet out of my jeans, searching for a condom.

"I don't have a rubber," I said, stepping away from her. If this wasn't going to be able to happen, I needed to be farther away from her. She followed after, throwing her arms around my neck.

"Pill," she said before kissing me. "I'm on the pill."

"I'll pull out," I offered instead, pulling her body flush against mine. I'd known of too many women who'd gotten pregnant while on contraception. My need had reached a desperation point, but I couldn't ruin her life on account of my pleasure.

"Pull out then. Just. Just put it in." She locked one leg around my hips and stood on the toes of her other foot, practically climbing my body to get where she needed me.

Where we both needed me.

Wrapping my hands under the curve of her ass, I lifted her up and backed up against the nearest wall. She threw her other leg around me, and a few short seconds later, I was inside her.

I was inside her, bare, with nothing between her and my cock, and she was heaven.

She was warm and wet and tight—so, so tight. It felt like I was stretching her wider than she'd ever been stretched. Like I was filling her better than she'd ever been filled. Like I was making her into a mold that fit me and only me.

She bucked her hips up, silently spurring me to move.

I became two men in that moment—the one who wanted to take his time and tease and taunt and make it last, another driven by blind lust and the need for satiety. Primal instincts won out, and I thrust into her at an unceasing tempo. I was crazed with my desire. I was the driving beat of a Metallica bassline. I was the prisoner in the yard, chasing the last bits of sunlight, realizing the day was fading into night. I was merciless and mad. I was filled with a love that I couldn't speak of, a love that drummed inside me, begging to be heard.

Audrey took what I gave her, clutching onto my neck as she gasped and moaned and interjected directions on how to fuck her. "Deeper," she'd demand. "Harder. Give me more."

I drilled into her over and over, my thighs slapping audibly against her ass as I gave her the deeper, harder, more she asked for, but still it wasn't enough for either of us. I couldn't get the right angle. Couldn't hit the end of her. Couldn't get deeper, harder, more enough.

Without pulling out of her, I carried her to the plastic-covered bed and dropped her on top. I climbed over her and took up that wicked pace again. It was easier here. I could really thrust in this position, and with my arms no longer holding the weight of her, my hands were free to play with her pussy.

She came right away. "Yes, yes, yessss," she cried, her body clamping so hard on my cock she almost pushed me out. Letting out a grunt, I forced my way back inside, shoving against her wet walls until I was in so far I was sure I was hitting the end of her. I held there, watching as her orgasm rolled over her like a severe thunderstorm, loud and wet and fierce.

I almost came at the sight.

Somehow, miraculously, I remembered in time and pulled out of her. I turned away from her and tugged at my cock a few times.

"No! On me! Come on me." She sat up and lifted her breasts with her hands, giving me a place to aim.

What a fucking turn-on she was—with those pouty, swollen lips and a freshly fucked glow on her cheeks, her legs still spread so I could see her juices gleaming on the folds of her pussy, her perfect, firm tits held up for me to mark.

I came immediately, spurting white ropes of cum across the peaks and valleys of her chest, decorating her with the baseness of my love. Making her dirty and defiled.

Fucking brilliant.

With my orgasm, my adrenaline was shot. We collapsed next to each other on the bed. Sweaty and spent, I closed my eyes and waited for my heart to settle. I could hear her next to me, her erratic breathing settling into a rhythm that matched my own.

"That was...wow," she said. "Just. Really. Wow."

I opened my eyes and looked, not at her, but at the wall in front of me. The wall that showcased her newly painted vines and flowers, as well as an imprint of her backside. I'd pushed her up against the blue wall when I'd finger-fucked her then pressed her to the other wall when I'd had my cock inside her.

"We made a mess of your art," I said, nodding toward the silhouette.

"I like it. I think I'll keep it." The plastic crinkled as she rolled to her side and studied me. "Was this why you were avoiding me? Because you were afraid we'd end up in bed together?"

I turned my head in her direction. There wasn't an easy answer to that question. Even a simple yes or no would be wrong. Neither word completely explained what I'd been avoiding, what I'd been afraid of. What I was *still* afraid of.

"I know I said I didn't want to confuse things. And I think

we've both felt the sexual tension building between us. So you stayed away, right? Because you wanted to keep this easy for me. Right?"

Just nod. Let that be the uncomplicated answer.

But all I could do was stare at her, my brow furrowed.

She smiled as though I'd responded. "I appreciate it. But I think it's a lost cause."

Considering that she was covered in my cum and now had sex art on her wall, I had to agree.

And apologize.

She'd made her wishes known the first night we'd bumped into each other in London, and while she was giving me credit for honoring her request to just be friends, I'd obviously failed at the task. Both because I'd fucked her anyway, but also because I'd developed feelings that were surely unwanted.

But before I could find the words—or the nerve—she scooted into me and nestled her head on my chest.

I put my arm around her, pulling her closer, without even thinking.

"I should have just told you I'd changed my mind." Her voice reverberated against me, causing my skin to buzz.

"What did you change your mind about exactly?" My pulse sped up again, hoping against all hope for something she couldn't be about to say.

"That I only wanted to be friends. Obviously."

She paused. The silence was filled with the hammering of my heart in my ears. Was she saying...? She couldn't want to be *more* than friends, could she?

"I mean, I still want to be friends," she continued. "But I think this is okay, too. Fooling around occasionally. It's kind of perfect, actually. Now I don't have to worry about my libido landing me in bed with a guy I don't actually want to go to bed with."

There was too much to process. Too much needed clarification. I didn't know where to start and ended up just choosing the last thing she'd said, the thing that also happened to be the one that hurt most.

"You still want to date other men, though?" I asked. I needed to be sure.

"Well, yeah. Of course. I still want the happy ending, and I know you aren't after that, but maybe that's what makes this so perfect. You already know that you can do a friends-with-benefits thing and not have it lead to a sticky, complicated mess. I'm the one who has to make sure I don't get attached—and I was worried I couldn't in the beginning, which was why I said that sleeping with you couldn't be an option, and maybe I'm fooling myself thinking I can keep sex and emotions separated, but I want to try."

She leaned up so she could look at my face.

"Do you trust me enough for that? I'm just really attracted to you, and you're really good in bed, and I can't bear the thought of constantly trying to talk myself out of jumping you, but I can't bear the thought of staying away from you either. So if I promise to try really hard, if I promise that any emotions developed are my responsibility and not yours, could we maybe keep doing this on occasion?"

She was anguished with this dilemma. It was written in her face, layered in her tone. It was a complicated predicament, to be fair, and she thought she understood it perfectly. She couldn't have surmised the situation as she knew it any better than she had.

But she was wrong in her breakdown of circumstances. She was wrong in assuming I couldn't have feelings for her too.

If I told her, what would it change? If I were another man, if I were a decade younger, if I weren't someone with enough experience to know that I could never be what she needed, how different would the next part of this conversation go? Would I be man enough to pretend I didn't care?

I wasn't another man, though. I was who I was and that limited my options for response. So, did I tell her I love her and that continuing to sleep with her could be very bad for my heart? Did I tell her and give her the chance to fall for me as well, knowing that as long as we were together, she'd drift farther away from her dream ending of marriage and kids and happiness?

The day's events had changed things, that was indisputable. But I still couldn't stand the idea of ever being the cause of her suffering.

I could only give her what I could, what she asked for, never mind what it did to me. Never mind how much it hurt.

"Don't be silly. I'm not even a little afraid of you falling for me. You have much better taste than that. As for doing *this* on occasion..." I glanced down at the erection that had started to grow again the minute she'd nuzzled up against me. "I think it's obvious I'm interested."

She followed the line of my gaze and a wide smile broke out across her face. "This arrangement is already working out better than I'd hoped."

That smile—that was what made any potential disaster to my heart inconsequential.

I brought my hand behind her head to guide her toward my mouth. Ignoring the tight ache in my chest, I kissed the grin off her lips.

TWENTY-TWO

Amy poked her head in my office and whisper-shouted across the room. "Is it happening?"

By "it," she meant the biweekly owner's meeting that was conducted over Skype. Often, she'd sit in the room during the videoconference, unbeknownst to my partners, just to provide mocking commentary.

I hit the button on my computer to mute my microphone. "Started about ten minutes ago and everyone's already arguing."

"Oh, tell me!" She hurried in, pulling one of the client chairs from in front of my desk to my side, just out of camera reach.

"Weston says our numbers are higher than they've ever been. Weston's *wife* thinks we should open a new office location in Europe. Sabrina thinks we should open a new office in the States. Donovan is preoccupied with something on his mobile, and Nate is..." I turned my head, examining the window on the screen with his face. It didn't seem like he was in his office, but I couldn't tell where he was instead. He was using a laptop at a kitchen table, maybe, and his focus seemed to be directed at something in his lap.

"I can't figure out what's going on with Nate."

"Got it. Turn it up, will you?"

I increased the computer volume.

"We have demand in Europe *right now*," Elizabeth said from the top right quadrant of my screen. "Clients are coming both to us and Dylan from Germany, which indicates a hole in the market."

"We have demand here too!" Sabrina argued back from the bottom left corner. "We have more than one client that comes from L.A. or Chicago or Atlanta to hire us. New York is farther from all of those places than either Paris or London are to Germany. The need is here." Sabrina nudged her husband. "Tell them, Donovan."

At her prodding, Donovan glanced up toward the camera. "Both Europe and the U.S. present good options for expansion."

Weston blinked as though he'd just caught up with the conversation. "Wait. So we're expanding? We're just deciding on a whim?"

"Honey," Elizabeth said through gritted teeth. "We've been talking about this for months."

"I thought we were just daydreaming, babe. Donovan wasn't involved so I didn't take it seriously."

"Nothing's ever serious until Donovan's involved," Nate said, as though he were part of the conversation, but the way he kept looking down suggested his attention was still devoted to something else.

"Donovan's involved now," Elizabeth said definitively. "The next move is to expand."

"And the expanse should be in the *United States*. Specifically, Los Angeles." Sabrina glared at her husband as if that was the way to coax support.

Donovan hesitated for half a second before looking up from his phone. "We need to see a lot more numbers and projections before deciding on a specific location. I'll hire a demographer to get us some more concrete information."

"He's neither disagreeing nor agreeing with her. That's a talent," Amy whispered next to me.

"Right? He's placating her. It's irritating. He's probably way ahead of us on this, anyway. I'm sure he's already done all the projections and settled on a location that he isn't ready to share with the rest of us yet." Normally I was fine with Donovan's puppeteer methods, but today I was annoyed. With all of them.

I'd tell them, too, if they ever gave me a chance to get a word in edgewise.

"Don't forget there are only five of us." Weston's voice had risen, calling my interest back to the screen. "Who's even going to run a new location? Are we going to start adding more people to this board?"

"Five of us? I count six here," his wife said, annoyed.

"I mean five owners of the company, Lizzie."

"There's seven then because Sabrina and I are now owners by marriage."

Amy and I exchanged an irritated eye roll.

"The point is, *darling*," Weston said, barely keeping an even tone, "that *we're* not going anywhere. We're settled in France. Are you willing to move, D? Or is it going to be you, Nate?"

When neither Donovan nor Nate answered, Sabrina stepped in. "We don't necessarily need an owner at every office location. Tokyo has been running without one of us for almost a year now."

"That's not exactly an ideal situation," Weston refuted.

"Is Cade ever coming back?" Elizabeth asked. It was the first time our fifth partner had been mentioned in weeks. The meetings where his name had come up previously had unraveled soon after. Cade's leave of absence was a touchy subject, particularly since no one knew details about his departure save for Donovan.

Sabrina once again nudged her husband from his mobile.

"Cade will be back," Donovan said without skipping a beat. "Eventually. When he's ready."

Weston leaned forward. "Are you ever going to tell us what's going on with him, D?"

"No." Donovan returned his gaze to his phone.

"I think there might be a woman involved..." Sabrina started, but if she knew more, she was too loyal to her husband to say more.

"Dylan, you've been quiet," Elizabeth said, sending my brows up in surprise. I was rarely called on in these situations. She had to feel desperate for support. "What are your thoughts?"

"Oh, this ought to be fun," Amy said, rubbing her hands together. "Make it good."

I turned the mic back on, and decided to do just that. "My thought, thank you very much for asking, is that there are entirely too many people involved in these conference calls. When did our team meetings turn into an episode of *The Newlywed Game*? Even you, Nate—am I wrong, or is that Trish's head in your lap?" If he was getting a blow job during our pathetic conference call, so help me God...

Nate's head shot up like a kid caught sleeping in class. "It's the day before Thanksgiving! I'm not even in the office, for Pete's sake. We really should have canceled this today."

"Ah, Thanksgiving. Right," I muttered. "Surely the rest of us should cease our normal business practices because of your bloody U.S. holiday."

"We're planning on celebrating here, actually," Elizabeth said smugly.

Weston's expression softened and he grinned. "We have a lot to be thankful for this year."

"We do," his wife agreed with a sigh.

Jesus fucking Christ.

It took all I had not to slam my fist on my desk. "This is what

I'm talking about—could we please keep the googly-eyed, lovey-dovey nonsense out of these meetings? This is a place of business, not a Netflix Christmas special."

Weston, that sad little goof, smirked. "Ah, poor Dylan. I bet it's tough seeing all your friends in relationships that worked out."

"Fuck you very much, King. For your information, I'm more concerned about having to be here when all the romance blows up in your faces." I'd never admit that his analysis of the situation was spot on.

Elizabeth stepped in, as always, to admonish us. "I don't think that was a very nice thing to say."

Her husband was offended. "Him or me?"

"Both of you. I'm not sure Dylan would take that kind of criticism from me, though. Since he's not my husband. And he's not happy." She tried to bite back a grin and failed.

"I'm right here, you know," I declared, glaring at Amy who was stifling a giggle of her own.

"All right, all right." Donovan stood up and leaned toward the camera, filling up the entire window in his quadrant. "That's enough from everyone. This meeting has officially gone off the rails. We can discuss expanding again at our next meeting in two weeks. Goodbye to all of you."

He and Sabrina disappeared from the screen. Without waiting for the others to bid farewell, I shut down Skype then sunk back in my chair in relief. The madness was over. Praise the lord.

"That went about as well as these things have lately," Amy said after a significant silence had passed. "I should have made popcorn."

"There are too many cooks in the kitchen. That's the problem." And too many emotions. Specifically of the affectionate variety.

Amy moved to perch on the edge of my desk and stared down

at me thoughtfully. "I know you don't want to hear this," she said cautiously, "but it seems that your partners have found the right women for them. They're annoying as fuck, and I feel sorry for each and every one of them, but they do all seem to be generally happier since they've settled down."

I narrowed my eyes and snapped. "You're right. I don't want to hear it."

"You do realize that your dim worldview on relationships has been tainted by one relationship."

"I'm a quick learner." I let my smirk fade. "You're also right about the rest. Their relationships are working out, and despite how it appears, I'm very happy for all of them."

"It's still hard to watch. I know. Especially when you're pining after someone you can't have. I definitely know about that." Her eyes glazed like she was remembering something or some*one*, and I wondered for a moment if there was a love story hidden in Amy's past I didn't know about.

But before I could ask, she shook her head and refocused on me. "You haven't been quite that grumpy this week, though, now that I think about it. Did something change between you and Audrey?"

"Not really." I frowned at the incompleteness of my answer. "Yes, something's changed, but also nothing's changed at all."

She nodded. "Ah. You're shagging."

"I didn't say... That's not..." I was flustered, both by her uncanny ability to read me and by the frankness of the observation. "How did you get that out of what I said?"

"We're the same person, Locke." She did a move with two fingers pointing at her eyes and then pointing at me, an eye check, as if to say *I see you*. "I get you."

"I'm glad somebody does." My tone was sarcastic, but in all honesty, I *was* glad that she understood me. Most of the time I felt like a man alone on a raft in open waters. It was an appropriate analogy, in most instances, but it was reassuring to be reminded that others were on the sea alone as well.

"I'm sure Audrey does too, in her own way. And good for you, I might add. Banging is certainly my go-to method of dealing with unwanted emotions."

"You have emotions?" I managed not to crack until she did. Then I joined her laughter wholeheartedly. It was a nice break to the tension. I could have gone on for a little longer with the joking, in fact, if the phone hadn't interrupted.

I looked at the telephone console. It was my direct line, the line that only three people knew—Ellen, Aaron, and my mother.

"We'll talk later," Amy said, slipping off my desk. She did the *I see you* gesture again as she walked out the door, and I picked up the phone. "This is Dylan."

"Audrey has been in London nearly two months, and still you haven't called me," Donovan Kincaid's voice blasted through the line. Apparently he knew the number as well.

And he wanted to talk about Audrey.

No doubt my outburst during our meeting had led to this confrontation. That hadn't been my intention at all. There were questions I should ask him, yes, but I wasn't ready to confront the answers. I'd been avoiding this discussion with him for that very reason.

I didn't intend to have it with him now, either, if I could help it. "Audrey's in town? Oh, really. That's interesting."

"She already told her sister the two of you are friends. But I understand why you're playing dumb." Fuck, right. Her sister would know that.

It didn't mean I had to confess anything. "I don't have the slightest idea what you're talking about."

"Look, Locke," Donovan's tone said he wasn't in a patient mood. "She's not going to be there forever if you don't take the bull by the horns."

I hesitated. What exactly did he mean by that?

It was probably just a general statement. Or it was a blind stab at trying to wind me up. If Audrey were leaving town, she would have told me. I clung to the same useless tactic. "Again, no idea what you're—"

He cut me off. "Do you need help with what action to take? Is that the problem here? Have you been too long out of the game to get how it's played? I told you this summer, I have ways."

I already had my suspicions about those ways, and since he'd brought it up... "Did you have a hand in her internship at the Gallery?" I asked point-blank.

"I might have dropped her portfolio and application into the email of some important people, but she wouldn't have gotten the job if she wasn't qualified, if that's what you're concerned about."

"Jesus, Donovan..." This was exactly what I didn't want to know. Though I was grateful for every minute that I got to spend in Audrey's presence, interfering in her life was the last thing I wanted to do.

"It's a much better opportunity than the Boston internship, if you ask me," he said, as though that made his intrusion better.

"You're the reason she didn't get that job, too?" The man was clearly out of control.

He bulldozed over my question as though I hadn't asked it. "And frankly, it's a little early in my marriage to have Sabrina's sister living in New York."

"New York?" I didn't try to hide my dismay. "Are you saying there was a job available in New York? Did you interfere with that as well?"

"Another job with limited opportunity. She was much better off in London, and she wouldn't have taken the leap if she didn't have a little push. I did what I could. Don't bother thanking me."

"I'm not planning on it." He'd be lucky if I didn't strangle him the next time I saw him. Audrey would have snatched a New

York City offer up in a second. I knew how hard it was for her to be so far away from her sister. Sabrina was her only family.

"You really are a sad sap, you know," Donovan said, changing his strategy. "It's pathetic. You weren't like this when we first met."

"That was over a decade ago. Things have changed. I'm a different person now."

"You are. You're a miserable person, and it's time that you did something about it." He waited a beat before adding, "Or I can do something about it…"

"No," I warned. "Do not do anything else. Do not. Do you hear me? You have done enough, thank you very much."

"I told you not to thank me."

"Donovan," I said, my temper flaring. "Don't interfere."

"I don't think you mean that." Before I could insist that I very much did mean that, he brought up something I hadn't thought of. "If she decides not to stay in London, you're going to want me to make sure she lands somewhere that's good for her."

Well, fuck. He had a point there. I did want the best for her. But did I want it enough to condone Donovan's methods? Now that involved a good hard think. What would be the best thing for me? For Audrey?

"Well, yes," I admitted. "That would be a kind thing for you to do. For Sabrina's sake." It wasn't me interfering, after all. It was Donovan.

"Speaking of my wife, she said Audrey's been dating a lot."

"Not a lot, really." Though, maybe he knew more about the situation than I did. "Did she say that exactly? That she's dating *a lot*?"

"Obviously it bothers you. I can help you with that."

Dammit, everything he said was a snare, and I'd walked right into this one.

"It doesn't bother me. Why would it bother me?" It was a sorry attempt at backpedaling. Even I knew it.

I let out a frustrated sigh. "I don't know where you got the idea that something is going on between us. I find the girl a breath of fresh air, and we have become friends, but that doesn't mean there is any scheme to try for more. You have to agree we are worlds apart, even if we do happen to live in the same location—temporarily, as you pointed out. I am fond of her, of course. I hope very much that she settles with someone who's good for her."

He paused, and for a moment I thought I'd managed to shut him down. But then he asked, "Are any of these guys that someone? Tell me honestly."

Honestly? That was tricky. I didn't like any of the men she'd told me about so far. None of them were good enough for her, but would anyone ever be? I didn't think it was possible.

What mattered was if she loved them, though. What mattered was if they made her happy. And so far, that wasn't happening.

"No," I answered, digging deep and telling the truth. "They're not."

"That's where I come in. There are ways to make those relationships—how do I put this? Not work out, so to say. Give me the word, and I'm all over it."

Was that how Donovan thought relationships worked? Disgusting.

On the other hand, it was tempting to consider. While no man would be good enough for her, there were at least men who were better than others. Did I want to be the one to decide who they were?

I did, but not this way.

"I think this is a journey she has to take for herself," I said, finally.

"If that's how you feel, then sure. Let her do that. But call me when you change your mind."

"I'm not going to—" He hung up before I finished my sentence. "I'm not going to change my mind," I said defiantly to the dial tone. Because I meant it.

I wasn't going to change my mind about interfering in Audrey's life.

I wasn't even going to think any more about it as an option.

Probably.

Oh, hell.

TWENTY-THREE

I watched as Audrey scrubbed the remnants of food off her dinner plate. She was careful in her handling of the piece, probably thinking that the china was fine—and it was. Some expensive set acquired during my marriage that I'd ended up with. I'd fought for it in the divorce, as I recalled, for no other reason than that it irritated Ellen to give it up.

The china itself didn't mean anything to me. It usually sat in a cabinet in my lounge, more decorative than functional. I couldn't even remember the last time I'd pulled it out and had only thought of using it today on a whim.

It had been a good inclination, in the end. Audrey couldn't be with her sister for their traditional Saturday post-Thanksgiving Italian dinner, and I'd been eager to do what I could to make the event special for her. The china had been a nice touch. She admired the set more than anyone else ever had.

And I admired *her*. Admired her ease around a kitchen, admired her sass and upbeat energy, admired how she looked just as beautiful standing behind a sink as she did covered with paint or dressed up to the nines or naked underneath me. Admired how one tiny person could make my flat feel not so overwhelmingly big and empty.

She glanced over and caught me staring. "What?" she asked with a grin.

I shrugged dismissively. "I'm regretting that second helping of dinner."

"I think you had thirds."

"I did. The third helping was marvelous. It's the second helping I regret." I waited for her to laugh before growing serious. "I know I said it already, but the meal was incredible."

"Nonna's lasagna never fails. I'm glad you liked it. It's literally the only dish I know how to make." She finished rinsing off the dish under the tap and handed it to me, sending a pleasant shock through my body when our fingers brushed. "Thank you so much, again."

"For what? Eating delicious food?" I stacked the plate in the drying rack. Normally, I'd leave this task for the housekeeper to do the following morning, but I didn't want Freja asking questions about who I'd dined with. And there were too many dishes to try to say it had just been me.

"Yes, for eating my food. For not leaving me to celebrate today alone. For giving me a magnificent kitchen to cook in." She turned the tap off and dried her hands on a towel before turning toward me and leaning her hip on the counter. "I'm incredibly appreciative."

It felt almost ridiculous to accept her gratitude. It had been a busy week at work for both of us, and though our daily calls had resumed, I hadn't seen her in person since we'd painted her bedroom. I'd missed her and wanted her in my home more than she realized.

I reached around her to dry my own hands on the towel. "I still feel bad that you didn't get a traditional feast on Thursday. If my schedule hadn't been so demanding, I would gladly have taken the day off and celebrated an American Thanksgiving with you."

"Meh. I was working too, and honestly? I couldn't give a flying fig about turkey and cranberry sauce. Today was the day that mattered most to me. You can't have any idea how much it means to me."

"I'm happy to hear that," I said, distracted until we met and locked eyes. I *was* happy to hear it, but it was hard to concentrate on the conversation when her gaze was so intense. And while I adored talking to her always, what I really wanted to do at the moment was turn her around, lift her up on the island behind us, and get under her skirt. I'd been thinking about it since she'd arrived, and had only refrained from jumping her because the dinner was a big deal.

Now, with the table cleared and the dishes done, there wasn't anything to prevent me from acting on the impulse except myself. We hadn't set terms for our relationship, whatever it was now, and I wasn't sure if there were rules. Was I allowed to touch her when I wanted to? Was I allowed to pull her in my arms? Fuck her against the worktop?

It wasn't like me to lack confidence in erotic matters. I refused to doubt myself now. I was going to do it. I was going to devour her. I was going to kiss her lips until they were swollen then go down on her pussy for dessert. Any second now.

In *five*

Four

Three

Audrey broke our gaze and gestured toward the television in the drawing room. "Do you have Amazon Video in here?" She was headed toward the media console before she finished the question, and my opportunity was lost.

I sighed quietly and stared after her. "I do. Is there something you want to watch?" I was content. Well, I could be. Watching my current view, enjoying her backside as she walked away. Maybe content wasn't the right word. She was killing me, literally killing me, with her sultry sway and short pleated skirt. She also wore black knee-high boots and a simple white blouse that made her look even younger than usual. Like a girl in secondary school. Like a girl I didn't have any business lusting after, which only made me want her more.

"It's the next part of the family tradition," she said. She found the remote and stood while she flipped through screens on the telly. "After dinner, we clean up then fall into a food coma on the couch while watching a classic old movie."

"Sounds lovely." The evening was about her, after all. I turned off the kitchen light and followed into the drawing room.

I eyed the sofa. It was too big, not for the room, but for my life. It curved around on one side, easily sitting ten. The most people I could remember having been over at one time was five when my mother, her latest husband, and Aaron had visited at the same time for Christmas. I'd invited Amy over for dinner, hoping my mother wouldn't bother me about my marital status with her at my side. Even then, there hadn't been a time that we'd all sat in front of the telly together. And now, Aaron didn't even come to London to see me very often.

Why had I even bought such a large flat? To show off to Ellen? Certainly I hadn't had ideas of entertaining. It was as though I'd imagined that I could sufficiently fill my life with fine art and furniture and square meterage, but it was all meaningless. I'd never noticed how much so until the vibrancy of Audrey in my space made everything around her pale and dull in comparison.

At the moment I hated how large the sofa was because of how many seating options that gave my guest. I wished for a loveseat instead, something small and cozy where Audrey would have no choice but to cuddle up close.

"What are we watching?" I asked, taking a seat right in front of the screen, the spot where I normally sat when I was alone. The next move was hers.

"One of my favorites. I hope you like it." The show was cued and on pause so I couldn't see what the title was when she spun around and surveyed the seating situation. "Oh good. You saved me a spot." She plopped down next to me, close enough to feel her warmth though not quite so close we were touching.

How did she do that? Deal with the sexual tension between us so easily? It was yet another trait that I admired about her. Another trait that made her irresistible.

She started the show and threw the remote down next to her. The credits started, but I was focused on watching her as she unzipped her boots, dropped them to the floor, and tucked her feet under her bottom.

Jesus. She was wearing plaid knee socks underneath. That basically completed the schoolgirl look. I couldn't look at her if she intended for me to actually get through the film.

I moved my eyes to the screen, a safer place for my attention, just as the title appeared. *When Harry Met Sally*.

"You call this an *old* movie? It's from the eighties." And it was a romantic comedy. She'd neglected to mention that.

She lifted one shoulder and dropped it. "It was made before I was born."

There again with the reminder of our age difference. As if I could forget. "Thank you. Thank you for that," I muttered sardonically.

She giggled, enjoying, as always, a joke at my expense. "Have you seen it?"

"I have not."

"You're going to love it." She side-eyed me as she reconsidered. "Maybe you won't love it, but *I'm* going to love watching it with you, and isn't that what really matters?"

"It seems that it is." And because she then sat back and leaned her head on my shoulder, I didn't have a single reason to argue.

We watched the movie like this for the first ten minutes or so, silent except for her soft chuckle at her favorite lines. The characters, Harry and Sally (who could have guessed), began as two recent college graduates who didn't really know each other but somehow ended up sharing a ride together to New York. They exchanged banter about this and that along the drive, as people do, until Harry stated that it was impossible for men and women to be friends if the man is attracted to the woman—sex always got in the way.

The muscles in my shoulders stiffened. The dialogue could be applied to the situation with me and Audrey. Or, at least, it brought up certain questions about our relationship, and I wasn't sure that I wanted those questions to be asked.

I didn't say anything, hoping that she wouldn't address the elephant if I didn't.

But it wasn't Audrey's style to be demure. "What do you think about that idea?" she asked, casually. "Can men and women be friends?"

"*We're* friends." Maybe she'd leave it at that.

"Buuuuuttt..." She drew the word out, forcing me to give her my attention. "I want to bang you. And I think you want to bang me..."

"Is that a question?"

"You want to bang me. It's not a question. Which pretty much proves Harry's point that men and women can't be friends without sex screwing it up."

"That's where I find his theory objectionable. He assumes that having sex will screw up a friendship-based relationship. I don't find that's true."

"Buuuuuttt..." Again she elongated the word and paused

after, as though what she wanted to say next wasn't something I necessarily wanted to hear.

"But what? Let me hear it." I leaned back to stare at her.

She pulled away so she could look at me directly too. "*But* you avoided me for a whole week. That had an impact on our friendship. If we hadn't put sex back on the table, would we be here right now?"

No. Probably not. But not for the reasons she thought.

"Yes, we'd be here," I lied. "Otherwise you're saying that men and women can only be friends if they're sleeping together. In which case, I really need to reevaluate all my female friendships." It was a joke, but if it weren't, there was really only Amy on that list, and I *had* slept with her in the past. Was she right?

"Except, then someone might develop feelings."

The back of my neck suddenly felt sweaty, and my throat felt tight. I swallowed. "People might develop feelings even without sex."

"True. It's just easier to encourage feelings when sex is involved because of the intimacy level. And what happens when one of the partners decides to end the sexual part of the relationship? Is it possible to go back to being just friends?"

The question felt important, as though it were a test, as though my answer said something significant about us. Amy and I had managed to maintain our friendship with or without benefits, but I was wary about saying yes to Audrey because I wasn't entirely certain that I could ever go back to being just friends with her.

But that wasn't because of sex. That was because I had already developed feelings for her. Not that she needed to know that. In fact, she really *didn't* need to know it.

I hesitated too long with an answer. "You don't think it's possible, do you?" she asked. "So when I eventually find a guy that I want to be with, are you and I just done?"

"No. Of course not." It was another lie.

"Buuuuutttt..."

I ran a hand through my hair. "We won't be *just done*. But a lot changes when you get involved with someone romantically. I'm sure you know that. Often, other relationships are not what they were. They take a backseat, whether there's a sexual history or not. So while I can promise that sex is not the glue holding our friendship together, I can't promise that we'll always be as close as we are now." It was more of a monologue than she'd wanted, perhaps, but it was honest, though maybe it wasn't the complete truth.

Because the complete truth was hard to say to someone like Audrey. The complete truth was that nothing lasts forever. Not even good things. *Especially* not good things.

Audrey settled back down next to my shoulder. "You're a real Debbie Downer sometimes, Dylan. You know that?"

"I do, in fact. It's an actual bullet point on my resume."

She pretended not to chuckle. "Do you need me to rewind?"

"No, I think I have the gist of what's going on."

The movie got better after that, or at least, less uncomfortable to watch. The writing was decent. The characters were well drawn, particularly the side characters. Some of the dialogue felt contrived, but it was enjoyable for the most part. I kept my comments to myself when it wasn't.

Until the public orgasm scene.

It was a famous bit. I'd seen clips of it before, but never in context. Harry was convinced that all the women who came into his bedroom through a revolving door, enjoyed themselves. In response, Sally faked an orgasm—in public—to prove that there was no way he could possibly tell.

"Oh, please," I mumbled.

Audrey sat up and narrowed her eyes in my direction. "You

have to expand on that comment. You can't possibly think women don't fake orgasms."

"I'm sure they fake them all the time, though I'm not entirely sure what the benefit is from that. If men think the woman they're with is satisfied, they're not going to put forth more effort." It was common sense. "But that's not what I find eye-rolling."

"They fake it sometimes because it's just easier. Like, it's not happening, and some men are so stubborn, they prolong the whole thing in an attempt to *make* it happen, and that's miserable for everyone."

"You sound like you speak from experience." If Audrey had similarly faked orgasms with the men she'd been with before me, no wonder there had been a problem in the bedroom.

"I do speak from experience. Not with you." Her cheeks pinked ever so slightly.

"Of course not with me."

And now I was thinking about making her orgasm. The sly smile on her lips suggested she was thinking the same thing.

But then her grin disappeared. "But tell me what you find eye-rolling."

I changed my seating position, adjusting myself discreetly, and sighed. It had been me who'd triggered the conversation. I had to back it up, no matter how smug I came across in doing so.

"While it's true that men can't always know if a woman is having an orgasm or not, there are a lot of tells that are easy to spot if one is simply paying attention. Non-vocal tells. Changes in breathing. Body quivering. Flexing of toes. Contractions of the...of the inner walls of..." If I said the word, if I mentioned her pussy, I was going to have to be inside it.

"You get what I'm saying."

Her blush deepened, as though she could read the thoughts

in my mind. She cocked her head to the side. "And you don't think a woman can fake all those things, sometimes?"

"She can, but it's my experience that most women don't even know what her tells are. It's difficult to fake something you don't know to fake."

"But if it's a one-night thing, the man doesn't know what her tells are, either."

"This is true. But if it's only one night you're spending together, why would the man even care?" It was terrible to say, but men could be terrible where sex was concerned. Men could be terrible, full stop.

"Harsh!" Audrey twisted her lips, pondering. "Are you saying you didn't care if I orgasmed that first time when you fingered me against the front door at your apartment?"

"It was different with you." My cock twitched in my trousers, remembering.

"Of course it was different with me." She repeated my words from a minute before.

"It was, though. You had specifically come to me with a request to have good sex. It didn't behoove either of us if I didn't put my best foot forward."

"Your best *finger* forward, you mean. Three of them, to be precise."

"I'm very flattered that you remember so well." Very flattered and very hard.

"It wouldn't have *behooved* me to forget." Her grin was so fucking sexy. I wanted to finger-fuck it off her face. With three fingers. "And I don't believe that you would ever not care about giving a woman an orgasm. You're very considerate like that. A true gentleman."

"And you're cheeky."

She moved to her knees, and faced me, the movie apparently forgotten. "What are my tells? Are they obvious?"

"You stop breathing." It was incredibly erotic. Her muscles would stiffen, her toes curl, and her quick breaths would all of a sudden stop, like she was bracing for the pleasure to hit. Then, when it finally did, she'd moan her release, her body stuttering as it rolled through her.

"Hmm. I guess I do." She was pensive suddenly, her eyes downcast. "I guess that's an easy thing to tell a new lover. 'Look for my breathing to stop, and then you know you've hit the spot.'"

My chest felt tight, like my insides were shrinking. Here I was thinking we were having a fun talk about us and what she was really thinking about was her future. About the guy she'd be with next, whoever he was.

But that was always the point of us, from the very beginning. Wasn't it?

I forced a weak smile. "There you go."

Her expression softened. "I don't have a new lover," she said quietly. "In case you were wondering. Besides you. I'd tell you if I did."

"Okay."

"I thought you should know that."

It was as though she knew what she'd said hurt me, as though she were trying to make it better. Which, of course, she wasn't. She couldn't know what was going on inside me. She was merely being considerate to her sexual partner. It was practical.

"I also have no other lover," I said, returning the consideration. "In case you were wondering."

"We'd stop this between us if anyone else came into the picture, right? Can we agree on that? Especially if we aren't going to use condoms. And we don't need to use condoms. I'm really good about the pill."

"We can agree on that." I didn't want to talk anymore about other lovers. I didn't want to think about her needing to be on birth control because of other men. I hoped this pact put an end to the subject.

Unfortunately, it only got worse. "I do have a third date with someone this week."

Discovering Ellen's affairs had felt like a dagger in my gut, and yet still these simple words from Audrey felt ten times worse. She'd been dating—I'd *known* she'd been dating—but this was the first time anything had ventured on being serious.

I played nonchalant. "Oh? A third date?"

I didn't want to hear more. I had to know everything at the same time.

"The first two dates were promising." She pushed a stray hair behind her ear and shifted to sit on her hip. "He's a decent enough guy. Catholic. Wants a big family. He's an architect, so that's a stable career. And he gets my artsy side. He has a really cute little Yorkshire terrier that he brought to our first date in the park. I'd marry him just to have that puppy. He seems really romantic, too. Says a lot of flowery things. Loves poetry. His name is Marco. He's the brother of one of the married guys I work with. He's Italian! Nonna would be over the moon if she were still alive."

Every word she said was bittersweet. Sweet because he sounded great. Bitter because I wanted to stab this Marco guy with a knife between the eyes. Several times. Twenty ought to do it. And I'd never been one for violence.

But I could see the bigger picture through the red. His qualities were perfect—perfect for Audrey, anyway. And wasn't that exactly what I wanted for her? A man who would give her everything she wanted, everything she needed. A man who loved her as much as she deserved to be loved. A man who could make her happy. If this was that guy, then I wanted it to work out for her.

Just, I wasn't ready to let her go.

"I'm not planning on sleeping with him," she said reassuringly. "So don't worry about that. Not yet anyway. I haven't even kissed him. So there's no reason for this to end." She gestured between the two of us.

"Okay."

So she wasn't done with us yet either, then. Not yet, and I meant to take advantage of that.

I turned again to the screen, not really watching it, but planning my move.

"That was an invitation, by the way," Audrey said at my side, always a step ahead of me.

I pushed her back on the couch and crawled over her, pinning her hands over her head. "Was it now? I'm allowed to stop watching this sappy chick flick then, but only if I instead turn my focus to draining every last drop of cum from your pussy?" My cock had softened during her talk of other lovers, but now it was back to full mast.

I bucked against her so she'd know.

"It's an invitation, not an obligation!" she giggled, and I kissed her. Kissed her hard.

"Your pussy is never an obligation," I said when I came up for air. "You're very naughty for even thinking it could be."

"I *am* naughty. I deserve to be punished, don't I? Are you going to spank me, Daddy?"

God, she was perfect. She'd probably meant to dress like a schoolgirl. She knew it would drive me mad, and it did.

She'd pay for that.

"Daddy has another punishment in mind, and you'll take it like a good girl, won't you?"

She squeaked out a *yes* that made me growl.

"Right answer. Take off your knickers." I slapped the side of her thigh then pushed off her and made quick work of unfastening my trousers and sliding my boxers down my thighs. I was too impatient to take them off any farther, and I had what I needed available and ready for her.

And she was ready for me, her knickers now discarded on the floor.

I sat back where I'd been sitting before and reached for her, intent on pulling her onto my cock, which was throbbing and red for want of her. But then I noticed her dazed expression. She wet her lips with her tongue and I followed her gaze to the swollen staff between my legs.

She wanted it in her mouth. It was all over her face. Those were the kinds of tells I was talking about.

I stroked my fist up and down my length. "You think you can suck me good, Audrey? You think you can take all of me and make it good?"

She blinked her lashes exaggeratedly. "I don't know if I can," she said, feigning innocence that she didn't truly possess. "It's so big. Would you let me try?"

A drop of cum leaked from my tip, I was so turned on.

"You may try."

Her eyes never left mine as she knelt on the sofa and bent over me. She had to turn her head to maintain the contact as she took my crown into her mouth, and God, it was perfect. So perfect. Her mouth was hot and wet and heaven. She wrapped her small hand around the base and eased the length of me back toward the inside of her cheek. My head rubbed against the inner wall of her mouth sending electric sparks of bliss down my spine. I let out a low hiss of pleasure.

Then she changed her angle, and this time when she sucked me back, she took me in deep. She hollowed out her cheeks, increasing the friction along my shaft and making me shudder.

She was so bloody sexy. So goddamned provocative. I was in near mindless ecstasy, but I needed to touch her. I needed to taste her.

I reached my hand around her backside and underneath her skirt. I smacked her once, and she yelped. The sound vibrated against my cock, sending another euphoric spasm through my body. I gritted my teeth and focused on not coming. She'd take my cum, she'd swallow all of it, I was sure, but I wanted to be wrapped in her pussy when I released. At the rate this was going, I'd need to make sure that happened soon.

I needed to get her ready.

My hand trailed along her slit until they found her hole. She was wet. Dripping wet. So wet that three fingers slid in easily.

"You're such a naughty girl, aren't you? Getting so aroused from sucking my cock. You love it, don't you? Tell me how much you love it."

She dragged her lips slowly up my erection. My crown fell out of her mouth with a loud pop. "I love it so much. I love how big you are. You make me so wet."

I had to have her mouth, that dirty mouth. Had to taste it and inhabit it. Had to be inside her with my tongue the way I needed to be inside her with my cock.

I clamped my palm behind her neck and drew her close. She came to me like a magnet, like we were meant to clash together. Like we couldn't be apart.

We kissed fiercely, our mouths twisting and slipping against each other while she climbed over me, her legs straddling my thighs. With one hand still braced behind her head, I used the other to guide myself inside her slick cunt. She trembled as she slid down my length, and I swallowed her accompanying cry.

I know, I told her with my kiss.

I know how good it feels. You make me feel that good too.

She rode me then, with vigor, her hips bouncing up and down over my cock like it was her vocation. I broke away from her mouth to watch her and nearly fell apart. She was a kinky little wretch, squeezing at her pert breasts through her blouse, her orange pleated skirt hitched high on her thighs. She looked like a goddamn Britney Spears video. A vixen of a schoolgirl, writhing on the plumpness of my cock.

"Don't pull out," she said, her breathing rapid. "I want you to fill me up."

I was going to burst any second, she was so fucking hot, but I needed her to go with me. My thumb reached under her skirt and found the button of nerves hidden under the hood of skin. It only took a handful of swipes before her muscles were tensing and her breathing turned rapid. Just as she stopped breathing all together, I gripped my hands on her thighs and ploughed up into her, fast and hard and insistent until we we were both there together, gasping and shattering apart as one.

I kissed her leisurely for a long time after, my cock half soft but still planted inside her. When she eventually crawled off of me, I groaned at the loss of her heat.

"My legs are asleep," she said, as though I deserved an explanation. As though there couldn't be any other reason why she'd want to get off my cock.

I liked believing that, anyway.

She curled up next to me, laying her head on my chest. I didn't want to move, didn't want to let her go, so I didn't tuck myself away. I just held her, placing soft kisses along her apple-scented hair. We didn't talk. We didn't say anything at all.

The movie had continued during our activity and was now near the end. I found myself caught up in its ending when Harry finally realizes Sally is the woman meant for him and runs to her, bursting into the party she's at on New Year's Eve so he can win her heart with a speech that could only have been written by a woman. It was so sappy and moving.

It wasn't a spoiler of an ending, even having missed a good portion of it. It was a rom-com. That was how all of these things ended, a blissful, happy myth. It was a lie, but instead of being annoyed like I usually was by it, I found I felt sad.

"I want that," Audrey said softly.

I wanted that too. Everyone did. That was what made it so easy to sell.

"It doesn't have to be a speech," she continued when I didn't say anything. "It doesn't have to be a party. It doesn't have to be any of that specifically. I just want the guy. I just feel like it's never going to happen some days."

She sounded as melancholy as I felt, and I hated that. It was one thing for me to be a scrooge, but not her. Not yet. She deserved years of living the fable before she discovered that endings were never happy. Hell, maybe she could even go through a separation without being broken. If I hadn't been so antagonistic with my ex-wife, maybe...but it didn't bear thinking about.

I kissed her on the top of her hair and summoned up the advice she needed, the advice I would have wanted when I was where she was in life, innocent and foolish and eager.

"That's a lot of pressure you're putting on the universe, to have things happen on *your* timeline, in *your* way. It doesn't give fate a chance to work the perfect ending you're waiting for. I think this is a case for that old adage—if you love something, set it free. If you believe that fate will bring you the guy you belong with, then stop trying to force it. Stop trying to predict it. Stop trying to rush it along. Let the idea of falling in love go. It will come back to you when the time is right."

She was quiet for several beats. Since she wasn't facing me, I couldn't see her eyes, but she made a noise that sounded like a sniffle, and I wondered if she was trying not to cry.

If she was, she managed to hold it in because her voice was clear when she spoke. "That's very optimistic of you, Dylan. I'm impressed."

I chuckled. "I fail to see how having no expectations is optimistic."

She shifted so she could see me. "No expectations? Do you really not expect anything from your future? I understand letting go, but giving up?"

Perhaps she felt my pep talk to her deserved one in return, but I was long past giving up. Her words of hope and encouragement were worthless, delivered in vain.

"Of course I have expectations," I said, kissing her on the nose. "I expect another round riding your pussy in about ten minutes."

Her eyes grew dark and hooded. "Why ten minutes?"

"Because first I'm ready for dessert." I pushed her onto her back and went down. She tasted like me and her together, and my dick hardened again, but I ignored my need and devoted myself to pleasing her. Only her. I ate her like I was a starving man. Like I was a man who still had a chance of being saved. Like I was a man who wasn't already dead inside.

TWENTY-FOUR

As Audrey's third date with Marco approached, I found myself more and more restless. More and more *jealous*, to be precise. It was easier to push aside when I was with her, when she was in my arms and my cock was lodged firmly inside her, but when we were apart, my mind latched onto thoughts of her with him, thoughts of him kissing her and seducing her. I had a solid picture of him in my head—dark unruly hair, thick biceps, a charming smile that persuaded unsuspecting young women like Audrey to hand over their knickers with a gift-wrapped bow.

Wanker.

It was ridiculous how much I thought about it. She'd been out on other dates, and I hadn't been so bothered. Mostly because my truth was that I was the man who got to talk to her before she left for her dinner or her play or her game of bowling, and I was the man who talked to her when she came home. Others had her for a few hours, but I was in her bed. And because of that, it had been hard to take her dating seriously.

But she had never had a third date.

She'd never even had a second date, and this new development haunted me. Marco became an obsession. Google became my enabler. I typed in combinations of what I knew—his name, his occupation, his religious denomination. I felt crazed as I searched for him. This wasn't me. Why was I acting like a stalker?

But I couldn't help myself. I was out of control.

Even as I told myself to stop, I couldn't. It wasn't like me, but then, nothing about Audrey was like anything I'd ever experienced.

I was a wanker, too.

When Google led to nothing, I had a chance to stop myself. I told myself to stop being a loon and focus on my work like a normal, rational person. I told myself to shut my browser and step away.

Then, somehow, like a mad man, I found myself on the Gallery website studying the staff listings. I paired the surname of every male on the roster with Marco's name, typing them into Google one at a time until I hit a match. Marco Ceresola. He was on Instagram.

Jesus, fuck, I muttered to myself. He was even worse than I imagined. His skin was flawless, his eyes large and piercing. Apparently a six-pack wasn't good enough for him. He had to go and get an eight-pack, which I only knew because of the countless images he'd posted of himself bare-chested. And that damn Yorkie was pussy-bait. There were more pictures of that ball of fur than of its owner. Adorable photos that made even the hardest of hearts melt. I was half convinced *I'd* drop trou for that puppy, and I neither cared for dogs nor men.

I couldn't go on like this.

I was barely sleeping. I was irritated and jittery from copious amounts of Earl Grey. I was out of my mind with envy. Yes, yes, I wanted the best for Audrey, and if the outside image was all there was to know about a person, then Marco Ceresola was absolute perfection, but in my experience, the story projected to the public was rarely the real story. Or at least, not the *whole* story.

Without any real proof, my gut said this guy was bad news. My head knew I was overreacting, but I didn't care. I had to do something about it before she made a mistake and fell in love. Before she got her heart crushed. Before I went insane.

Thursday afternoon, one day before the big date, I settled on exactly what that something was—I had to ring Donovan. He'd take care of my dilemma. He'd offered often enough, but I hadn't been desperate to take him up on it. Marco, though... Marco made me desperate.

I shut my office door for privacy and pulled out my mobile. I flipped through my contacts and found Donovan's information.

My thumb hovered over the call button as I hesitated. Once Donovan was involved, there was no turning back. He wasn't the kind of man who tolerated flakiness. I considered what I wanted my friend to do, exactly. Set a tail on Audrey to be there in case she got in trouble? Get rid of this boyfriend altogether? Get rid of all her boyfriends?

That was the rub, wasn't it? As soon as I got involved once, it made the line of interference immovable. I was always going to be That Guy. Either I had to let Audrey live her own life and make her own mistakes, or I'd be in this endless pursuit of trying to make her life perfect for her.

And I already knew there was no such thing as a happy ending. So what was I expecting from that course of action?

I couldn't do it, couldn't intrude. But I couldn't just wait around and obsess while she lived her life, either. A distraction was necessary.

I put my mobile down and returned to the Gallery's staff webpage. A few clicks and I had the number I was looking for. I picked up my phone again and made the call.

MIDWAY through my dinner the next night, I realized I'd made a big mistake.

As painful as it was to sit at home while she went on a date with Marco, going on a date of my own was even more miserable. Especially going on a date with Jana Spruce.

I'd thought it had been a rather practical idea when I'd had it. If Audrey was going to be dating, I should too. Not because I was looking for the same thing that she was—I wasn't. But it seemed like a good way to occupy my mind while she was off trying to find her happily ever after. If I only went out on one date, two at the most with the same woman, no one could become attached. I wouldn't bed them. I might even gain something from it—a nice meal, good company and conversation. The plan sounded perfect.

It was only a coincidence that I chose Audrey's boss to be my first date. Since I hadn't been looking for a woman to ask out, my choices had been limited, and Jana Spruce had hit on me the night I'd met her at the fundraiser anyway. It had only barely crossed my mind that Jana might tell her subordinate about our evening out. I hadn't fancied that Audrey would find herself in the same jealous torment that I was in.

Well, I hadn't *overly* fancied it anyway.

The evening with Jana had started well enough. The restaurant had been my choice, so the food was excellent. The service was above satisfactory. Jana was punctual and looked nice. She was smart and interesting and attractive and was a superb storyteller. She was a divorcee with two kids who were near Aaron's age, and that gave us a lot to talk about. I didn't normally date women who had parenting in common with me, and it was, it turned out, a pleasant change. She was also very funny, though I failed to laugh at most of her jokes. That had nothing to do with her—it was a *me* problem. I saw the humor, saw the wit in her jokes, but I saw Marco and Audrey far more vividly. Even in the midst of engaging conversation, Audrey's date was foremost in my mind.

Which was why the entire night was a disaster. I hadn't distracted myself from anything at all. I'd only proven that I was very capable of multitasking my agony.

And agony was much better performed with no distractions for optimal wallowing.

As soon as Jana excused herself to use the loo, I reached for my phone in hopes of a message from Audrey. I'd been itching to look since dinner began. Though Audrey usually didn't contact me during her dates, I hoped that this time was different. Hoped that Marco had bailed on her or that she'd bailed on him or that she was bored or dismayed or *something. Anything.*

There was nothing. Not a single notification from anyone. My stomach sank at the implications. She didn't need me. She didn't want me. She was having a nice night. And it didn't involve me.

I pocketed my phone, but pulled it out twice more to look again before Jana returned. The last time I even rebooted it, just in case there was an issue with my mobile or the service connection.

"Is there something you need to attend to?" Jana asked when she returned and found me staring at my screen.

"No. Sorry. Just checking my messages." With a sag of my shoulders, I put my phone away, but even with it back in my jacket pocket, I could feel it burning against my chest, ceaselessly nagging for my attention.

Jana was quiet as she took a swallow of the brandied latte she'd ordered in lieu of dessert. I'd hoped she would have skipped the course all together so I could get back to my pining. I'm not sure I didn't sigh audibly when she asked to see the coffee menu.

It would be over soon enough. Another ten minutes, probably, at most. I could be patient.

"Can I ask you something?" Jana asked studying me.

I nodded, afraid if I actually spoke that she'd hear the irritation in my tone.

"Why am I here?"

"I beg your pardon?"

She shook her head dismissively. "A better question is why are *you* here? I'm sure you realize that I fancied you that night we met, and I was excited when you reached out. I didn't think for a minute that you were interested in anything serious. A smart, sexy man like you would have a woman if he wanted one. I assumed when you called that you were looking for the same thing that I am—companionship. I'm certainly not keen on marrying again or even getting involved in a relationship, but I do enjoy a good lay as much as the next woman. If that's why you're here, then all we need to work out is your place or mine.

"However, you've seemed distracted all evening. So you tell me—am I reading you wrong? Why are you here?"

My brow furrowed. I'd already realized that I was here for all the wrong reasons, but now I felt like a total heel as well. It hadn't occurred to me she'd recognize my angst. I *wasn't* interested in pursuing a relationship, but I did know that people came to a date with something to offer. I'd figured a paid meal and engaging company was enough—and it likely would have been, had I actually been engaging.

But that wasn't the reason I hesitated in my response.

I hesitated because it finally hit me how fucked up I was over Audrey. A handful of months before, I wasn't actively dating, but I would have welcomed a no-strings attached physical relationship with an attractive woman like Jana. I would have gladly taken her home and put out.

I still could. I could invite her to my flat and fuck her on the couch and against the kitchen sink and over the dining table and everywhere else that Audrey had been and touched. Maybe that would be the distraction I needed. Maybe if I fucked someone else, I'd remember that there were other cunts in the universe, that there were other attractive women worthy of spending physical time with.

But I didn't want to take Jana home.

I didn't want to use another woman to fuck away thoughts of Audrey. It wouldn't be fair to either of them. And it was new to me to have such a thought. Fair wasn't a concept I typically considered.

"I'm not sure why I'm here," I said finally. "I fear I've been a terrible waste of your time. I apologize sincerely, and please, rest assured that as cliché as it sounds, it's not you. It's most definitely me."

"Please," she teased. "I know it's not me. I'm a hell of a catch." She was a confident woman, and I usually found that a turn-on. What a waste of a good evening, for both of us.

"You *are* a catch. At another time in my life, maybe..." I trailed away because it wasn't polite to offer hopes I couldn't back up.

Jana tilted her head. "What *are* you looking for at this time in your life? If you don't mind me asking. I'm not trying to change your mind, I'm simply curious."

"Well, that's a good question." I ran my hand along my trouser leg under the table as I decided how to answer. "I suppose I'm like you, looking for some companionship now and then. Nothing permanent. No committed relationships for me anymore. Been there, done that."

"Your marriage ended as badly as mine did, did it?"

"It did." *Bad* was an understatement. *Permanently scarring* was a better term. *Completely destructive* was another. "Yes, I know one bad experience doesn't mean they're all going to be terrible, but it was *really* terrible. And painful. And a hassle, in the end, arguing over custody and record albums that neither of us are ever going to listen to again. It killed something in me, I think. I was an awful person through it all and a horrible father. I was mean and distracted and sad. So very sad. I had to go numb inside in order to survive it."

I was *still* numb. Or I had been until Audrey.

"If I did ever fall in love again," I said, omitting the part that I was already in love with someone we both knew, "I'm afraid I'd never be able to fully commit, even if I wanted to. I'd constantly be bracing for the other shoe to drop. I'd be guarding myself, waiting for the end to come. I don't believe that I'd ever be able to give my whole heart, and I know enough about successful relationships to know that's one of the most important ingredients."

I stayed caught in the thought for a moment when I was done talking, letting the things I'd said sink in. I'd been more truthful than I'd intended to be. It was the most honest I'd been with another person about the subject. It was the most honest I'd ever been with *myself*.

Jana put her mug down and scooted it away. "You know. After you came to the fundraiser with Audrey and gave that generous donation that secured a position for her, I thought the two of you might be involved."

"No, no, no." I realized I'd been too eager with my denial, both to Jana and to myself. And as long as we were being truthful... "It's one-sided, anyway. She's a very special young lady, as you surely know, and I am tremendously fond of her. I wouldn't ever put that upon her because she's looking for the whole romantic picture—the groom and the picket fence and the children—and that's obviously not something I'm able to offer. But I do care for her, greatly. I wish her to receive every opportunity available, and I suppose I crossed a line in donating that money. I simply wanted her to be able to stay here if she liked, and I let my affection for her get the better of me."

"I understand. She is very special." *And too young for you.* She didn't say it, but she had to be thinking it. "Has she said that she wants to stay here?"

I frowned. "No, she hasn't." We hadn't actually talked about it. I'd simply assumed. "Has she said something to you?"

"No. But she hasn't accepted the job either. And if she doesn't, I wondered if you expected the money to be returned or if you would allow us to allocate it elsewhere."

"Oh. I didn't realize that." It felt like an anvil was suddenly pressing against my chest. It was hard enough getting used to the idea of sharing Audrey with other men. It was much harder to accept if I didn't get to have any part of her at all.

I didn't want to accept it. I wanted her here. I wanted to tell Jana that she had to make the offer more attractive. I'd double the donation. Whatever it took.

But that was interfering too, wasn't it? When I'd decided that I wasn't going to do that.

I let out a heavy sigh. "Of course you can use the money how you please. I only wanted to give her the opportunity. Is there a deadline for her acceptance?"

"The show she was brought on to help with opens tomorrow, so her internship is winding down. I told her I needed to know by December tenth."

It was the last day of November. That gave me ten days. Ten days to hope she'd decide to stay. Maybe she'd stay for Marco. My stomach twisted at the thought, and I bit my tongue so hard I tasted blood.

But at least she'd still be here, I told myself. Surely that was worth the anguish.

It was. It had to be.

My dinner date was over, and I was even more miserable

than I'd been when it had begun. I paid the bill, and we walked outside together where I hailed Jana a cab.

"You sure you don't want to come over? I'm a great nightcap."

I was tempted this time more than I had been before. My interest level hadn't changed, but I was sure it would be good for me. I needed to fuck away my Audrey attachment, even if I didn't *want* to.

But that didn't feel fair to anyone. I wasn't even sure I could get it up.

I thanked her again and sent her away before hailing another cab for myself. I checked my phone as soon as I was on the road and found nothing had changed since the last time I'd checked. I stared out the window at the Christmas lights and composed a hundred different messages to Audrey that I never planned to send.

How did your date go?
Are you happy with him?
Will you stay in London for him?
Will you stay?

It turned out I didn't have to send a single text to get at least some of my answers. Because as soon as I walked through the lobby of my building on the way to the lift, I spotted her sitting on the stairs. Her shoulders were slumped and the corners of her mouth were bent into a frown.

"My phone died," she said, her voice thick. "I didn't have anywhere else to go so I just waited for you here."

She was obviously upset. I immediately tensed, ready to take action. "Did the asshole hurt you?"

"No. I think I might have hurt *him*."

"Physically?"

She shook her head. "He wanted more. But he's not The Guy, so I can't give him more. I can't force it."

I didn't know how it was possible to be elated and hurt for her at the same time, but I very much was both.

"I'm taking your advice, Dylan. Letting go of the idea of love. Here's to hoping it comes back."

My feelings for her bubbled abruptly inside my chest, rising through my throat, pressing to escape in the form of words. *I'm here. I love you.*

But it wasn't the kind of love she wanted, and even if it was, it wasn't the love she deserved.

I held out my hand and offered her the only thing I could give instead. "Want to go upstairs and get fucked for being such a good little girl, making such a grown-up decision?"

She took my hand. "Yes. Yes, I do."

TWENTY-FIVE

"Fantastic show, Audrey," I said as we walked out of The National Gallery. "Simply splendid. Brava." It was opening day of the Christmas exhibition she'd been working on, and she'd just finished taking me through the display. It had truly been awe-inspiring to see her in her environment. I couldn't stop grinning.

Her cheeks flushed the way they did when I was balls deep inside her. "I don't really deserve any credit for it. It wasn't *my* show. Mostly I pulled things from the archive room and got people coffee."

I looked at her curiously. False modesty wasn't like Audrey. Either she truly hadn't done much or she believed that she hadn't. "Nonsense," I said sincerely. "You knew each and every piece inside and out. Your commentary was the highlight of the exhibit. You can't have that much knowledge about the project if you weren't deeply involved."

She hesitated, as though she wanted to accept my words, but wasn't so sure. "No, honestly. I'm just an intern. Anyone could have done what I did."

"But not anyone did. You did, and they hired you for a

reason." And they'd offered her another position as well. Was that the real reason she hadn't accepted? Because she didn't feel confident?

She considered. "I suppose that's true. And I really did love the work. And the people at the museum. It's definitely been a dream job, even though it was mostly gruntwork."

Then take the offer, I thought. *Stay and climb the ranks.*

I didn't say it though. She didn't know that I knew she hadn't accepted, and while I could just ask her what she was doing next, I was too afraid of the answer.

There were still ten days until she had to give her decision to Jana. Nine and a half now. I planned on making them the best days possible, hoping she'd be happy enough to want to stay.

"You'll let me take you to dinner now to celebrate, won't you?" My mind was already working through the restaurants I knew in the area that didn't need a reservation. We'd want to go someplace close or else get a cab. It hadn't started snowing yet, but the forecast had called for it and the afternoon air was cold and crisp.

"I'd love that. But I have something I'd like to do first, if you don't mind."

"What is it?"

She tugged at the collar of my coat. "It's a surprise!"

"Well, then I can't honestly tell you if I mind," I teased. I couldn't imagine a single thing I'd mind doing as long as I was with her. Even if she suggested something as outrageous as ice skating, which was definitely at the top of the list of things I suspected she'd be interested in.

"Are you trying to wind me up?" She wrinkled her nose, and it looked so adorable I nearly had to kiss it.

Somehow I resisted the temptation, but just barely. "I am. Of course I don't mind. Take me where you will."

"Good because I already bought us tickets. Give me a

second." She pulled out her mobile and made a few swipes. Then she slipped her arm through mine and tugged me toward the stairs. "This way. Our Uber will be here in five."

Less than twenty minutes later, we'd gotten in our car, crossed the Thames, and had been dropped off in front of Jubilee Gardens. There were many things around here that required tickets, but one option was especially obvious.

"We're going on the London Eye?" I asked nodding up at the cantilevered observation wheel in front of us.

"Yes! Have you ever been?"

"Not in years." Ellen and I had been newlyweds when it had opened. We'd come in the summer and it was hot and the queue had been long, but the thrill of floating more than four hundred feet about the river with my bride at my side had been unforgettable. All of London had been stretched out before us, and it had felt symbolic of our lives.

I'd come again with Aaron soon after my divorce, and the magic of the first time was nowhere to be found. He'd only been seven, and the view only interested him for about five minutes before he was ready for it to be over so we could go play at the playground. I'd been irritated and impatient and unimpressed. The whole thing had felt like an overpriced, overlong ferris wheel ride, and I'd vowed to never go on the bloody contraption again.

"Want to go again? With me?" Her eyes were big and intense as she stared at me for my answer.

"Yes. I do."

We made our way down the sidewalk toward the Queen's Walk and found the queue for the flexi tickets she'd bought. There were about fifty or so people ahead of us and the young lady who scanned Audrey's mobile to let us in said it would probably only be ten to fifteen minutes before we could get on.

"I thought about getting the fast pass," Audrey said as we waited. "But I didn't know what time we'd be done at the

Gallery. I'm glad I didn't since it doesn't look like we'll need it. I'd expected it to be more crowded for being in the So Many Children and Tourists part of town."

I chuckled at her reference to the stereotypes map she'd used to familiarize herself with London. "It's not the season for tourists or children. You should see this place in the summer months. On second thought, you shouldn't. This is much better. Though clear skies would be ideal."

She looked up at the clouds, as though she hadn't noticed them before. "I would have thought you were a fan of this broody, gray weather."

"Oh, I am. But it doesn't do well for visibility."

"No visibility is a plus as far as I'm concerned."

"The whole point of this wheel is the views."

"I know, but I'm afraid of heights."

Somehow I'd forgotten this fact, or really never believed it in the first place. It was still so odd to think of her frightened of anything. But if she insisted... "Then why are we doing this?"

"Because I'm afraid of heights." She laughed at my confused expression. "Fear is so annoying. It keeps people from doing and having things they might really want. It's usually stupid and unwarranted, too, the things that scare us. I know I'm not going to fall out of the sky. I know it, and yet my heart starts pounding, and I start sweating when I even think about going up there. Look at my hands!" She held out her palms for me to see. "Sweaty."

She stuffed her hands into her coat pockets. "But the London Eye is one of the most famous tourist attractions in London. I don't want to tell people back home I never rode because I was too scared. I'd rather face the fear head-on. Personally, I think it's the better way to live."

She was right. Of course she was right. And still I felt like arguing for some reason. "Facing your fears makes for a good life, yes, but that only works when you really don't want to be afraid any longer. It's possible that some people like to stay afraid."

"Why would anyone want to stay afraid?"

"I don't know. Because it's familiar, I suppose. You already know what to guard yourself from. You have all your safety nets set in place. And when you get over those fears, you open yourself up to becoming afraid of something else. Sometimes it's easier to live with the fears you know." This speech had come too easily to me. As though it was something I'd said before or was already formed inside me, waiting for a chance to be spoken.

She pressed her lips together tightly. "Well, that's just silly. I think holding onto fears makes it *easier* to be afraid of new things, not the other way around. It's like wagon wheels in a rut—once you've trained your neural pathways to react with anxiety about one thing, it isn't long before a lot of things scare you. I can't imagine living like that. Is it even living at all?"

I didn't want to answer, so I just shrugged. It seemed like a pointed question, like she was trying to confront me about my fears and how I lived my life—or *didn't* live my life, according to her.

Or maybe she hadn't meant it personally, and I just took it that way. I considered asking outright, but in the end, I was a coward.

"I do know this," I said genuinely. "You're a brave woman, Audrey Lind." Certainly she was braver than me. About all sorts of things.

The queue moved fast as the ticket attendant had assured, and we were led into a capsule shortly with nearly two dozen other people. That was one of the admirable features of the Eye's boarding process—though it was a popular attraction, the actual ride wasn't ever crowded. It would have been near intolerable to be stuck for thirty minutes on the wheel otherwise, even with the air conditioning.

I stepped in after Audrey who walked immediately to a spot against the window. "There's a bench here," I pointed out. "If you'd rather have some distance between you and the glass."

She shook her head. "This is good for now. I find it's better to dive right into these kinds of things. Tiptoeing around the fear only makes it worse."

"That it does." I moved next to her, placing my hands on the rail like she had done. The ride was already in motion, another one of its highlights. The wheel rarely stopped, even as passengers got on and off, making for one smooth trip.

But that also meant we were already rising, already climbing higher in the sky.

"Are you doing okay?" I asked. Audrey was feeling the anxiety of it. I could hear her shallow breaths and her knuckles were white as they gripped the railing.

"Fine," she said, her voice tight and high. "I'll be fine."

Though the clouds covered the sky, there was still a lot to see. Big Ben, Westminster Abbey, the Shard, but I was more interested in watching Audrey, looking for any cue she might give for help.

Not that there was much I could do for her now that we were in the air. I did my best to distract her, giving her the history of the wheel and offering tidbits of trivia about the city below us.

She didn't say anything, only blinked and nodded. Her gaze never moved, as though she'd anchored her eyes to some landmark below and was clutching on for dear life. There was something oddly inspiring about watching her. Her delicate throat swallowed. Her lip quivered. She reminded me of the Mark Twain quote that said something about courage being the master of fear and not the absence of fear.

Audrey was definitely afraid, and as awed as I was by her, I also felt helpless. And that made me terrified. It was how I often felt watching Aaron grow up and embark on scary new adventures. I knew he had to experience both the good and the bad to learn, that I couldn't intervene and learn for him. It was one of the hardest things to do as a parent, stand by and let this person I loved go through something trying.

It was just as hard watching Audrey. Not necessarily watching her on the wheel, but in her life. I wanted to wrap her in my arms and keep her safe from everything and everyone. Wanted to make sure she had every happiness, but I couldn't hand her the romantic, unambiguous future wrapped in a bow that she wanted. I had to let her get to her ending on her own.

It was a good thing she was courageous. It made it easier. For me, anyway.

"We're at the top now," I said encouragingly. "Look! You've done it! Gone to the top of the London Eye. It's all down from here."

She closed her eyes and let out a long deep sigh. Then she turned and rested her elbows on the rail behind her. "That's better."

I peered over my shoulder, following her sight lines. There was a small family speaking in Korean and snapping pictures in front of the opposite window, blocking Audrey's view. "You can't see a single thing this way."

She grinned. "Just how I want it. I told you—it's not about seeing anything."

A memory of the apartment hunting with her the first week we'd met popped into my mind. "You'd said you were afraid of heights before, but you didn't seem all that frightened by the windows in the New York flat."

"Because when we were there together, I was preoccupied with other things, if you remember. It's hard to be worried about your fears when you're on the verge of orgasm." Her eyes twinkled as she glanced at me, checking out my reaction. Trying to wind me up, most likely.

It was definitely working.

"Maybe that's what would make this better—if you got under my skirt." Her voice was low now, so that there was no way anyone could hear but me. "I could turn back to the window, and you could come right behind me, embracing me. You could hitch up my skirt, push my panties aside, stick your cock inside me. Make me feel real good. Distract me from the fall. I'm already wet from talking about it. You'd slip right in. Too bad we didn't book a private ride."

Such a fucking tease. I was instantly hard.

I put my hand around her shoulder and swiftly pulled her closer so I could whisper greedily into her ear. "I'm going to finger-fuck you under the table at dinner, I'm warning you now. Three fingers, deep and merciless, until you're shivering and boneless."

She turned her face so her mouth was inches from mine. "And then later, will you meet me in the bathroom so you can do me in a stall?"

Damn, she was perfect. Sensual and sassy and smart and strong. I could write books about all the amazing things she was. I could write sequels about all the amazing things she made me feel, and in that moment I was drowning in the awe of her. I was grasping for something to hold onto, gasping for air, and it didn't matter what I knew I *should* do because all I could think about was how much I wanted her with me. Always.

"Why haven't you accepted the permanent position at the museum?" I asked pointedly.

Her smile faded, and she stepped out of my embrace. "How do you know about that?"

"Jana told me. Answer the question." I sounded harsh and demanding, and I hated myself for it, but I couldn't help it.

Her brow knitted as she crossed her arms defensively over her chest. "Why are you talking to my boss about me?" Her features shifted as she seemed to realize something. "It was *you*, wasn't it? You donated the money for the job. Jana admitted there was a single donor. Why would you do that for me?"

My mouth went dry and my mind raced to come up with the most convincing lie. "Because I believe in the arts," I stated defiantly. That sounded good.

She stuck out her chin. "That's not why."

"Because I believe in supporting young artists," I amended.

"Would you have supported *any* young artist, or just me?"

The capsule was descending at a slow even keel, but I felt like I was tumbling from space without a parachute. I didn't want the tables turned on me. I didn't want her examining my motives—I wanted her to explain her own.

"I know you personally," I said defiantly. "It makes sense to want to help out a friend."

"You wanted to help out a friend," she repeated, unconvinced. "You donated the amount of a full-time salary for a *friend*." Her gaze bore into me as though she were trying to see *into* me. As though she thought she could find the truth and pull it out of me with just a look.

"Yes. I'm generous like that." I stared back at her, refusing to back down. She maintained eye contact, just as stubborn as I was. Whatever she wanted me to say, I wasn't going to say it. Not only did I not know what she was looking for, but didn't she realize yet that I wasn't that brave?

The tension between us was so tautly strung, it became unbearable.

I looked away first, staring out at the winter evening. Snowflakes were beginning to fall, and they glistened in the river lights. It was surreal and beautiful and sad, too, for some reason.

"I don't know why it matters now," I said quietly to the cold glass. "It doesn't seem you want the help, since you aren't choosing to take it."

"I haven't chosen to go either," she whispered, stepping into me. I could feel the heat radiating off her body, could feel it beckoning me closer.

I didn't move. "What are you waiting for?"

She turned toward the window, mirroring me. "A reason to stay."

I could give it to her, I thought. I wanted to give it to her, a reason to stay. I wanted to keep her and trap her and love her, selfishly. For me.

But...

But, but, but.

But that meant standing up to my fears. That meant possibly finding new fears. And it was easier to live with the fears I knew.

So instead of saying anything, I took the advice I'd given her and let her go.

TWENTY-SIX

A curtain came between us, brought down by my own hand. The countdown to the date Audrey was to accept or decline the job was foremost in my mind, and I hoped beyond hope that she'd decide to stay, but in the very real case that she didn't, I put up my walls. We still talked constantly. I spent the next several days with her, taking her around London, showing her my favorite parts of the town. We fucked nightly. Every morning she woke up next to me, but the increased time together was very superficial. I had to protect my heart. I kept her at arm's-length. I didn't let her in any more than she already was.

It was difficult at first, watching her flit around, preparing her wings for flight while I stayed tight and secure within my cage. I was familiar with the feeling of being tethered and bound. I'd been here before, and I dealt with it in the same way I had in the past. I closed down my emotions. I went numb.

I prepared to let her go.

Thursday night, four days to go on the countdown, I was just getting out of the shower when there was a knock on the door. I glanced at the time. Audrey was due to arrive in half an hour for our evening plans. She should have been off of work by now, but she'd said she needed to go home to get ready before coming over.

Dripping wet, with a towel wrapped around my waist, I checked the peephole. "You're early," I said as I opened the door.

My chest tightened when I really got a look at Audrey. She hadn't changed after work—she was still in tights and a jumper under her coat, the outfit she'd worn when I'd left her flat this morning. What concerned me, though, was her face. Her skin was splotchy, her eyes red and puffy, her makeup smeared. She'd been crying.

I went on alert. "What is it? What's wrong? What happened?" Whoever had hurt her, I had to know. I'd fix it. I'd hurt him back.

She shook her head dismissively. "I just had a bad day is all. Do you mind if we cancel the theater? I know you already got tickets, but I don't really feel like sitting through something right now."

"Don't worry about the show. Do you want to go somewhere else? Anywhere you want is fine with me. I'll even go ice skating, if that's what you'd prefer." The desperation to make her better was overwhelming.

"Can I just come in and maybe talk a little?"

"Of course, of course." I stepped aside for her to come in, then I opened my arms, expecting her to come in for an embrace.

Instead she stuffed her hands in her pockets and stepped away. "I don't really feel like being touched right now, if that's okay with you."

The rejection was unexpected and stung sharply. Was she upset with *me*?

Before I got too panicked about the possibility I talked myself down. I'd never seen her upset at all. Perhaps this was her usual method of coping.

"I'll..." I didn't know what to do. What I *should* do. She was standing in my entryway looking sullen and sad, and all I could do was stare at her. "Let me take your coat," I said finally.

"I'd rather keep it on for now, thank you. Could I maybe have some water?"

"Yes. Sure. I could put the kettle on, if you prefer."

"Water's fine."

She followed me into the kitchen and took a seat in one of the high chairs at the island. I grabbed a glass from the cabinet and filled it with water from the refrigerator then set it down in front of her.

I watched while she brought it to her lips and took a swallow. She was so quiet and pale. Not like her usual self at all. I yearned to wrap my arms around her and kiss her better. I couldn't stand seeing her like this, and not being able to touch her made me feel even worse.

"I hope I didn't pull you out of the shower," she said after a long silent minute, gesturing to the towel, loose at my hips.

"I was already getting out." It did feel awkward to be naked in front of her when she was like this. "Will you be okay for a minute while I throw some trousers on?"

She gave me a yes and a tight smile, and I took off to my bedroom in search of something to wear, but when I got there, I stood in the doorway for several seconds, thinking. My mind raced, imagining every scenario that would put Audrey in such a glum state. Something at work, probably. Or something back home? Was it Sabrina? Again, I wondered, was it me? I couldn't think of anything I'd done to offend her, but I was stuck to guessing, and didn't have many other ideas.

I wanted to *fix* it.

But I couldn't. I knew I couldn't. Even if I knew what was bothering her, I likely wouldn't be able to do anything but simply be there for her.

It was maddening.

With a frustrated sigh, I pushed myself into the task at hand, grabbing a pair of sweats from my dresser and hastily putting them on before returning to the kitchen.

She was where I'd left her, her coat still on, a classic beret beanie winter hat on her head. Ready to leave at a moment's notice. It distressed me—all of it, her posture, her unwillingness to share, her refusal to make herself comfortable.

I eyed the seat next to her, but moved around to the other side of the island instead. It was too tempting to touch her if I was close, and I needed to wait for her invitation.

Bracing my hands on the worktop behind me, I tilted my head and studied her with concern. "Do you want to talk about it? I know a compassionate nature isn't one of my better traits, but I assure you, I can listen."

She almost chuckled. Then she let out a long breath. "I just...I found out something today and it..." She shook her head, as though to erase her beginning. Then she started again. "I've decided to tell Jana that I'm not going to accept the job."

Her voice cracked, or my heart did. It felt suddenly hard to breathe. I'd seen this coming. I'd prepared. And yet, I wasn't ready.

I blinked several times, searching for a foothold on the ground that was quickly slipping out from underneath me. I wanted to demand she change her mind, but I had no place to. She *wanted* to stay, though. I could hear it in her tone.

"Is this why you're upset? If it's worked you up like this, then why go? You love your job. I know you do."

"I do. I do love it." Her brow furrowed. "But I love what I do. I can do it anywhere. I like the staff at the Gallery, but it's not like I've formed any real bonds there. This is the crossroads. This is when I decide what happens next in the bigger plan, and staying here is a big decision. It's planting roots. It's dealing with Visas and establishing myself here, and it's so far from Sabrina, and she's my only family left. It's one thing to go overseas and do something temporary, but it's not practical without..." She trailed off, disappearing into some private thought.

Audrey twisted her lip and stared absentmindedly at a spot on the island worktop. She was more in her head than in the room, and I longed to be there with her, but I waited for her to be ready to go on, not wanting to prod or poke while simultaneously wanting to shake her sharply and yell in her face to fuck practicality. My grip on the worktop behind me tightened as I held in my restraint, my nails digging into the underside of the silestone.

"I guess that's why I was so eager to try to find The Guy," she said eventually. "I know I said I'd let it go, and I have, but it would have made it easier to stay. I could justify everything I'd be losing with so much gained."

Her eyes reached for mine. "I really don't know why I couldn't find him. It wasn't like I was being picky. I just wanted someone who would make me laugh. And challenge me. Is fun to be around. Gives good orgasms." She let out a quick laugh and then grew somber again. "Someone who thinks about me when I'm not with him. Someone I look up to, but doesn't make me feel small. Someone who takes care of me. Someone who puts me first. Someone who runs to me when I need him. Someone who just...loves me. Why is that so impossible to find?"

As she spoke, I could feel words forming inside of me, bubbling up within my chest, building toward explosion. They shaped in the back of my throat, they slid to the tip of my tongue, and no matter anymore if I believed them or that they weren't the words I wanted. They were solid and familiar, and they detonated with a roar. "You can't find it because it isn't real! None of it is. No one loves anyone more than themselves. Fate doesn't intervene to bring people together. True love is a fairy tale. It's a myth. Stop fooling yourself that it isn't and grow the fuck up!"

Audrey lifted her chin and fired back. "Or maybe I have

found him but the man I'm in love with is a coward who has abandoned the possibility of anything good so he can be a cynic."

I already regretted my words. They'd come from a cold, shadowy place inside me, and I wanted to retract them and apologize immediately once they'd been said.

But now I was stunned into silence.

"Yes, it's you, you asshole. I'm in love with *you*." She'd never sworn before in my presence, and the word was a blunt display of how angry she was. How filled with frustration.

And still I couldn't say anything, could only stare at her with incredulity. She was *in love* with *me*? Impossible. She was too smart for that. Too levelheaded to waste her heart on a shit like me.

"I know I told you I wouldn't fall for you," she continued. "Or I promised that I would try not to, and I *did* try. I thought I'd done a pretty good job of it, too, when we parted in New York. But then I saw you again here, and I think I realized then that I'd been in love with you from that very first kiss. But I knew you didn't want that. So I tried to be your friend. I tried to not think about you like that. I tried." She was worked up and animated, saying words that felt unimaginable and also plucked from my own head.

"But you went on those dates..." I was sorting it out. Slowly processing.

"I did! All those crappy dates, hoping I'd find someone else who'd make me forget you. I wasn't going to sit around believing that you'd change how you felt about love and marriage and babies for *me*. But then you'd do these things—stupid, wonderful things, like donate the money for my job and help me paint my freaking apartment—and I started to think *maybe*. Maybe something's there. And I didn't want to push, so I just nudged you when I could, and everytime I hit a brick wall, and so I'd back down because I knew you'd put it there for a reason."

She stood up suddenly, too agitated to stay sitting. "But then you know what I realized? I realized that you weren't behind that wall because you really thought life was better there. You were *hiding*. Because you're scared. And I get it. You don't want to be hurt, and I could be patient with that, because I think there's a part of you that really wants to come out. And I'm *not* Ellen. I wouldn't cheat. Ever. I'm fiercely loyal, and if you'd give me a chance to prove it..."

Her eyes sparked hot. "Except then! Then I find out today you went *on a date* with Jana, and maybe it's not fair, but that hurt. It hurt a lot, Dylan. It broke my heart, because you said that didn't interest you. And I believed you. Was that not true? Or is it just that you aren't interested in dating *me*? Because I can't believe that's the case. You feel something for me. You have to. I know you do. Don't you?"

She stared into me, her chest rising and falling with shallow, riled breaths, her cheeks pink with emotion. "Say something!"

There were so many things to say. I wanted to tell her that I *did* feel something for her. That Jana meant nothing. That I was deeply and hopelessly in love with her. That I could give her all those things she wanted. That I could be The Guy, the someone who ran to her and took care of her and put her first. All I had to do was open the door to my cage and step out. I could taste the nearness to freedom, could feel it beckoning to me like sunshine streaming through the bars of my prison. Could vividly imagine taking flight with her in the sky.

But I'd hesitated too long.

"I guess that's my answer," she said, her eyes brimming. She spun on her heel and headed toward the door.

She was walking away. I didn't want her walking away, and that sprung me into action.

"No, Audrey." The house phone started ringing, but I ignored it to chase after her. "Wait. Please, wait."

She didn't turn around. "I can't talk to you right now," she said in a choked voice. "Answer your phone."

I didn't give a fuck about the bloody phone. She was at the door now, opening it with haste and slamming it shut, just as I got to it. Cursing, I opened it and called again to her as she jogged down the hall toward the lift.

Janice Morgan, my next door neighbor, stepped out of her flat with her two German shepherds, blocking my path.

I danced this way and that, trying to get around the threesome. Finally, I put my hands on her shoulders and scooted her out of the way.

"Mr. Locke!" she said sharply at my back.

I stopped to see if I'd hurt her in some way, but found her pinched expression was directed at my clothing—or lack thereof.

A glance back at Audrey told me I wasn't going to catch her in the lift, and I couldn't go running down the icy sidewalk with no shoes and no shirt.

"Bloody hell," I muttered, turning back to my flat. I opened the cupboard next to the front door and pulled out a coat and slipped on a pair of loafers. Then I grabbed my mobile and my wallet (in case I needed to catch a cab and go directly to her house) and renewed my pursuit.

I took the stairs, pulling up Audrey's number on my phone as I raced down. It rang three times before her outgoing message picked up.

"Fuck." I tried again. This time it went immediately to her voicemail. She was avoiding me. I redialed, ignoring the annoyed look of the doorman as I blustered past him to the street. When the buoyant sound of her recorded voice filled my ear, I left a message. "Audrey, pick up. Ring me. Let's talk. Please."

Outside, I searched in both directions, trying to guess if she'd gone toward the underground station, and if so, which one, since

I lived squarely between two. I couldn't see her either way so I scanned instead for a cab. None were in sight.

I picked a direction and started walking, typing out a text as I walked.

> You surprised me. That's all.

An incoming call interrupted my message, but I cursed when I saw Ellen's name instead of Audrey's. I sent my ex to voicemail and was about to go back to typing when I heard a car. I looked up to see it was a cab. Too late, I reached out to summon it and let out another string of swearing when it drove on by.

I went back to my message.

> Please come back. Please let me tell you everything in my heart.

I pushed SEND as my mobile vibrated with another call. Ellen, again.

"Jesus, what?" I roared.

"Dylan, I'm at the hospital. You have to come. It's Aaron."

TWENTY-SEVEN

I moved in a fog back into my flat. Thoughts raced through my mind, but I couldn't grasp any of them, like they were on the Autobahn and I was a pedestrian standing on the side of the road, watching them fly by. Simple words and phrases sped by like fuzzy blobs, the emotions and meanings impossible to fully comprehend: *Infection. Pain. It's serious. Hurry.*

There was only one thing I could cling to, letting it drive me through the haze—*get to New York. Get to my son.*

The next half hour was spent on the phone. With my assistant, mainly. She took over the major task of booking me on the next flight over the pond and arranging a car both to take me to Heathrow and another to pick me up at LaGuardia. Next, I talked to Amy, putting the reins of the company in her hands until who knew when. A call to Donovan followed, apprising him of the situation. Finally, my mother, who cried even when I assured her it was too soon to panic.

It was a lie anyway. If it were really too soon to panic, Ellen wouldn't have said I should come. But I couldn't think about that right now. I could barely think at all.

I didn't pack a bag. Even if I didn't have clothes and essentials in my New York apartment, I would have left empty-handed. My flight took off too soon—I was going to be scrambling through security to make it as it was—and I wouldn't have been able to concentrate on what I needed, what I didn't need. I had no idea how long I'd be gone. I was barely thinking clearly enough to remember to grab my passport.

I was in the cab on my way to the airport before I could identify the one thing I *did* need—Audrey. I was devastated when I got her voicemail again and was sure she hadn't turned her phone back on, but I tried over and over, hanging up each time the recording was finished. It was comforting to hear her voice, even if all she said was *I'm obviously not available or I'm avoiding you. If you don't leave a message after the tone, you'll never find out which.*

Finally, when I was checked in and boarded, I left a brief message telling her what was going on. Then I typed out a text, knowing she'd see it sooner.

> Aaron has a serious infection and is in hospital. I'm about to take off to the U.S. now. Please, call. I need you. I need to tell you

I stared at the screen, trying to figure out what I needed to tell her.

Everything. That's what. Every bloody thing I'd never told her. That I loved her. That I wanted her. That I wanted to talk this through.

It was too much of a declaration over message. I deleted the last lines and ended with

> Please, call.

Then I put the phone on airplane mode and buckled in for the eight-hour flight.

There was a lot of time to think in the air, without internet connection. I thought about Aaron, of course, replaying Ellen's words in my mind.

"I took him into the clinic yesterday because he was complaining that his face hurt," she'd said. *"They diagnosed him with a sinus infection and gave us antibiotics. His upper lip was a little bit swollen when he went to bed. When he woke up today, he was in a lot of pain and the swelling had spread down to his chin and up to the middle of his cheeks. I called the doctor again, and they said to take him to the E.R. They admitted him immediately, and Dylan, it's serious. You have to hurry and get here. He's getting an MRI now so they can try to determine the cause, and they're putting him on IV antibiotics and pain meds, but if they don't stop the infection, if the swelling moves past his eyes and to his brain..."*

She hadn't finished her sentence, but she hadn't needed to. I understood clearly what she was saying even without hearing the words.

I didn't like thinking about that for too long, but almost every time I batted the thought aside, it immediately returned to buzz in my brain like an unwanted fly. The few times I managed to shoo it away for any significant amount of time, my head was filled instead with Audrey. Beautiful Audrey. Sweet, saucy Audrey. Bold and unafraid Audrey. Owner-of-my-heart Audrey. What to do about Audrey?

I never made it beyond the past. I retraced every step of our relationship, every encounter, every fragment of conversation I could recall. I saw her in her underthings, standing in front of the windows in my New York flat. I heard her humming as she painted her bedroom walls. I felt the pit in my stomach as she called me a coward. I watched her running out my door, two steps ahead of me, leaving me behind.

If Ellen hadn't called, I would have gone to her place and waited on her doorstep until she let me in. I could picture that far, but what happened when I saw her, what I said, what I did—that was beyond my imagination. I didn't know what to do about Audrey, and with Aaron tied up to a hospital IV in another country, it was impossible to consider seriously.

It was just after midnight when I landed at LaGuardia, and my mobile was dead. I hadn't thought to grab a charger, and while it was possible there might be one for sale in the airport, I was too eager to get to hospital. Asking Ellen for an update on Aaron could wait until then, and if Audrey had called, I wasn't sure I wanted to know. My priority right now had to be my son. I didn't have room for distractions, as sweet as that particular distraction might be.

The ride into the city was smooth and quick, a benefit of my late arrival. There weren't too many cars, and the warm front the region was experiencing after the prior week's snow had cleared up any lingering ice from the roads.

Getting past hospital security was a lengthier process. Visiting hours were over, and even though there were exceptions for minors, I couldn't ring Ellen to approve my relation to Aaron without my mobile phone. The main entrance was closed and the only way in was through the ER, which was filled with the typical late-night medical emergencies. It took more than thirty minutes to find someone who had the time to talk to me, but eventually I was given a pass and sent to the children's ward. Then there was another door to be buzzed through and a paper to sign at the Pediatric desk, but finally, I was directed to my son's room.

The door was ajar, and I stood outside it for a moment to catch my breath, then pushed it open. The lights were dim, and a curtain hid the bed where, I presumed, Aaron was sleeping. I'd expected to find Ellen stretched out in the recliner next to him, but instead, she was standing just inside the room with her arms crossed over her chest while she talked to a man in a lab coat.

"Oh, good. You're here," my ex-wife said quietly when I walked in. Her voice sounded a bit raspier than usual, and her eyes looked heavy and tired, but otherwise, she seemed as she always did—poised, collected. Cold. Clinical.

There had been a part of me that had wanted to reach for her the minute I saw her. While we spent most of our interactions these days in battle mode, none of our fights felt relevant at the moment. She was the mother of my child, a woman I still loved fiercely for that reason alone. There was no one who could better know what I was feeling, how distressed and out of my mind with worry.

But even with the man next to her, she seemed too detached for an embrace. Too withdrawn. It reminded me vividly of a night long ago, another cold night spent in hospital fretting over a child. *Her* child. Amanda hadn't made it through that night, and Ellen had shut down the minute her daughter's time of death had been declared. She'd become unapproachable. Distant. Aloof. It had felt impossible to try to comfort her.

I'd resented her for that then, and that resentment was a barrier around her now, preventing me from pulling her into my arms.

"He's sleeping right now," she said, before I could ask. "This is Dr. Sharma. Aaron's going into surgery tomorrow morning, and Dr. Sharma's associate is to be the surgeon."

I shook the doctor's hand. He had a firm grip, and that reassured me for some reason. "I'm Dylan, Aaron's father. I'm sorry I don't know what's going on—I just arrived from London. Could you possibly get me up to speed? About everything."

"Yes, Mr. Locke. I'm sorry to meet you under such serious

circumstances. I was actually only hanging around to update you."

My chest constricted like it had been gripped with a large hand, squeezing all the air out of my lungs. It hadn't even occurred to me that medical doctors didn't usually visit patients in the middle of the night until he'd said something. If he'd been waiting this late specifically to update me, then Aaron's condition had to have taken a turn for the worse.

Ellen read the panic on my face. "No, no, it's not what you think. Donovan hired Dr. Sharma to be available when you arrived. He knew you'd want to talk to a medical professional directly."

Bless Donovan Kincaid. Sometimes his overreaching really was appreciated.

Dr. Sharma explained to me the situation in detail. The MRI they'd conducted while I was in flight indicated that he had a dental abscess, and the infection had moved to his skin. "It's called cellulitis and is mainly treated by heavy antibiotics. Unfortunately, it's difficult to get the medicine exactly where we need it. The veins in the face are small, and it can take some time before the IV meds get into that area. The surgeon will scrape out as much of the infection as possible tomorrow morning, which should help speed up the process, but the most important component for fighting this is the antibiotics."

"They've already changed which antibiotic they were giving him once since this morning," Ellen added.

I didn't like the implications of that. "What was the reasoning for the change? It's been less than twenty-four hours. Surely that couldn't have been enough time to determine the first medicine wasn't working."

"It's not as concerning as it sounds," Dr. Sharma assured me. "We put him on one antibiotic when he checked in, and after watching him for a few hours and seeing the infection was spreading at a faster rate than we'd originally suspected, we decided to move him to a more powerful medicine."

"It's spread?" I sounded more alarmed than I wanted to.

Ellen met my worried gaze. "It's just under his eyes now, Dylan. And it's moving down his neck."

"That's bad, isn't it? You don't want it to move past his eyes." I was only repeating the information she'd given me earlier.

"That is correct, Mr. Locke. Once the infection gets past the orbital bone, it can easily enter the brain. Encephalitis is quite serious, but I don't want to worry about that until it reaches that point."

"And if it gets into his lymph nodes. That's bad too." Ellen wanted me to know all the worst-case scenarios, it seemed.

I appreciated this. I'd spent most of the flight imagining what they could be. I needed to know what the reality was. "What happens if it gets into his lymph nodes?" I asked.

"The lymph nodes can easily deliver the infection through the bloodstream, spreading the bacteria throughout the body. There is a possibility that could lead to sepsis."

The vice grip around my chest tightened. "Aunt Edna died of sepsis."

"That's exactly what I thought," Ellen said. Her lip trembled, the only indication of the desperate emotions that had to be raging inside her.

Dr. Sharma tried to soothe us. "Again, that's not something we should worry about until necessary. Right now we have a clear path of attack. Let's give the antibiotics time to work."

I thanked the doctor for his time and for staying so late and giving us reassurance. The minute he left the room, though, the anxiety of the possibilities pressed heavier on my shoulders. I caught Ellen's eye. Her features were smooth, but I knew her well enough to see the agitation simmering underneath. She was still closed off, her arms wrapped around herself. Nothing about her posture was inviting.

But I pulled her into my arms and clung to her anyway, something I maybe should have done more of when her child had died, because this time it was also *my* child, and I needed *her*, even if she didn't need me.

She didn't pull away, and after a while, I could feel her body soften in my embrace. We stood there for a long time, talking to each other only through touch, sharing the weight of this hardship as well as we could. When she finally broke away, her eyes were brimming, and she excused herself to go to the ensuite bathroom.

Alone, I took a beat to get myself together. Then I stepped around the curtain to see my son. He was sleeping on his back, his body twisted as though he wanted to be on his side, but couldn't manage it with the various hookups to machines. Or possibly, the pressure of laying that way hurt too much, which was understandable. His entire face, from his eye sockets down, was swollen. Much more swollen than I'd imagined. I couldn't even tell where his cheekbones were. Even his nose was misshaped with edema. He looked like a puffed-up marshmallow, and I didn't doubt he was in incredible pain.

I stood over him and gripped the bedrail until my knuckles were white. He looked so small and fragile, and I suddenly remembered standing over Amanda's bed. Remembered how she'd seemed small and fragile. Remembered how much it hurt to watch her slip away from this life and into the next.

It had been unbearable, really.

More unbearable than all the things that happened next—Ellen's complete shutdown, her string of affairs, our divorce. Amanda had been thirteen when I'd married her mother, and six years later, when she'd sat on her deathbed, I'd grown to love her as though she were my own. Losing her had ripped me apart. It had destroyed parts of me that could never be recovered. It was her death, not the end of my marriage, that had taught me the lesson I held onto so resolutely now—*love leads to loss.*

And I never wanted to feel that kind of loss again. If Aaron died…if he was no longer in my world…

A sob escaped from my throat.

I couldn't lose him. I wouldn't. Whatever I had to do, whatever I had to pay, Aaron had to stay alive. He was lodged inside me so deeply, that I was sure I couldn't exist without him. I was helpless at his side, but I silently vowed to do anything within my power to keep him here.

And I renewed an older vow too, the vow I'd made when I closed down my heart after Amanda—*never let anyone else inside.* No one. Not even Audrey. She'd worked her way past my walls, but not all of them, not yet, and it couldn't be too late to build more. If I didn't let Audrey in any farther than she already was, if I pushed her out of my heart all together, then there would be less chance that I'd ever be here again, standing on the brink of sanity while my world crumbled to pieces in front of me.

Losing her now would hurt, yes, but not like it could. Not like the possibility of losing Aaron hurt. Not like it would hurt if I let myself love her—*really* love her—and *then* lost her.

So I wouldn't love her. Not *really* love her. Or anyone, ever again.

Sure, it was a cruel, cynical way to live, but as far as I was concerned, it was the only way to survive.

TWENTY-EIGHT

The rest of the night crept by slowly. I parked myself in a steel-framed upholstered chair while Ellen curled up in a lounger that converted to a bed. The room was dim, only a small light shone from a lamp next to the bed, but neither of us bothered to try to sleep. We knew it would be impossible.

For much of the time, we sat silently, listening to the chirps of the automated equipment hooked up to our son. I was thankful for the quiet, too weighed down with the enormity of the situation to manage an abundance of conversation. Even my thoughts were sparse and scattered. I thought about the milk container I left on the kitchen worktop and the Christmas gifts I had for my mother that I hadn't bothered to send off and impressed myself by remembering the song order of all the Metallica CDs I'd listened to in high school. Trivial things. Things that didn't have an emotional residue. Things that didn't make me want to find the nearest stairwell and scream until my voice gave out.

I imagined Ellen was in a similar fog. When she did make the effort to engage, her statements were just as random. "The green in that painting reminds me of the shag carpet in your flat in Southampton," she said once. And another time, "I still haven't finished reading the *Outlander* series. I should get on that."

Each instance, I murmured something appropriate and meaningless and soon we'd fall back into taciturnity. The long stretches of silence were familiar and comfortable. We'd done this before—existed in separate cocoons of shared grief. This was something we knew how to do well.

"I have to remember to cancel my appointment with the internet company later today," she said just a little past four in the morning.

I blinked a couple of times, processing the simple statement. It was the kind of thing that didn't require a response, but I was beginning to bore of the stupor and this felt like a safe, mindless conversation to embark on. "Do you have a problem with your service?"

"I've had a terrible time with our old provider. Aaron complains every day when he tries to do his homework that he can't get the sites he needs to load."

I hmphed. "Sites he *needs*? Or YouTube videos?"

"I know, right? Though, it's both, I'm sure. So much of the education at his school is provided in other learning formats such as video and podcasts. I like it. I just swear the internet company is throttling download speeds. It's gotten progressively worse over this year. The irritating part is that it will be another three weeks before I can get a new appointment, even on a wait list."

I scowled at the annoyance she must feel. "Don't you have someone who can meet them for you? Aaron is always telling me that you're dating. Is there no one?"

"No one significant. No one who would meet the cable guy for me, anyway. No one who would come sit at the hospital with me while my son is in surgery."

We'd been conversing without eye contact, but now I turned my head toward her. "*I'm* here."

"For Aaron."

"And for you." I was grateful that I wasn't sitting at his bedside alone, and assumed she'd felt the same. It was a typical problem from our past—I assumed too much when I should have tried harder to really communicate.

I assumed too much about people in general.

I decided to make the effort now. "I mean that, Ellen. You're the only person who gets what I feel about him."

She looked at me while she considered. "No one can love your creation as much as you do except a co-creator, I suppose."

I started to nod in agreement, then thought about it more. "Although...I really loved Amanda."

Her eyes widened, surprised, perhaps, by the declaration. When she turned away, she wrapped her arms tighter around herself, and I knew I'd taken a wrong turn.

"I'll ring Donovan later," I said, steering us back to safer topics. "He can get someone over to your apartment to meet the technician."

"Thank you." She stared at an unidentifiable spot before her, and I figured she'd slipped back into a daze. Then, abruptly, she asked, "How about you? Do you have anyone you're dating?"

The question felt shocking, like a bucket of ice cold water thrown over my head. It was too close to talking about Audrey —*thinking* about Audrey—and I didn't want to do that.

But not answering all together would only draw more attention to the topic, so I responded with succinct honesty. "Not really. I don't do that sort of thing anymore."

Ellen shifted again to study me. "You don't do *what*? Have sex? Spend time in other people's company?"

I glanced quickly at Aaron. He was still sleeping, but I

lowered my voice anyway. "My bed isn't cold. But I've found it's...easier...to live without any unnecessary attachments."

She let out a sigh laced with pity. "Oh, Dylan. When did you become so bitter? Did *I* do that? That's an awful lot of power to give me."

I frowned. I didn't like how it felt like she was turning the tables on what really happened. As though it were my fault that I'd loved her enough to be affected by her infidelity. "I'm not sure I'm comfortable discussing this with you," I said, hopefully putting an end to the matter.

"That's too bad. There was a time you'd tell me anything. I don't expect you to anymore, of course, not after...well. It's just sad to hear that you don't have someone in your life now. I always saw you as a man who needed to love to be alive. I never imagined you'd become so hard-hearted."

"I was also very young when we met. Now I've grown up."

We fell back into silence then for the bulk of the next hour, until the commotion of shift change stirred us again. A nurse came in, turning on the overhead before he introduced himself.

At the light and the sound of the new, louder voice, Aaron shifted in his bed. "Dad? You're here. It's not Christmas already, is it?"

I took the two steps to his side and leaned down over him, taking his hand in mine. "Hi, kid. Not Christmas yet. I came early. Flew all night. Boy are my arms tired."

He smiled then let out a groan. "Ow. It hurts to smile."

"It was a terrible joke anyway."

"A dad joke for sure."

My grip on his hand tightened. He was hurting, and there was nothing I could do about it. Parental helplessness: one of the worst feelings in the world. I would carry all his burdens for him if I could. I'd suffer all his pain.

"I'm okay, Dad," he said, as though I were the one who needed soothing. "I mean, I feel like I'm dying, but I'm okay."

My heart pinched. He was a far cry from death, but the possibility lurked too close for comfort, and if I continued to stand there and think about it, I was going to lose it in front of him.

Thank God the nurse stepped in to take his vitals, giving me a reason to step away. And then it was time to prepare for surgery. A slew of doctors and nurses came through in turns, discussing anesthesia and Aaron's allergies, administering new IV's and inspecting the extent of his swelling.

Another hour of this and then his entire bed was wheeled away, leaving Ellen and me alone to wait.

"Do you want any coffee?" I asked, needing something to do besides worry.

"I'm good. The machine out there is terrible."

"Oh." I didn't really want coffee anyway. I only wanted this whole nightmare to be over.

"Remember the last time he had anesthesia?" Ellen said when I didn't get up to leave. "After his adenoid surgery. He took forever to wake up."

"I remember. And those faces he made while we were trying to rouse him. Those were the funniest expressions I've ever seen on a human."

"He's always made those faces in his sleep. Since he was born."

I chuckled. "And the sounds he makes. He snores like he's an old man."

"At least that improved after the adenoid removal. It was nearly impossible to be in a room with him while he slept before that."

We exchanged a smile. This was better than waiting in silence or sitting in the dark with our thoughts.

"Remember how he always moved the s's at the front of words to the end of the word?" Ellen asked. "Like *stop*. He always said *tops*. And he loved riding on the *leds* instead of *sled*."

I'd forgotten that he'd done that. It used to delight us to no end.

"That stupid stuffed pig he had. What was its name?"

"Stumpy," I said, the name coming easily despite not having said it in years.

"That's right. He called it *Tumpys*."

"He loved the twinkle, twinkle *tars*." I smiled as it came back to me.

"He always said you were so marts. 'Daddy is so *marts*. You're only a little bit *marts*, Mommy.'"

I chuckled. "*Marts*. I forgot that one." God, I loved the kid. "He's grown up to be very *marts* himself."

"Very," Ellen said with pride. "And sweet. A very sweet boy."

"Don't you mean a *weets* boy?"

She laughed, but it quickly faded. "Sweet, but never cuddly. I thought I'd done something wrong with him in the beginning because he never wanted me to hold him the way Amanda did."

I was taken aback. She'd never mentioned this fear when we'd been together. "That's just his personality. He's still not very touchy. How is that your fault?"

"I don't know. I wondered if it was because I wasn't as clingy to him as I had been with Amanda. He was a second child, and that is what it is, but I couldn't help feeling guilty about it. Aaron always slept in his crib, from the minute he came into the world, but Amanda was always in my bed. I remember the day she was born, holding her in my arms, wrapped up like a little burrito, and I just didn't want to let her go, even as I fell asleep. The nurse came in and asked if she could take her for me, put her in her bassinet at least, and I said no. I didn't want to let her go. I loved holding her."

"She was always an affectionate girl." It hurt to remember that, how warm Amanda had been. She had been nearly a teenager when I'd met her, but her biological father had never been in the picture, except to write a child support check every month. I'd quickly filled the spot of patriarch, even though I'd only been a dozen years older than her. Maybe she accepted me so easily *because* we were so close in age. I'd understood the girl better than the men her mother had dated that were closer to her own age. Ellen had always joked it was one of the perks of marrying a younger man, saying I bridged the culture gap between her and her teen.

Thinking about that made me think of Audrey and how she'd been so good at communicating with Aaron the couple of times they'd interacted.

But I didn't want to think about Audrey.

I wasn't so sure I wanted to keep thinking about Amanda, either. It was too painful. Yet, it was cathartic talking about her with Ellen. We'd waited too long to reminisce together about her, and it felt like progress between us, despite the emotions it drudged up.

"Remember how she always begged us to let her sleep with Aaron?" I asked. "I always felt so bad for saying no."

"He was a baby," Ellen laughed. "It was because she never liked to sleep alone. Remember how often she snuck in our bed? When she was really little, she used to sleep so close to me that I'd wake up and her head would be *on* my head. Like I was her pillow. I couldn't imagine how she found that comfortable."

"She was still doing that when I met her. We'd watch telly together, and she'd be fused into my side. She had zero personal boundaries. Anytime I had any food or drink, she'd take it without even asking. She truly believed in the 'mine is yours, yours is mine' philosophy of co-living."

"It was annoying sometimes."

"It was annoying a lot of the time," I agreed. "And also...also not." It was hard to look back at the nuisances, things she'd done that had been exasperating at the time when I'd give everything in my bank account to have her back and bothering me just one more time. Losing a child was the true definition of hell. The worst part was that it never went away. It burned and burned forever. Eternal damnation.

It was such serious pain that it made a person want to do anything to avoid feeling ever again.

"She looked up to you. So very much." Ellen's voice caught, and when I glanced over at her, I saw a tear rolling down her cheek.

I wiped at my own eyes. I couldn't do this anymore. I couldn't continue with this excruciating flood of emotions, remembering my dead stepdaughter, worrying about my ill son. "You know what? This isn't helping. Trips down memory lane are supposed to be bittersweet, but this feels more like a haunting. Like a visit from the Ghost of Christmas Past."

Ellen sat up and peered sharply in my direction. "If this is a haunting, I think I'm actually the Ghost of Christmas Future. Look at me. I've lost everything I've ever loved in this world. My parents. My daughter. Then you—the love of my life. And I'll never get those things back."

I was speechless. I'd been the love of her life? I'd believed that once upon a time, but she still felt that way?

"I'm alone now," she went on. "And lonely, with nothing and no one in my life but Aaron, and even if he does pull through this—"

"He's going to pull through this, Ellen," I interjected forcefully.

"*If and when* he pulls through this, I've got...what? Another handful of years before he goes off to college. What will I have in my life then?"

My scowl deepened. "Stop it. It's not too late for...I don't know, for anything you want. You're fifty-three. Not one hundred. You have a lot of life to look forward to." As much as I'd hated her at times, I'd also loved her. I'd hated her *because* I'd loved her so much. I still loved her in a way, and I sincerely wanted nothing but good things for her.

"A lot of life to look forward to *alone,* if I can't turn myself around." She settled back into her chair. "I know my issues, what I have to work through, but it's unbearable to me that you, of all people, might be following in my footsteps. Especially if I had anything to do with it, which I'm sure I did. Don't be *me*, Dylan. Don't stop getting attached. Let people into your heart. Cherish the love you have while you have it. Otherwise, what's the point in even living?"

It was a bloody conundrum. A catch twenty-two. Live a life with love and risk being destroyed. Live a life without and never really live. I thought I'd worked it out—earlier tonight, earlier in my life—but Ellen sparked something in me when she referred to me as the love of her life. I'd felt that way about her once, too. I certainly didn't feel that way anymore. I'd grown out of her. Grown past her.

And it struck me then that the loneliness that she talked about, familiar as it was, didn't accurately describe my current state of living. Sure, I'd been as miserable as she was now, living the same old bland routine with no color in my world. I'd walked through my life in a bubble, sealed off from any contamination of sorrow or happiness and joy and hope, and there had been no point.

But then Audrey had walked into my life and changed everything. She'd made me a better person. She'd made me happy and hopeful and now, without any promise of her in my future, I was back to being a wretched curmudgeon, and if I was honest with myself, I didn't feel safer from sorrow than I had with her at my side. In fact, she made me feel *more* protected from heartbreak.

She made the risks seem worth it. And selfishly, I wanted her here with me now, comforting me. Reassuring me. Sitting by my side while my son went through surgery.

I wanted her with me after that too. I wanted her with me for always. And when I tried to think the phrase "love of my life," it was her face that popped up. Her eyes. Her laugh. Her everything. Why would I let her slip away? Why would I, as Ellen had said, give that much power to a miserable, lamentable past? Why would I not take every chance to avoid the future that she presented, a future that was sure to be my fate if I didn't make a change now?

I stood up suddenly and looked at the clock on the wall. It was just past seven in the morning. That meant afternoon in London. Audrey probably already told Jana she didn't want the job, but if I got to her in time, she could change her mind. I had to change her mind.

"What's wrong?" Ellen asked.

I pulled out my phone from my pocket and tried to turn it on before remembering it was dead. I kicked myself for not asking around earlier for a charger. "I need to make a call. Can I borrow your mobile?"

"Sure." She stood up and crossed to the small table where her mobile was charging. After tapping in the password, she handed it over. "Zero, seven, two, nine is the code if it locks up again."

The numbers were familiar. "Our anniversary?"

Her cheeks flushed. "It's memorable, that's all."

For the second time since I'd arrived, I pulled her into my arms, hugging her tight. So much had passed between us, so much good and so much bad, and I didn't regret any of it. I didn't even regret having loved her as deeply as I had. As I *still* did.

But it was finally time to move on. It was time to let go of her and Amanda and all the hurts of the past that I'd held so tightly for so long. It was time to stop living so bloody scared.

I kissed her head before I pulled away. "I'm still here with you, don't doubt that for a second," I reassured her. "I'm just going to be out in the waiting room, making this call."

"Go," she said. "I'm going to pace the room, anyway. It's less embarrassing to do it when there's no one else around."

I didn't want to leave her alone, but I had to take care of this before it was too late, and while Aaron was in surgery was the best time to step away.

Without my own phone, it was harder to do what I needed. I didn't have Audrey's number memorized, and when I called the staff number listed for her department on the Gallery website, I was told she'd called off for the day.

I was sure she wasn't ill. She was likely upset, and I hated myself for being the one who'd caused that.

I had to get a hold of her.

Donovan would be able to get me her number. My thumb hovered over his name in Ellen's directory. Then I had another idea and dialed the number to my office instead.

"I need you to do something for me," I said when I'd been transferred to Amy's line and she'd answered.

"Dylan! How are you holding up? What's going on with Aaron?"

"He's fine. Or, not fine yet. He's in surgery, but I'm praying he's going to be fine, and that's not why I'm calling. I'll give you an update on him as soon as I have it. I need something else in the meantime." I spoke rapidly, running my free hand through my hair as I paced the length of the waiting room.

"Uh, okay. What can I do?"

"I'm not sure exactly. Something big, but I'm not very good at this so I don't know quite what that is."

"This isn't something I can work with, Locke."

"Right, right." I tried to pull my frantic thoughts into something cohesive. "I need you to go to Audrey's for me. I'll give you the address. I need you to go over there with flowers and chocolates and...I don't know...balloons! Balloons are good. Heart-shaped balloons. And lots of flowers."

"I think you have the holidays mixed up. It's Christmas season, not Valentine's. I'm not sure I can find chocolates and heart-shaped balloons."

"Do the best you can, then. Get whatever you think might be romantic. The biggest romantic things you can find, and then tell her I love her. Tell her I don't want her to go, and that I love her, and that I'm not going to be scared anymore." I paused, wondering if there was something else to add, but couldn't think of anything. "Is that good? Do you think that's good? Do you think she'll think that's good?"

"I think she'll think that's quite wonderful. But she isn't home right now."

The voice wasn't Amy's, and it came from behind me, not from Ellen's phone. With the mobile still pressed to my ear, I turned around and suddenly the light in the room was brighter and my knees went weak and my heart was pounding like it would jump out of my chest.

Because there she was. There was Audrey. Bundled up like an eskimo, her cheeks flushed, her eyes shining.

"Never mind," I told Amy, never taking my eyes off the woman in front of me. "Cancel it. Cancel all of it."

I ended the call without saying goodbye, and let the mobile slip out of my grasp to the carpet so I could have both hands free as I took Audrey into my arms.

She threw her hands around my neck and pulled my head down toward hers. My mouth found hers easily, like it was made for this, made to only kiss her. I kissed her like it had been decades since I'd last seen her. I kissed her like I hadn't been alive until now.

I kissed her like I would die if I didn't kiss her.

Breathless, I pressed my forehead against hers. "Stay in London. Let me be the reason you stay."

She nodded, tears sliding down her face. "Okay."

Then I kissed her again, like I'd never let her go.

TWENTY-NINE

With my arms still around her, I pulled back to look at her. The enormity of what she'd done for me struck me suddenly. She'd gotten on a plane, flown across an ocean at the drop of a dime. The price of the ticket alone had to be an obstacle. "I can't believe you came."

She pushed my chest lightly with her palm. "Of course I came. It's your son, you ninny." She searched my features, seemingly as in awe of me as I was of her at the moment. "Did you think I didn't really mean it when I said I loved you? As soon as I got your message, I had to be here."

My breath felt trapped inside my chest. She'd said the words before, but I hadn't been ready to hear them then. *Really* hear them. There was a great deal of things to say, things I should have said the first time she'd said them.

But I hadn't lost complete sight of where we were and what was going on. "Audrey, there are things I want to tell you, just..."

She cut me off with a shake of her head. "It can wait. What's going on with Aaron?"

"He's in surgery right now." Suddenly I remembered my ex-wife. "I need to go back to his room to wait for him."

"Do you want me to come with you? Do you want me to go? Whatever you need..."

I tightened my grip on her waist. "Don't go. I want you to stay. Please?"

"I want to stay, too. Thank you for letting me stay." She sounded relieved, and I almost laughed at how ridiculous it was that she wasn't sure that I'd want her with me, when I wanted her as acutely as I did.

I was so grateful, in fact, that I couldn't begin to tell her. I wasn't sure I could speak at all, actually. I cleared my throat. "Would you...may I introduce you to Ellen?"

Her lips turned up in a soft smile. "I'd like that."

I kissed her once more, quickly, simply because I couldn't *not* kiss her, then grabbed the phone off the floor and held it in one hand and Audrey's hand in the other as we walked to the hospital room. Along the way, I updated her on Aaron's condition telling her about the abscess and the swelling and the possibilities of encephalitis and sepsis. All of it sounded just as awful as it had when I'd heard it from Dr. Sharma, but somehow the situation seemed a little more hopeful, just because she was here.

At Aaron's room, I unexpectedly became nervous. I'd never introduced another woman to Ellen, and something about that felt significant. More significant, even, than introducing a woman to my mother.

I dropped Audrey's hand so I could go in first. "Um, Ellen..."

She was standing at the window, staring outside at the street below.

I waited for her to shake out of her thoughts before I went on. "I sort of lied earlier, when I said I wasn't dating anyone." I reached behind me and pulled Audrey to my side.

"Hi," she said, offering her free hand to Ellen before I could complete the introduction. "I'm Audrey."

Ellen's eyes went wide. She blinked a couple of times, a faint smile appearing on her face. She shook Audrey's hand. "Ellen Wallace."

"I'm very glad to meet you, though I'm so sorry it has to be under such terrible circumstances."

"Nice to meet you as well." She was surprised, I was sure, and why wouldn't she be? I'd given her no reason to see it coming. She narrowed her eyes and looked curiously in my direction. "Dylan, have you been hiding her from me?"

"No! No. Not at all." Though I was at a loss of what to say to explain our relationship.

Thank God Audrey was better at these things than I. "It's not his fault," she explained. "We've known each other for more than a year, but..." She looked at me, her cheeks pinking. "We're only just now sorting out what we are to each other."

God, she was perfect.

Ellen's forehead was still knotted in confusion. "Do you live here? Or in London?"

"I'm American, obviously," she giggled. "And we met here. But I've been living in London for the past several months. I flew out here as soon as I heard about Aaron. Dylan didn't know I was coming."

Ellen's features relaxed. "Ah." She gave me a knowing look that I couldn't interpret. Not for lack of trying.

She returned her focus to Audrey. "Dylan has always had a thing for American girls."

"Really? I guess I never put that together. It works out, because I have a thing for this British man."

Now I was the one to blush.

It was time to change the subject. "Did you hear anything while I was gone?"

Ellen's sober expression returned. "Nothing yet. It should be soon. I hope. I'm going crazy with the waiting."

"I can't even imagine." Audrey's tone was genuinely sympathetic. A beat passed. "If you'll excuse me, I could use some tea. I spotted a coffee station in the waiting room. Can I bring you both something?"

Ellen declined, while I asked for Earl Grey, if they had it.

As soon as she left the room, my ex-wife smirked. "Dylan, you dog. I can't believe you didn't mention her. She's adorable."

"She's young." I was prodding her, trying to provoke her into admitting what she had to really be thinking.

Ellen just rolled her eyes. "*You're* young."

"She's *younger*." Maybe it was silly to expect my ex-wife to be shocked by the age difference, seeing as how she was ten years older than me.

It was probably even sillier that I worried about the gap at all. I loved Audrey exactly as she was, and for some insane reason, she loved me.

Ellen seemed to sense I needed more reassurance. "I'll tell you the same thing my mother said to me when I brought you home for the first time: Right on."

She winked, and anxiety rolled off my shoulders. "I've still got it," I said, boastfully, embracing the lightness of the moment, as fleeting as it might be. "It's probably because I'm in a band. She's an artist. She appreciates other artists."

Ellen full out laughed. "Oh, is that what she appreciates about you?" Her smile lingered. "Seriously, though. You have someone who will sit at the hospital with you. You better keep her."

That had been the knowing look she'd given me, I realized now.

"I'm working on that." I wasn't sure how I'd expected Ellen to react to me having a girlfriend—was that what Audrey was? I hadn't imagined bringing a woman around her since she'd cheated on me. Then, I'd fantasized an insane amount about the idea, about having a sexy, young, intelligent bombshell on my arm, about flaunting it in her face. I'd wanted to hurt her, make her jealous. Make her regret giving me up.

This was nothing like what I'd imagined. It was so much better.

A few minutes later, Audrey returned with the tea, then a few minutes after that, the shift nurse came in. "Mr. Locke, Ms. Wallace, I'm happy to report that Aaron is out of surgery. He's in the recovery room now. Would you like to be taken down to see him? The surgeon can talk to you both there."

"Yes," Ellen answered immediately.

"I'd like to go as well." We'd already been told only parents were allowed in recovery. I knew Audrey would understand, but I looked at her for confirmation.

"I'll be here when you get back, if that's okay?"

I wasn't sure if she was asking me or the nurse. "Can she stay in the room while we're gone?"

"Sure. I'll bring another chair. And your relation is...?" The nurse studied Audrey, trying to find a resemblance, perhaps.

I waited for Audrey to play her usual game and claim to be my daughter or a niece, but she didn't. She reached out and took my hand. "I'm his girlfriend."

So she *was* my girlfriend.

I liked the sound of it, but also, it didn't feel right. It wasn't enough of a word to describe everything she was to me. Everything I wanted her to be.

But right now I needed to see my son. The rest could wait until later.

THE PROCEDURE HAD GONE WELL. Aaron would need a root canal and debridement once he got out of the hospital, but the surgeon was confident he'd gotten the bulk of the infection out. Now it was a matter of waiting for the IV antibiotics to take care of the rest. He expected we'd see progress within the next twenty-four hours or so.

Like the last time our son had undergone anesthesia, Aaron took a while rousing. It was nearly two hours later before he was ready to return to his floor. He was still fairly out of it as they wheeled him into the room, and I debated whether or not I should wait to re-introduce him to Audrey.

Turned out Aaron made the decision himself. "I know you," he said, looking Audrey over. "You're my dad's girlfriend, aren't you?"

I grinned over at the woman I loved. "Seems he figured it out faster than we did."

"I knew the minute we first met that you were a smart one," she said directly to Aaron. "I hope you don't mind that I'm here right now. I don't want to invade your family time."

"I don't mind. You're nice." His eyes closed. "And pretty," he added before drifting back to sleep.

I didn't say it out loud, but I had to agree. That kid really was *smarts*.

The rest of the day was spent at his bedside. Audrey became more than a comfort; she was also extremely helpful. She brought us food when we got tired of the cafeteria options. Ellen gave her the keys to her apartment and Audrey met the cable guy. She bought me a charger for my phone so I could distract myself with internet surfing. She engaged in idle conversation with each of us. She sat by my side.

Through it all it became more and more clear how much I needed her, how perfectly she fit into my world, how completely she belonged to me. And even as my main focus was my son and his illness, the wheels worked in the back of my mind. Ellen's advice played over and over on repeat—*you better keep her*. Little by little, I broke down what I'd have to do, what I'd have to become to make that happen. Little by little, I unraveled the knots that had previously been barriers to letting Audrey in permanently.

As evening approached, she encouraged me to consider some self-care. There had been no changes in Aaron's status, but no indication that it would worsen. Reluctantly, I left the hospital for the night. I was exhausted and needed a shower, a bed, a change of clothes. Audrey was just as tired. We collapsed into sleep as soon as we got to the flat.

We returned to hospital Saturday morning for a repeat of the prior day, with one difference—Aaron's swelling was receding. The latest antibiotic seemed to be working. It was easier to leave that night, and Sunday when we arrived at hospital, the doctor informed us that Aaron would be able to go home later in the day.

The news was so overwhelming, I lost it. I had to make an excuse to step out of the room so Aaron wouldn't see me overcome with emotion. Audrey followed, and I buried my head in her neck and sobbed with relief.

After the episode passed, my head was clearer, as though a long lying fog had finally lifted. The foolishness of the vows I'd made the first night at Aaron's bedside became apparent. Silently, I made new ones. I vowed to make Aaron my priority and to be the best father possible. The first step in doing that was to be the best man possible. Audrey made me that kind of man.

I slipped out again soon after to make another phone call.

"I need your help," I said to Donovan when he answered the line.

"It's about goddamned time."

AARON WAS DISCHARGED a few hours later. Audrey and I helped get him home. He'd had several gifts sent by friends and family members while he'd been ill—flowers, balloons and the like. Too much for Ellen to manage by herself. I also wanted to personally see him back in his normal environment. Even though he went immediately to bed, it was reassuring to see him in his own room rather than the clinical surroundings of the hospital.

And I had reasons for not wanting to go back to my own apartment quite yet.

We stayed for dinner, delivery pizza at Aaron's request, and by late evening, I was finally ready to leave. I was more than ready, actually. There was nothing more I could do for my son. He was on the road to recovery. He was tucked in and medicated. He'd listened to me tell him I loved him countless times without protesting too much.

Now I turned my focus to the woman who'd sat patiently on the backburner throughout the ordeal. I wanted her. I needed her in a very different way than I had the past few days, and with the furtive glances she'd been giving me for much of the day, I was pretty sure she needed me in the same way.

By the time we walked out of Ellen's building to meet my car, the air around us was charged with arousal. My body felt too hot, even in the winter air. My fingers ached with the craving to touch.

The driver held the back door open while Audrey slid across the backseat of the saloon. Seeing there wasn't a window separating the front seat from the back, I turned to him before I got in myself. "I'm sorry for what's about to happen," I said.

Though I wasn't really *that* sorry.

Audrey was on the same wavelength. As soon as the door shut beside me, she crawled on top of me, straddling her legs over mine.

"This is familiar." I gripped her hips and pulled her pelvis forward so she could feel the thickening pressure of my cock beneath her. "Are you going to ask me for some sort of lessons now?"

She raised her chin so I could place open-mouthed kisses along her neck. "Actually, I'm going to give you a lesson."

"Color me intrigued." I slipped my hands inside her leggings and palmed her ass. My mouth found hers and I sucked on her bottom lip, making it plump and swollen.

When I went in to kiss her more completely, however, she pulled just out of reach. "Lesson time, Dylan."

I gave her a mock frown. I was eager for her lips, eager to taste her, eager for the talking to be over.

But I did enjoy the idea of reversing our usual roles. "All right, then, Ms. Lind. School me."

"You have been a bad boy, Dylan Locke."

"Yes, yes. A very bad boy."

"I'm here with you right now because I love you, but I almost wasn't here. You almost let me slip away. You almost lost me all together."

Oh. So this was a serious lesson then.

Except, the whole while she scolded me, Audrey rocked up and down along the length of my cock.

"I know, I know," I said, distracted by the fire she stoked in my lower regions. "I fucked up." I reached again for her lips.

Once again she darted away. "If you want to keep me with you, you can't play this scared routine anymore. I already called Jana and accepted the job at the Gallery, but you can't be closed off if you want me to really stay. You can't keep building these walls. You have to tell me how you're feeling. You have to start trusting me with your heart. You hurt me, Dylan."

Guilt won over lust. I brushed her cheek with my knuckle. "I know, and I'm incredibly sorry. I never wanted to hurt you. If it helps, I hurt us both."

She cupped my face with her hands and lifted it toward hers. "It *doesn't* help. I don't like you hurting. I don't like either of us hurting. Don't do it again."

"I won't," I promised. But it came out on a groan as she drew a lazy circle over my crotch with her hips.

"I mean it." She drew another circle. Then a third.

My eyelids threatened to close from the agonizing sparks of pleasure shooting through my dick. "I can't tell if you're trying to punish me or please me."

"My favorite kind of punishment." She was such a vixen, that woman. Such a bloody tease.

She bent her forehead to mine as she continued to grind on my cock. "Tell me you understand what I'm asking from you."

"I understand."

"Promise me you're going to do better."

"I promise," I moaned.

"Promise that you aren't going to assume I'm going to be someone different than I am based on your experiences with other people."

"Audrey." I pulled her pelvis tight against me so her movements would still and I could concentrate for a moment. Then I looked her directly in the eyes. "I understand that I have been an incredibly daft wanker where you are concerned, that I hurt you, and that you are more mature than I could ever hope to be, and I vow on my very life that I will endeavor to be a man who deserves to have your love and affection for as long as I shall be allowed to receive it. Now, let me kiss you."

A grin broke out on her face as she brought her lips to mine. My mouth latched onto hers and held there, savoring the connection. I took my time with my tongue, licking into her with shallow strokes before fully stretching out to inhabit her completely. Her hands came up to tangle in my hair. Our breaths came rapid and synched. I bucked my hips to press against her, wishing she wasn't wearing trousers. Wishing she wasn't dressed at all.

With a soft moan, she tilted her head up, offering her neck. I licked her along the curve of her chin and nibbled down the exposed skin.

"Are we going to talk about what it means that you asked me to stay in London?" she asked, panting.

"No." My palms found her tits and squeezed them together. I was going to fuck her here. I hadn't done that yet, and I definitely needed to add it to my to-do list.

"No?" The sharpness in her tone forced me to give more attention to the question.

"I mean, yes. We will. But not right now." I leaned for her mouth, but she turned away so my kiss landed on the side of her lips. She wanted a more committed answer. "I promise we'll talk about it, Audrey. Soon."

She let me kiss her then, but it was brief. "Like, in Dylan-time soon? Or in regular-people-time soon?"

I had to chuckle at the necessity for the clarification. Still, I only responded with, "Soon."

"Sir? We're here." Something in the driver's tone suggested we might have been parked at the curb for several minutes. I hadn't even noticed the car had stopped moving.

Audrey and I broke apart. Immediately I felt cold without her warmth. I ushered her in through the lobby as quickly as I could. Once the doors were shut in the lift and we were alone again, I pushed her against the wall and pinned her hands behind her back.

My mouth hovered over hers. "I'm going to lick your pussy so long tonight, you won't have any sensation anymore by the time I'm done."

She whimpered.

"And then I'm going to fuck you. I'm going to fuck you everywhere. I'm going to fuck your mouth and your tits. I'm going to fuck your sweet cunt until you come so hard. You won't be able to stand tomorrow."

"Dylan..." she gasped. I cut her off with a greedy kiss.

The doors opened on our floor, and we were so into each other, they closed again before we were able to untangle ourselves. Laughing, I pushed the DOOR OPEN button. She darted out ahead of me, and I chased her like she was a bitch in heat, and I was the tramp that had caught her scent. At my flat, she stroked me through my trousers while I kissed her and dug in my coat pocket for my key. Finally, I had the lock undone and the door open.

"Don't turn on the lights," I said when I stood back to let her go in before me. Then I said a silent prayer that everything was as it should be inside.

I was still in the foyer when I heard her gasp. My pulse quickened. My heart hammered against my chest like it was trying to escape. Quickly, I hung up my coat in the cupboard and followed in after her.

The room had been beautifully transformed. I almost gasped as well. Rose petals had been scattered across the wood floor. Red and white poinsettias were strewn in bunches around the furniture. White electric tea lights and evergreen garland weaved through the plants and tangled up the small cart that had been wheeled in for the occasion. At the top, several electric candles glowed next to a silver champagne bucket. Two long-stemmed glasses were set next to it along with a tray of fresh strawberries.

Audrey's back faced me as she slowly took in every detail of the scene. I watched her reflection in the window. One hand was clapped over her heart, another over her mouth in awe. Her voice was quivering when she exclaimed, "This is so unbelievably romantic!"

It *was* very romantic. Donovan Kincaid was much better at this than I was, it seemed. I'd have to take notes.

Then she saw it.

I knew by the way her breath hitched, and her knees started to sway. She reached a shaky hand out to pick up the object from the arrangement on the cart, and when she turned around to me, she held it between her thumb and index finger, and I saw it too. It was as perfect as the image on Tiffany's website had indicated. The two carat round diamond sparkled with the candlelights and appeared to be floating in its setting above a radiant rose gold band.

I got down on my knee and reached my hand out to the sweet girl in front of me. To my surprise, she fell down on her knees with me. She slipped the ring on the first knuckle of her thumb and clutched onto my jumper.

"But you don't believe in commitment. You don't want a relationship," she said, tears streaming down her cheeks. Despite her words, her tone was hopeful. "You said…" She was too choked up to go on.

I cupped one hand against her face. "I'm a liar, Audrey. I want a relationship. With you. I want it all with you. I am madly drowning in love for you. I have been since that first week in New York, I was just too chickenshit to admit it."

Her eyes widened. "Since then? Why didn't you…?"

She didn't have to finish the question for me to understand what she was asking. "I *couldn't* tell you. I could barely tell myself, at first, and when I figured it out, I couldn't bring myself to share that with you. I wanted you to be happy, and I was convinced I couldn't possibly be the person to give that to you."

Gently, I loosened her hand from my jumper so I could take the ring off her thumb. I held it up in between us, letting it be the underline for everything I had to tell her. "I've spent all this last year reminding myself of all the reasons why I'm not good for you,

Audrey. But I never stopped to list all the reasons why *you're* good for *me*, and when I try, it's such an incredible job to even begin to catalog. The long and short of it, though, is that you make me a better man. You make me believe in things I never thought possible. You make me love when I thought I was no longer capable. You make me want a very different future than the one laid out for me at present."

I took her left hand in mine and eased the ring on the appropriate finger. It fit perfectly. Sabrina was to thank for that.

Audrey blinked at the diamond on her hand before peering up at me.

With my thumbs, I brushed tears off her face. "I'm beguiled by you, Audrey. And when you said you loved me, when you flew across an ocean to be at my side when I needed you most, a selfish hollow in my heart ached to believe that I might have something that I could give you, even if I could never balance the scale between us. Marry me and let me spend the rest of my life trying."

Her lips rolled inward as she tried to suppress a sob and she flapped her hand in front of her face, as though that would dry up her tears. Nodding profusely she managed to squeak out her response. "Yes. I say yes."

A wave of relief rolled through my shoulders. I hadn't realized how worried I'd been about her answer until I heard the one I so desperately wanted. "Thank God," I sighed. With my palms braced on each side of her face, I kissed her, and kissed her. Kissed her with sweet, shallow kisses.

"*This* is what I meant when I asked you to stay in London with me," I said in between kisses. "Is this discussing it soon enough for you?"

She burst into laughter, and her eyes twinkled as bright as her diamond. "I'd been preparing myself for a long road ahead. My next goal was to get you to see the convenience of living together.

I didn't think...I wasn't sure that marriage would ever be on the table. Are you sure this is what you want? I can go slow. We don't have to commit to—"

I cut her off. "I *want* to marry you, Audrey. I know that with every fiber of my being, and going slow isn't going to make me any more committed than I am right now, because I am utterly and hopelessly devoted to you. Surely you know that by now. So unless *you* don't want to get married..."

"I do! I told you the next guy was going to be The One, and I meant it. Because either the next guy was you or it didn't matter who he was. I only ever wanted you. Since that first week in this apartment, it's only been you."

"Thank fuck, because I was likely going to murder another man if he were to touch you. You're mine." I kissed her again, deeper this time, a primal possessive kiss. The kind that was meant to lead to the removal of clothes.

But before I'd managed to strip more than her coat off her shoulders, she broke away. "And babies?" she asked hopefully. "It's not a deal-breaker. I love you too much. I'm willing to make concessions."

It pulled my heart to hear her suggest she'd give up something she wanted so much just to be with me.

But she didn't need to concede anything on this front. I desperately wanted to see her round and swollen with my child. Wanted to look down at my infant's tiny face and see the perfect blend of features of hers with mine.

Though, I did wince a bit at the prospect of sleepless nights and dirty nappies. "Could we maybe just start with one and see how it goes?"

"We can definitely *start* with one," she said, with a devilish grin. The kind of grin that told me she knew I was wrapped around her little finger and all she had to do was get me to agree to *start* and from there I'd be a goner. "We could start practicing right now even, if you like."

"I'd like that very much."

We lost ourselves in each other then, making love right there on the lounge floor. When we'd finished, we broke open the champagne and fed each other strawberries before I carried her into the bedroom for another round.

Later, as we drifted on the edge of consciousness, it hit me again how close I'd been to losing her. How stupid I'd been and how determined I was to hold onto her now. "How is it possible that you're even here?" I asked, kissing her temple as she lay in my arms. "I tried so hard to set you free."

"And I came back," she replied sleepily. "You know what that means, right?"

"It's kismet."

EPILOGUE
AUDREY

Dylan ran his palm along my outer thigh, his gaze pinned on our reflection in the full-length mirror. "You're so fucking sexy. Look at you take my cock like that. Such a good girl."

I let out a breathy moan. Wow, he felt good. Better than ever.

I was bent over the end of the bed, one of the few positions I found comfortable these days, and my husband was pushing into me from behind. We'd recently discovered we could watch ourselves in the mirror from here, and Dylan loved that.

I loved it too, but I was such a horny sex kitten lately that I didn't care where we were doing it, as long as we were doing it. Dylan had yet to complain.

"Stop teasing," I whined, urging him to go faster. "Give it to me already."

Despite my pleas, he dragged his cock out of my body all the way to the tip.

"Patience, my love. This is too good to rush."

I glanced at him in the reflection. His eyes were dark and focused as he slid back into me, just as slow as before.

"Are you watching this, Audrey? Look how wet you are. You can see it on my dick."

This time when he pulled out, I could see the gleam of dripping moisture on his cock.

"Unf," I gasped. "That *is* hot." I stared magnetically as he repeated his leisure thrust and drag. My belly tightened deep inside as the beginnings of an orgasm formed just from watching the erotic scene.

It was followed by a cramp that wrapped from my lower back around to the front of my torso. That was the downside of pregnant sex—many of my orgasms had been accompanied by uterus contractions since twenty-four weeks.

Which was why Dylan needed to hurry up, titillating as it was to watch the current pace. "But I'm not going to be able to keep this up long, and I need you to bang me good."

"Yes, yes, you're right." He dug his fingers into my hips and notched up the tempo to a steady, moderate pulse.

The tingling knot of arousal began to build and spread at an agonizingly sluggish rate. "Harder," I begged. "Really pound into me."

I wasn't usually so bossy during sex. Dylan knew how to read me without me having to say the words. As I'd neared the end of my pregnancy, though, he'd become more tentative.

"I don't want to hurt you. Are you sure this is okay for the babies?" But he thrust faster anyway, pounding into me so hard, our thighs slapped together.

That was hot too. So hot.

"The babies are fine. Keep this up and Mama will be fine too." More than fine. I sighed with pleasure. A sigh that quickly turned into a whimper as a cramp jolted across my middle. I clutched my hand to the side of my expansive belly.

Dylan noticed and immediately halted. "What's wrong?"

"A cramp. That's all. Keep going."

"Do you want me to—?"

I cut him off. "Don't you *dare* stop!" I pushed my hips back, bouncing on his erection. If he wasn't going to take my need seriously, I was going to do it myself.

"Fuuuuccccckkkk. That's so hot, chasing after my cock like that. Your tits look so fucking fantastic right now. Such a dirty, sweet girl." He was so turned on, he forgot about his concern and drove into me like I wanted. Like I needed. Hammering into me until we exploded simultaneously into orgasm.

Dylan leaned over my backside, and placed light kisses over my shoulders. "I'm going to miss this. We need to get in as much of this as possible before Aaron gets here for Christmas, because after the girls are born, who knows when we'll get to be intimate."

"Oh, please." I shrugged him off so I could roll over and collapse on my back on the bed. "We're still going to have sex after the babies are born. I don't know how many times I have to tell you this. I can't live without it."

He stretched out on the bed next to me on his side and rubbed a hand over my stomach. "I'm not disagreeing that you are a greedy girl when it comes to fucking, but you are vastly underestimating the exhaustion of one baby, let alone twins. I don't know how many times I have to tell you this."

His playful smirk was irresistible, and I couldn't help giggling. "So we'll have to figure out ways to work it in. Sex when we shower. Half-asleep sex. Is it too weird to try to bang while nursing?"

"I am not fucking you while you nurse our daughters. I'm not ever going to be even close to naked around them. That's just...I can't..." His eyes narrowed suddenly. "Ah, I see. You're winding me up."

I lifted up to press a kiss on his lips. "Yes. I'm winding you up. I know it's going to be hard. But I'm young. I'm tough. I'm not worried about it." I stroked the side of his cheek with my fingertips. "Are you worried about it for reals?"

He shook his head. "Not at all."

"And you really don't regret this pregnancy, even though it's two instead of one?"

It was his turn to kiss me. "No regrets. I know better than to argue with what fate has in store for us."

"Good answer." I closed my eyes, relishing the feel of his palm sweeping over my belly. Relishing the awesomeness that was our lives.

Fate really had been good to us. I had never doubted that it would be, but there had definitely been a time when Dylan had. It had been difficult for me to be patient at times. Not all the time, but some of the time. I'd thought about him so much after our Thanksgiving tryst in New York City. Wondered about him. Fantasized about him. He'd made a mark in my life, and I'd figured that was all there would ever be. That we'd be two ships that had crossed in the night, never to meet again.

But then, when I'd found out I'd gotten an internship in the same city he lived in—an internship I hadn't even remembered applying for—I'd been sure that fate had a plan for us. I wasn't sure what the plan was, though, and after countless speeches from Sabrina about how easily I fell in love, I'd tried to steer a course that protected my heart. Dylan had been more than clear that he didn't want a future with anyone, let alone me, and not being willing to lose him from my life all together, I'd believed friendship was the best option for us.

Truth be told, if he'd asked me back to his flat that first night after our reunion, I would have gone in an instant.

But he didn't. His goals hadn't changed, and I'd been determined to accept that. I'd tried *so hard* to accept it.

Except, how could I when he didn't act like that was what he really wanted? He'd jump when I'd call. His gaze would linger.

He'd react when we accidentally touched. He'd go out of his way to make sure we accidentally touched.

Maybe it had been wrong to start dating in front of him. I'd been a total tease about it, too, throwing the random guys I encountered in his face, as though they'd meant something to me. As though they could ever possibly mean something to me. I'd wanted him jealous. I'd wanted him as crazed over me as I was becoming over him, whether there was a happy ending for us or not.

When he'd pulled away from our friendship, I'd had to face reality—yes, Dylan was affected by me, but not enough to do anything about it. I figured his attraction must have been physical only. I told myself I should let it go, let him walk away. I told myself to find another guy for real.

I couldn't do it. I'd already become too hung up on him. So I tempted fate. I offered him the one thing that I knew would confuse my heart the most—I offered him a sexual relationship. And while I fell more and more in love with him, all I could do was hope beyond hope that the stars had something in store for us that I couldn't begin to imagine.

The universe delivered tenfold.

We were married in May, in between shows at the Gallery, just five months after he'd proposed. Unbeknownst to us, I was already one month pregnant at the time. We didn't find out until after our honeymoon, a week spent in the beautiful countryside of Southampton where Dylan had been born. We didn't find out we were expecting two girls until late July. To my delight, my husband took the news beautifully. *"I could never imagine being so happy and blessed,"* he'd said.

I couldn't have agreed more.

Still rubbing my stomach, Dylan's lips pressed against my temple. "Do you realize today is the one-year anniversary of our engagement? And here we are getting ready for our girls to arrive in another month. So much has changed in this year, hasn't it?"

I opened my eyes to look at him. At exactly the same moment, my belly tightened with another cramp, and I winced.

His hand stilled. "Damn. I felt that. Is that a contraction?"

"No," I said dismissively. "I mean, yes, but just Braxton Hicks. You know I get these after sex all the time."

Another cramp shot across my middle, winding around my torso. "Oh my fudge," I groaned. This one was painful.

"Are you sure that—"

Before he could finish his thought, a gush of water ran down my legs.

"Your water just broke. Oh, my God, Audrey! Your water just broke!"

Oh, huh. Hadn't been expecting that.

I sat up to look at the mess between my legs. My pulse quickened excitedly and my eyes went wide. "It's time! Oh, my gosh, Dylan! It's time!"

Dylan jumped up and ran to the bathroom, returning a second later with a towel. "This isn't good," he muttered as he cleaned me up. "I knew sex was a bad idea. I shouldn't have gone so hard. We shouldn't have been fucking at all this close to the due date! It's too early. They aren't due for another four weeks!"

"Honey," I said patiently. I said it again when he didn't give me his attention. And a third time. I put my hand on his forearm to get his attention. When he finally looked at me, his eyes blinking rapidly, I continued. "Due in three and a half weeks, actually. We're almost at thirty-seven weeks. The doctor said if we made it to thirty-six weeks with twins it would be fine. We're fine."

"We're fine," he repeated unconvincingly.

"We're going to be fine."

"It's fine." He seemed somewhat calmer. As calm as to be expected, anyway.

"Now, could you maybe move so I can get up and we can both throw some clothes on and head to the hospital?"

"Right, right. Hospital. Right." He started for the dresser, but then immediately turned around and came back to me. He took my face in his hands and kissed me. "I love you. All three of you, but right now I especially love you."

I beamed up at him. "I love you too. So much. Are you scared?" I was. Well, excited *and* scared.

He grinned back at me. "Terrified. Now let's go do this. Let's go meet our daughters. It can't be a coincidence that they've decided to come on this anniversary."

"Of course it's not. It's kismet."

The Dirty Universe Continues with Dirty Wild Trilogy

We were supposed to run away after high school.
When she didn't show up at our meeting place, I gathered my courage and went after her.
It was a mistake.
I left bloodied and bruised.
My heart didn't fare half as well.

I had no choice but to walk away.

Years passed. A decade. More.
I traveled, settled halfway around the world, made myself a name and enough money that I didn't have to look back.
But I never got over her.

And when my memories got the best of me, I went looking. Put all my effort behind the search.
Even the best of the best private eyes couldn't find the woman I'd deeply loved.

Then, out of the blue, she calls.

And, what she asks for, the favor that she wants?
I never thought I'd be willing to take a life.
But the truth is, and always has been: I'd do anything for her.

**Start reading the
Dirty Wild Trilogy on the next page.**

THE DIRTY UNIVERSE CONTINUES...

Meet all my Dirty Men.
Dirty Universe reading order

The Dirty Duet - Donovan Kincaid

Dirty Games Duet - Weston King

Dirty Filthy Fix - Nate Sinclair

Dirty Sweet Duet - Dylan Locke

Dirty Wild Trilogy - Cade Warren

Dirty Sweet Valentine & Other Filthy Tales of Love

Ten Dirty Demands - Donovan Kincaid

Kincaid - Donovan Kincaid

ALSO BY LAURELIN PAIGE
WONDERING WHAT TO READ NEXT? I CAN HELP!

Visit www.laurelinpaige.com for content warnings and a more detailed reading order.

Brutal Billionaires

Brutal Billionaire - a standalone (Holt Sebastian)

Dirty Filthy Billionaire - a novella (Steele Sebastian)

Brutal Secret - a standalone (Reid Sebastian)

Brutal Arrangement - a standalone (Alex Sebastian)

Brutal Bargain - a standalone (Axle Morgan)

Brutal Bastard - a standalone (Hunter Sebastian)

The Dirty Universe

Dirty Duet (Donovan Kincaid)

Dirty Filthy Rich Men | Dirty Filthy Rich Love

Kincaid

Dirty Games Duet (Weston King)

Dirty Sexy Player | Dirty Sexy Games

Dirty Sweet Duet (Dylan Locke)

Sweet Liar | Sweet Fate

(Nate Sinclair) Dirty Filthy Fix (a spinoff novella)

Dirty Wild Trilogy (Cade Warren)

Wild Rebel | Wild War | Wild Heart

Men in Charge
Man in Charge
Man for Me (a spinoff novella)

The Fixed Universe
Fixed Series (Hudson & Alayna)
Fixed on You | Found in You | Forever with You | Hudson | Fixed Forever

Found Duet (Gwen & JC) Free Me | Find Me

(Chandler & Genevieve) Chandler (a spinoff novel)

(Norma & Boyd) Falling Under You (a spinoff novella)

(Nate & Trish) Dirty Filthy Fix (a spinoff novella)

Slay Series (Celia & Edward)
Rivalry | Ruin | Revenge | Rising

(Gwen & JC) The Open Door (a spinoff novella)

(Camilla & Hendrix) Slash (a spinoff novella)

First and Last
First Touch | Last Kiss

Hollywood Standalones
One More Time

Close

Sex Symbol

Star Struck

Dating Season
Spring Fling | Summer Rebound | Fall Hard

Winter Bloom | Spring Fever | Summer Lovin

Also written with Kayti McGee under the name Laurelin McGee
Miss Match | Love Struck | MisTaken | Holiday for Hire

Written with Sierra Simone
Porn Star | Hot Cop

ABOUT LAURELIN PAIGE

With millions of books sold, Laurelin Paige is the NY Times, Wall Street Journal, and USA Today Bestselling Author of the Fixed Trilogy. She's a sucker for a good romance and gets giddy anytime there's kissing, much to the embarrassment of her three daughters. Her husband doesn't seem to complain, however. When she isn't reading or writing sexy stories, she's probably singing, watching shows like Billions and Peaky Blinders or dreaming of Michael Fassbender. She's also a proud member of Mensa International though she doesn't do anything with the organization except use it as material for her bio.

www.laurelinpaige.com
laurelinpaigeauthor@gmail.com